Maps

A Visual Survey and Design Guide

By Michael and Susan Southworth

A New York Graphic Society Book
Little, Brown and Company, Boston

Acknowledgments

Copyright © 1982 by Michael
and Susan Southworth

All rights reserved. No part of
this book may be reproduced in
any form or by any electronic or
mechanical means including information storage and retrieval
systems without permission in
writing from the publisher, except by a reviewer who may
quote brief passages in a re-
view.

First edition

Southworth, Michael.
Maps, a visual survey and design guide.

Bibliography: p. 218
Includes index.
1. Maps. I. Southworth, Susan.
II. Title.
GA105.3.S67   912   82-3403
ISBN 0-8212-1503-5   AACR2

Designed by
Logowitz + Moore Associates

New York Graphic Society
books are published by Little,
Brown and Company
Published simultaneously in
Canada by Little, Brown and
Company (Canada) Limited
Printed in Italy
by Arnoldo Mondadori Editore, Verona

Our fascination with maps began long ago as part of our work in urban planning and architecture. Through the years our collection of maps has grown steadily, along with our conception of what makes a good map. Too often we have found the map to be a barrier to communication of a design or planning concept, or worse, a misrepresentation of what would result if the proposal were implemented. And we have seen people confused and frustrated in learning about and using their environment because of poor maps. It was the inspiration and enthusiasm of Dr. Craig Fields of the Defense Advanced Research Projects Agency that finally encouraged us to write this book. His generous and intelligent advice has been essential and his quest for innovative maps has opened our eyes to new possibilities.

Several other people have contributed their time and their maps. Dr. Gershon Weltman of Perceptronics, Inc. helped establish the direction of the project and contributed several interesting maps from his research and development work in new computer applications. Richard Saul Wurman, who has made important contributions to map design and graphics, as well as environmental design and education, kindly allowed us to include many of his delightful and provocative creations. We have benefited from the insights of Dr. Alison Fields, and Dr. Kristina Hooper of the University of California, Santa Cruz, shared with us her experimental map research. And we thank Joel Katz for the many innovative maps he provided. The supportive encouragement of Floyd Yearout of New York Graphic Society and the editorial assistance of Betsy Pitha have been gratifying and important. Finally, we thank the many individual map collectors, mapmakers, and institutions throughout the world that have been helpful to us during our search.

Also by Michael and Susan Southworth
Ornamental Ironwork

Contents

Part I:
Maps, Man, and Space

1
Maps, Map Users, and the Milieu, 8
The Uses of Maps, 10
How Do We Use A Map?, 12
Design Characteristics of Successful Maps, 16
2
Landmarks in Mapmaking, 18
Maps and World View, 20
Changing Images of the Earth, 22
The World Map Expands, 30

Part II:
Mapping Techniques

3
Land Form, 36
4
Built Form, 62
5
Networks and Routes, 104
6
Quantity, Density, and Distribution, 142
7
Relation and Comparison, 156
8
Time, Change, and Movement, 172
9
Behavior and Personal Imagery, 184
10
Simulation and Interaction, 204

References, 218
List of Maps and Illustrations, 219
Index, 221

Part I
Maps, Man, and Space

1.1
Anthropomorphic Map
This satirical map of 1870 turns
the geographic shapes of countries into robust, imaginative figures that vividly portray national
characters and political attitudes. England holds the fierce
puppy, Ireland, on a leash, while
Doña Spain reclines on a sullen
Portugal. With the spade of
Switzerland, France fights off
the encroachment of Prussia,
who has hands on Holland, a
knee on Austria, and a foot on
Italy. Turkey lolls on pillows,
smoking her nargileh, while the
bogeyman Russia advances on
Europe with an empty basket
on his back. *Courtesy Biblio-
thèque Nationale, Paris.*

L'ANGLETERRE, isolée, peste de rage et en oublie presque l'IRLANDE qu'elle tient en laisse. L'ESPAGNE fume, appuyée sur le PORTUGAL. La FRANCE repousse les envahissements de la PRUSSE, qui avance une main sur la HOLLANDE l'autre sur l'AUTRICHE. L'ITALIE, aussi, dit à Bismarck : Ote donc tes pieds de là. La CORSE et la SARDAIGNE... un vrai Gavroche qui rit de tout. Le DANEMARCK, qui a perdu ses jambes dans le HOLSTEIN, espère les reprendre. La TURQUIE d'EUROPE baille et s'éveille. La TURQUIE d'ASIE aspire la fumée de son narguilhé. La SUÈDE fait des bonds de panthère. Et la RUSSIE ressemble à un croquemitaine qui voudrait remplir sa hotte.

What is a map? A signpost in Entebbe, Uganda, points to great cities of the world—Khartoum, 1074 miles; Zanzibar, 640; New York, 7065. Place-names familiar and exotic radiate from the post, which fixes our position on the earth's surface. A signpost, yes—but, in fact, a map (1.2).

For most of us, accustomed to the idea of a map as a sheet of paper printed with a pattern of roads and geographic features, calling this signpost a map may seem unwarranted. But a good definition of *map* should include not only that signpost but also the conventional diagram, not only the stick chart of the Marshall Islanders, but also the computer simulation of topography.

The Latin word *mappa* originally meant signal cloth, napkin, or towel—probably because early, portable maps were drawn on cloth and used as signals or guides for armies moving across unknown terrain. In medieval times, the word *mundi*, "world," was added, to form *mappa mundi*. Most definitions in use today suggest flat, two-dimensional formats, excluding many important innovations in mapping techniques:

A map is a conventionalized picture of the earth's pattern as seen from above, to which lettering is added for identification. (Erwin Raisz, 1948)

[A map is] a representation of the earth's surface or a part of it, its physical and political features, etc., or of the heavens, delineated on a flat surface of paper or other material, each point in the drawing corresponding to a geographical or celestial position according to a definite scale or projection. (Oxford English Dictionary, *1971)*

A map is a representation normally to scale and on a flat medium, of a selection of material or abstract features on, or in relation to, the surface of the Earth or of a celestial body. (International Cartographic Association, 1973)

A map is a graphic representation of the milieu. (Arthur Robinson and Barbara Petchenik, 1976)

In this book we seek to broaden the concept of what a map can be. Our examples go far beyond the conventional road map or atlas to include maps that use new media, that allow user input, or that have been responsive to map users with special needs—the traveler, the blind, the child. Our emphasis throughout is on innovative techniques—both historical and contemporary—for making maps useful, informative, and exciting. From globes and topographic models to highway signs and pointing fingers, from street directories to underwater diving guides, from photographic panoramas to maps that talk, our search uncovers an array of approaches to map design.

Yet despite diversity of physical expression, all maps are basically *representations* of a set of *spatial or temporal relationships.* A map's essential elements are few. Almost without exception, maps communicate information about *locations* and *connections* among locations. Locations and their connections have *attributes* that may be the *quantity* or *quality* of certain variables, or their *change* over time. These variables may be objective and measurable, such as population or production; subjective, such as personal interpretations of scenic appeal; or cultural, such as place-names, which are facts of tradition. Within our definition, then, a map may be two- or three- or even four-dimensional—it may portray time as well as space. It may be verbal, numerical, graphic, photographic, sculptural, small- or large-scale, static or changing. It may represent things, places, people, ideas, qualities, or activities in space or in time. Anything that can be spatially or temporally conceived can be mapped.

The Uses of Maps

Imagine what it would be like to live without maps! Suppose you were attending a convention in a strange country where maps were unknown. You would feel uncertain about your location, and you would have no sense of the distance between your hotel and your meeting place, the time it might take you to travel that distance, or the relationships among the various places described in your convention program.

Probably you would become much more attentive to orientation cues—landmarks, street names, terrain, verbal directions, descriptions by other people. You would try to make mental maps of where you were now, where you would be going tomorrow; but your chief feeling would be one of confusion. Lack of organized knowledge about the layout of the environment can make the world beyond one's personal territory puzzling, even threatening. It is not surprising that in many ancient cultures banishment to strange lands was viewed as punishment in the extreme.

Maps provide us with a structure for storing geographic knowledge and experience. Without them, we would find it difficult, if not impossible, to orient ourselves in larger environments. We would be dependent upon the close, familiar world of personal experience and would be hesitant—since many of us lack the explorer's intrepid sense of adventure—to strike out into unknown, uncharted terrain. Moreover, maps give us a means not only for storing information, but for analyzing it, comparing it, generalizing or abstracting from it. From thousands of separate experiences of places, we create larger spatial clusters that become neighborhoods, districts, routes, regions, countries, all in relation to one another.

Orientation and Travel

One of the primary purposes of a map is to guide us from one place to another. In familiar places, orientation is accomplished without conscious effort, simply by following familiar routes and landmarks. Usually we resort to maps only to avoid becoming lost or to become reoriented once we are lost. An anguished telephone call to a friend may help to rescue us—that verbal communication is itself a kind of map. Or we look at a map, trying to find out where we are, where we want to go. Sailors, pilots, motorists, hikers, divers, bicyclists, tourists all rely on maps.

Besides providing mere route information, maps can tell us something about the character and quality of places, making the stranger feel more at home in foreign territory. From them we can glean a sense of what there is to see and do and can plan our exploration of a new era. A selective map can identify those spots of special interest to the user—hotels, restaurants, museums, parks, airports, historic sites, scenic views, shops—thus eliminating time-consuming, possibly difficult, expensive, or frustrating exploration by trial and error. It is an easily and cheaply acquired savoir-faire.

A map can be a surrogate journey, too, an epitome of a trip. We may sit comfortably by the fire, map in hand, and take a trip in our imagination to places we have never been. "Journey over all the universe in a map, without the expense and fatigue of traveling, without suffering the inconveniences of heat, cold, hunger, and thirst," said Cervantes. For the armchair traveler, the more evocative and informative

1.2
Signs as Maps
Cities of the world radiate from this fascinating signpost in Entebbe, Uganda: Moscow, Sydney, Dar-es-Salaam, Timbuktu . . . At first glance one may not consider it to be a map, but by communi- cating spatial relationships it permits the viewer to build a mental picture of his location in the world. *Photograph © J. Mullender, Paris, 1964.*

the map, the better. Maps can kindle the imagination, sustain trips through time and space, make real the milieux of fantasy or fiction or history—the lands in Tolkien's Middle Earth, the trail of clues in a mystery, the routes followed by Alexander the Great.

Comparative Study, Planning, and Strategy

Since anything spatial can be mapped, maps can simplify comparative study of spatial patterns and are useful in many disciplines, from linguistics and history to demography and anthropology, from economics and sociology to biology and political science. Developers, planners, military strategists use them in analyzing and planning courses of action. By studying spatial and temporal patterns on maps, geologists can predict earthquakes, meteorologists the weather, environmentalists the effects of rainfall and drought (3.6, 3.24).

Data Storage

Another use of maps is the storage of spatial data for future retrieval. Insurance atlases record parcel size and construction type (4.41); assessor's maps give lot dimensions, addresses, property valuations. Land records, or cadastral maps, were, in fact, among the first map types. The earliest evidence of mapping dates from about 2500 B.C., in Babylonia, where cadastral surveys were made on clay tablets and used in taxation (1.3). Maps were used in a similar way in ancient Egypt and by the Aztecs.

Decoration and Symbolism

Besides their purely utilitarian functions, maps have served decorative and symbolic purposes since ancient times. Sometimes maps were ornaments in illuminated manuscripts of the Middle Ages (1.4). Large, beautiful ones, such as the Ebstorf and Hereford maps, were used as altarpieces in cathedrals (2.10). The Ducal Palace in Venice once contained a room called the "Sala delle due mappe," decorated on all four walls with map murals by Giacomo Gastaldi in 1549-1550. And today we often see large maps used to decorate interiors of public buildings.

Propaganda

Maps can symbolize the character of a place and its people or the power of a country; they can also serve as propaganda. Since people generally believe maps are accurate guides to the unknown, their great power can be used as well to mislead or to misinform in the hands of the artful. Frederick the Great, for example, had maps of Silesia printed with erroneous information in order to confound his enemies. Nearly every country has produced propaganda or political maps to impress others with its power or strategic position (9.17).

Simulation

Simulation of real-world experience is still another function of maps. Special kinds of maps are used to train navigators, pilots, or soldiers to give them the feeling of "being there" without the costs and risks of the real world. Computer fly-through maps present the pilot with all the data and images of the actual airspace over an airport in order to practice takeoffs and landings (10.2). Computerized movie maps enable military personnel to become familiar with unknown enemy territory and to rehearse various tactics (10.1). A walk-through model of a city, reducing distances from miles to feet, yet preserving the three-dimensional aspect, can make immediate and vivid the problems to be faced in urban planning and redevelopment (10.6).

How Do We Use A Map?

The Map and the User

The user of a map may be anyone—he may be planning, predicting, relocating, comparing, traveling, or just trying to visualize a verbal description. Whatever he is doing, he will have certain goals and needs and certain levels of skill and experience in using maps. In addition, he will have an internal, mental map of the environment, however primitive or inaccurate, based upon his past experiences with it and with other maps and information sources. Our mental maps consist of more than geographic data; they may include information about distances, travel times, danger points, social values, driving procedures; or they may be simply a muddle of images elicited by a verbal description of, say, cease-fire lines running from unknown point to unknown point.

Success in using a map, then, is in a large measure determined by the congruence of the map with the needs, skills, and knowledge of its user. A map for children must take into account their limited experience with both maps and the environment and their relative difficulty with abstractions (5.1). It should be simple and direct, using as few learned conventions as possible. Maps for the blind obviously must

1.3
Ancient Babylonian Map
The earliest known map, this clay fragment, 7 centimeters wide, was part of a cadastral survey used for taxation. A river runs from the bottom to the top, flanked by mountains. The fragment was found at Nuzi near Kirkuk in northern Mesopotamia, twenty miles north of Babylon, and dates from the dynasty of Sargon of Akkad, c. 2500 B.C. *Courtesy of Harvard Semitic Museum.*

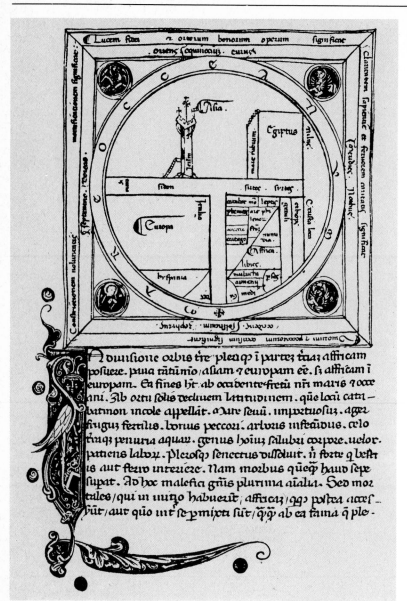

1.4
Illuminated T-in-O Map
Medieval maps were often
more ornamental and symbolic
than functional, as in this deco-
rative T-in-O map from a four-
teenth-century Sallust manu-
script, now in the Biblioteca
Marciana, Venice. *Leo Bagrow,
R. A. Skelton,* Meister der
Kartographie *(Berlin:* © *1973
Safari Verlag).*

be nonvisual; most likely they will be tactile or auditory or even both (4.45, 4.46, 4.47, 10.10). They must
use orientation cues that are meaningful to the
blind—not the visible landmarks of the sighted but the
feel of paving textures or slopes or walls, or sounds
that reveal spatial character and activity. For each map
user a specific set of map needs can be identified.

The Map and the Milieu
    Just as the map must be suited to the
user, so it must be congruent with the environment it
portrays. Most maps convey information about the
earth's surface, often in connection with other information such as weather, social facts, road networks,
ocean currents, vegetation. All this information must
be presented accurately and understandably. To do
this, the map must use a language that the user can
comprehend. A travel or training map especially must
accurately represent the environment mapped so that
the user can make valid connections between the
map and the real world. Maps fail when users cannot
find needed information, cannot "read" the map's language, or cannot relate the map to the real world; the
user becomes upset, disoriented, lost.

    Symbolism, orientation, and scale are
some elements of map language. Somehow the real
features of the environment must be represented on
the map—by lines, circles, stars, colors, textures, pictograms, whatever. The mapmaker must make these
symbols clear, accurate, and understandable. The
symbols used are usually set out somewhere on the
map *legend*, which tells the map user what this vo-
cabulary means.

    Orientation of the map tells how to relate
the map to the earth. Convention has determined that
north is usually at the top of a two-dimensional map,
although historically east, or sometimes south or
west, was uppermost. This convention can become
too rigid; as we shall see, a change in orientation can
often provide a better sense of the mapped environment.

    The *scale* of the map indicates its size in
relation to the environment portrayed. Obviously, a
map must reduce the spatial dimensions of the earth.
Thus, a given unit of measurement, such as an inch or
a centimeter on the map, stands for a larger unit on
the earth, such as a mile or kilometer. Scale is particularly important when time and distance are critical, as
in travel or military operations. Maps made without
scale can lead to misconceptions about the size, importance, or accessibility of places, and the distances
between them.

Scales generally are of three types: *graphic,* where a given line segment is equal to a particular distance (——————— equals 1 mile); *proportional,* where a unit on the map is some fraction of like units on the earth (1 : 250,000); or *inch-to-mile,* where a given numerical measure equals another measure on the earth (1 inch = 100 miles). Graphic scales remain valid when the map is enlarged or reduced, while proportional and inch-to-mile scales must be adjusted if the map changes size. A map is said to be *large-scale* when a small earth area appears quite large on the map; it is *small-scale* when it shows a large geographic area in a small space. The scale system of determining distance on maps is sometimes not valid or at least is difficult to calculate. Scales may fail on maps of vast territories or of the whole earth because of distortions inherent in map projections. On the Mercator projection, for example, areas near the poles expand far beyond their actual size. Irregular, complex road patterns cannot be measured accurately for travel distance without an opisometer (map meter). Similarly, route distances in moutainous regions cannot be determined easily by studying a flat topographic map. Here, a time-distance map is valuable (8.4). The vertical dimension is obviously difficult to represent on flat maps; contour lines, hatch lines or hachures, and shading are some methods used.

The Process of Map Use

Map use, then, can be conceived as a three-way process of communication between the *user,* who has particular needs, skills, and conceptions; the *map,* which represents a spatial or temporal pattern of places and qualities of the real world; and the *real world* itself.

Why do many people find maps baffling and all but unusable? Usually it is because they cannot connect the map with the environment the map represents. The lines, symbols, pictures, words, or numbers are a puzzle that seems unrelated to the path and scene before them. It may be that their map-reading skills are inadequate, or it may be that the map is presented in too abstract a language, or it may also be that the intuitive or conceptual leap required to relate an abstract, small-scale representation to the real world is difficult.

In using a map, especially for travel, a person must think at both the abstract level of the map and the concrete level of the real world and continuously make mental connections between them. We must first establish a point of reference or connection between the world and the map. Where am I now? We search the map for the orientation cues we see before us—place-names, landmarks, hills, rivers, railroad tracks—or, vice versa, we search the environment for the features shown on the map and at the same time seek to understand the scale of the map. And we must relate the orientation of the entire map to the direction we are going. For the ground traveler this is often perplexing, since what we see in the environment is a perspective view, but what we see on the map is usually the view from above. Then we must locate our destination, which usually isn't going to be visible until we get there, but must be found on the map in order to plot a route to it. Following that route means frequent checking back and forth from map to milieu for cues to confirm that we are still on the right path. When the map fails to match what we see, we become concerned, study the map and environment, and carefully search for additional cues. Backup cues help here; redundant information on the map is very reassuring.

When a map is used for analysis or planning or prediction, the process of use is somewhat different. Here the fit between the geographic points and the map is usually not as important; indeed, too much local information may interfere with one's aim. The need is rather for maps that facilitate comparison of data. Ideal maps for this purpose allow the user to select the variables he wishes to study and eliminate extraneous information. Maps for comparison should usually be at the same scale and in the same "language"; maps for the study of change should show the same data at several points in time. The ideal map for analysis and planning should allow the user to add his own input—to summarize, annotate, manipulate, or add new data. Computer technology has greatly increased the potential of analytical maps by permitting user selection and manipulation of map data.

Design Characteristics of Successful Maps

A map should be suited to the needs of its users. No one map can serve the needs of all users. The best maps are directed toward specific groups and are tailored to their needs. Knowing what to exclude is difficult but important—the unsuccessful map tries to present too much information. The purpose of the map must be narrowly and precisely defined and then every bit of data that is not essential to this purpose must be strictly excluded.

A map should be easy to use. The ideal map requires a minimum of special skills or learning time, and should be as culture-free as possible. This criterion is becoming more difficult to meet, as maps become more scientific and make use of abstruse technical data and jargon. Still, simplicity of use should be a guiding principle. Also, the map designer should be concerned not only with the verbal and graphic language of the map but with the convenience of the medium the map is presented in. For example, with paper maps one would be concerned with size, folding, storage, and handling. With a computer-video map, ease of understanding and using the controls and the minimizing of visual fatigue are important considerations.

Maps should be accurate, presenting information without error, distortion, or misrepresentation. When a new map is made, data should be checked for accuracy as much as possible rather than simply lifted from older maps, as is often the case. Similarly, spatial relations—particularly time distances—between data points should not be distorted. Highway maps often exaggerate road patterns in congested areas simply to accommodate the tangle of lines and words, a practice that misleads and confuses the map user. Exceptions to the criterion of accuracy, of course, are maps that mislead intentionally, such as those made for propaganda purposes, personal image maps that represent individual geographic experience as shaped by one's own values and use patterns, or maps that are purely decorative.

The fit between the map and the environment represented should be good. The map user should be able to connect map to environment and environment to map. Thus, prominent orientation features or important routes and places one actually sees should be equally prominent in the map and should be represented in such a way as to require a minimum of translation. To meet this criterion, the mapmaker should study how map users see the environment in question. Just as different types of users require certain mapping techniques, so do different environments. This criterion is particularly important in travel and orientation maps, military maps, or construction and development maps, where action in the environment is tied directly to the map. More remote environment-map connections are less dependent upon the requirement of fit, but cannot totally escape it.

The language of the map should relate to the elements or qualities represented. For example, in a graphic map, symbols and colors should use a commonly understood graphic language. Patterns and symbols for areas of vegetation should look more like trees or plants than water or desert. Major highways should look major, large towns should look large, important landmarks should look important. Totally abstract symbols are particularly difficult because, having no conventional associations, they require more time to learn and interpret and can be forbidding to the uninitiated map user. Even abstract shapes often suggest elements of the real world; these associations should be considered in developing a symbol system.

A map should be clear, legible, and attractive. In a graphic map, the language should be made up of compatible symbols, colors, or pictures that will work with, rather than against, each other. Similarly, style and size of typefaces should be selected to promote clarity and ease of use. Scale, point of view, and orientation are also important design decisions. Main bodies of information should be distinct and clear. Color is often used to convey information, but it may be used simply for decorative purposes, and distraction or confusion may result. Since color is so compelling, often taking precedence over shape or pattern, words or numbers, it must be used with great care and should communicate truly significant information, with its visual dominance proportional to its informational importance. A designer should remember that the general public can reliably distinguish only a handful of colors, perhaps five or six.

Many maps would ideally permit interaction with the user, allowing change, updating, or personalization. Interactive maps allow the user to focus on a particular area in more detail, to add personal observations to a map, or to study one or two types of information, letting everything else drop out or become subdued. The traditional printed map is made interactive only with difficulty and imagination: informational overlays or allowance for the user to make notations are possibilities. The potential of truly interactive maps has only recently been realized with developments in computer and video technology that promise new and intriguing directions for maps of the future.

Besides theorizing about what the ideal map might be, mapmakers and designers can learn from study of actual maps. In the following chapters, we shall examine an array of mapping techniques designed for varied users and purposes. Beginning with a look at maps of other eras and cultures, we will be particularly interested in how maps have been made to fulfill particular needs. Our aim throughout is to stimulate creative map design and use through understanding how maps function and the range of choices available to the mapmaker.

2.1
Coastal Profile
Coastline elevations or ''recognition views'' were often included in sailing charts and manuals as navigation aids. This one, dated 1538, is from Pierre Garce, *Le grand routier de la mèr*, Paris. *Leo Bagrow, R. A. Skelton*, Meister der Kartographie (*Berlin:* © *1973 Safari Verlag).*

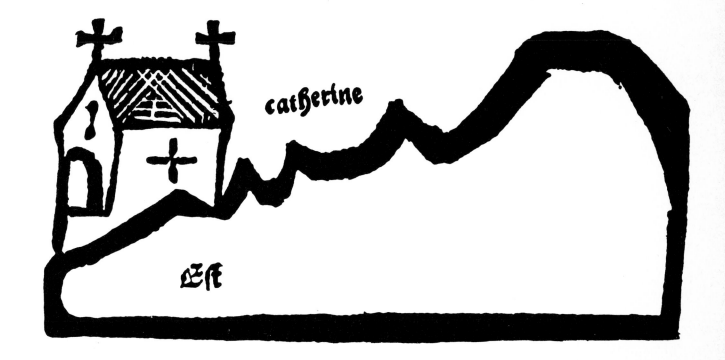

Maps and World View

Maps are cultural mirrors. Since ancient times they have helped man organize this ideas and activities and at the same time have reflected the thought and technology of the time. From naive representations of the flat earth to sophisticated satellite or computer maps, art, technology, and culture unite in the making of a map. They express the values and geographic knowledge of the mapmaker and the society of which he is a part.

The mapmaker puts on his map those places and references that he feels are most relevant to the map user, because he knows of them, uses them, or values them symbolically. In the past, distortions of continents and bodies of water reflected mistaken theories of geographic relationships, limited exploration, and lack of long-distance surveying techniques. Then and now, map inaccuracies and distortions may express cultural values as well. A body of water that is rather small but highly valued may be exaggerated in size to communicate its cultural importance. The mapmaker's familiar territory was typically featured more prominently and in more detail than other areas of his town or country. Features that he used for orientation might have been stressed, and confusing areas might have been given less detail because of the mapmaker's failure to grasp them. Scientific studies have repeatedly confirmed this characteristic of mental mapping. Local exaggeration is even found at the scale of whole countries, as in the seventeenth-century maps of France. Louis XIV is said to have told his cartographer, Jean Dominique Cassini, that his new and more accurate map of France, drawn on the floor of the Paris Observatory in 1682, had taken more away from France than had been added by all the king's conquests!

2.2
Dutch Map of Africa
Dutch cartographers of the sixteenth and seventeenth centuries were known for their inventiveness. When information was lacking, they often filled the empty spaces with imaginary place-names, rivers, or monsters. Africa, supposedly the kingdom of the legendary ruler Prester John, was the locus for much of this creative geography. *Abraham Ortelius (1527 - 1598),* Epitome Theatri Orteliani, *1595. Courtesy of the Trustees of the Boston Public Library.*

Some early maps contain considerable fanciful geography. Seventeenth-century Dutch cartographers, for example, had the habit of filling unknown areas with invented information—towns, rivers, monsters, or strange savages (2.2). Thus Africa, one of the less explored continents at that time, appears to be one of the more developed areas of the world! It was in reference to such maps that Jonathan Swift wrote:

> *So geographers, in Afric maps,*
> *With savage pictures fill their gaps,*
> *And o'er unhabitable downs*
> *Place elephants for want of towns.*

When imagining or drawing maps of our own neighborhood or town, all of us distort the geography, usually unintentionally, reflecting our own patterns, of travel, activity, and values (see 9.18, for example). Intuitive mapping expresses a great deal more than just geographic knowledge. Our entire social and psychological response to our environmental experience colors our interpretation of geography. Favorite spots grow in size and detail and are represented as much closer to us, while relatively unknown or disliked areas shrink, recede into the distance, are devoid of information. The proverbial conceptual map of Bostonians focuses on Massachusetts Bay and the giant hook of Cape Cod (2.3). New England is pictured in great detail, but the rest of the country has, as the map itself warns, "some inaccuracies." The Californian's view has similar distortions, including a very parochial sun. And imagine what a map by a Texan would look like! Such geographic caricatures are amusing, but contain bits of truth.

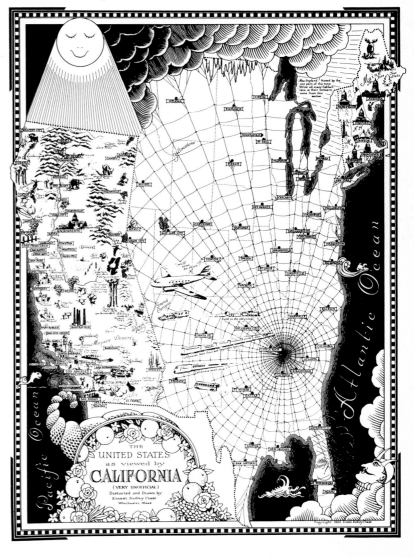

2.3
Mental Maps
Geographic reality is distorted in our minds by our experiences and values. While some regions of our mental maps grow in importance, others shrink or completely disappear. These satirical maps make the point that the United States of the Bostonian is quite different from that of the Californian. *J. B. Post, An Atlas of Fantasy (Baltimore: Mirage Press, Ltd., 1973): "A Bostonian's Idea of the USA," copyright by Daniel K. Wallingford. "The United States as Viewed by California," copyright 1940 by Ernest Dudley Chase.*

Just as maps reflect our culture, they have the great power to shape our concepts of the world. How large is it? What shape is it? What are its parts? What countries or cities are near or far, easy or difficult to reach? What are their relative sizes, power, wealth? Maps substitute for experience, particularly at the scale of continents, world, or universe where real experience is difficult or impossible. Our conceptions of the geography of continents and oceans, for example, are largely developed from seeing them on maps, not through firsthand travel. If we traveled the length and breadth of Italy, we would not be aware of its boot shape, but once we see it on a map, it is a strong and compelling image. Concepts of neighbors or power relations, of national strength or security can be greatly affected by choice of viewpoint in a map. The scientist Athelstan Spilhaus, born in South Africa, so resented seeing maps that always had the North Pole on top that as a child he pinned world maps upside down on his wall or stood on his head to look at them. Equally disturbing is the sense that north-flowing rivers must go uphill, since north is almost always at the top of the map. And how many adults seem forever disoriented because the map in their elementary school was on the wrong wall in relation to real world directions?

Our own difficulties with intuitively producing accurate maps based on firsthand experience alone, without measurement or knowledge of the correct map image of an area, demonstrate the historical difficulties people have had in comprehending and representing the world.

Changing Images of the Earth
Egocentric Disk Maps

Before the size, shape, and geography of the earth were known, maps usually portrayed only a small territory centered on the location of the mapmaker and were based on his own personal experience and knowledge. His country was most of his world, and he put most information in the area he knew best—his own locale. Representational systems were often mixed, combining plan, elevation, or perspective in one map. The few known foreign places appeared on the periphery along with legendary places and strange or terrifying creatures. These were often surrounded by a ring of ocean that defined the end of known territory and led into darkness.

This egocentric world view is expressed in an ancient Babylonian map of the universe (c. 500 B.C.) inscribed on a clay tablet with Babylon shown in the center as a disk floating in the sea (2.4). Similarly, in accordance with Taoist beliefs that China occupied 1/81 of the earth's surface and was surrounded by ocean, Taoist maps of China show it as a disk surrounded by alternating, concentric rings of ocean and land. Even into the seventeenth and eighteenth centuries the concentric ring concept is found; in a Korean map, known territory is surrounded by a ring inhabited by mythical people and animals (2.5).

2.4
Babylonian World Map
In this Babylonian clay map from the sixth century B.C. the world is shown as a disk surrounded by a ring of water. *Leo Bagrow, R. A. Skelton,* Meister der Kartographie.

*Philosophers' Earth Concepts: Pillars,
Cylinders, Planes, Spheres*

Maps in the classical world reflected the
orientation of the ancient Greeks, who considered geography to be a part of philosophy. Largely schematic,
maps were used mainly for theoretical discussions of
the world. In fact, they were so lacking in specific data
that they were ridiculed by the historian Herodotus
and by practical-minded sailors.

The Greeks developed numerous theories
about the form of the earth. Homer speculated that
the earth was a plane disk surrounded by the con-
stantly moving ocean-river Oceanus, while heaven
was an inverted hemisphere resting on the edge of
the disk and held up by tall, invisible pillars entrusted
to Atlas. Hyperion, the sun god, rose daily from
Oceanus. Thales, too, conceived of the earth as a
disk, but one floating in water rather than fixed and
surrounded by it. Anaximander of Miletus, an astronomer and geographer, believed the earth was a cylin-
der, with the habitable part a disk resting on top and
the Aegean Sea in the center. On the other hand,
Anaximenes, a student of Anaximander, held that the
earth was a rectangle supported by compressed air;
in fact, he believed everything was made of air of
varying densities.

These fanciful notions were dispelled,
however, by a developing world view that coupled
philosophy with scientific observation. Indeed, it was
the Greeks who laid the foundations for modern
mapping—the concept of the spherical earth, lines of
latitude and longitude, and surveying. Pythagoras
(c. 523 B.C.) is considered by many to be the first to
have conceived of the earth as a sphere, although we
do not know how he reached this conclusion. About
350 B.C. Aristotle formulated arguments to prove the
earth was a sphere, basing his thinking on observation
of the partial eclipse of the moon and the fact that
certain stars visible in Egypt and Cyprus were not visible farther north.

Orientation

In the fourth century B.C. Dicaearcus of
Messana, Sicily, a follower of Aristotle, introduced the
scientific approach to mapping when he suggested
the need for an orienting line on world maps. His line
ran east-west through Gibraltar and Rhodes. Following his precedent, Eratosthenes of Cyrene (c. 276-
196 B.C.), head of the library at Alexandria for Ptolemy
III, added several more lines—seven parallels and
seven meridians, including a meridian passing through
Alexandria. These were not spaced equally and simply

**2.5
Korean World Map**
Similar to Buddhist and Taoist
maps, this Korean map of the
seventeenth or eighteenth century depicts the world as an island surrounded by a ring of water and then an outer ring of
land inhabited by forbidding
mythical creatures. *Leo
Bagrow, R. A. Skelton,* Meister
der Kartographie.

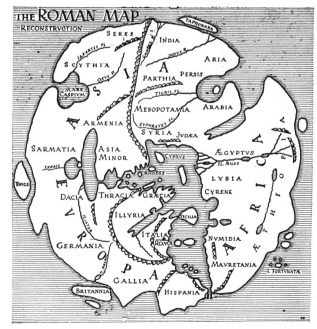

**2.6
Roman World Map**
Romans of the first century B.C.
thought of the Roman Empire
as occupying most of the world.
Rome was at the center, with
Asia at the top, Europe to the
left, and Africa to the right.
Erwin Raisz, General Cartography *(New York, Toronto, London: McGraw-Hill, 1948).*

ran through familiar places. Such abstract references were a considerable advance over total reliance on topographic landmarks, especially in open sea or vast undifferentiated deserts or forests. But both Hipparchus the astronomer (c. 150 B.C.) and Strabo the geographer (c. 63 B.C.-A.D. 24) criticized the arbitrary nature of Eratosthenes' reference lines. In his diatribe, *Against Eratosthenes,* Hipparchus became the first to suggest equally spaced parallels and meridians, and went even further in proposing that these lines be located by astronomical measurement.

North was not standardized at the top for centuries. The tendency was to put the direction that was most important at the top. The Arabs liked south at the top, while some early American maps put west up. Roman and medieval maps put east—the Orient—at the top. Thus, we now say we are ''oriented'' or discuss the ''orientation'' of a map or view. It was not until the fifteenth century that north orientation of maps appeared, and it did not become universal until centuries later.

Eratosthenes carried the spherical notion further by calculating the size of the earth correctly within 14 percent by measuring the distance between Alexandria and Syenê (Aswan)—500 miles—and then the sun's angle at midday at both points during summer solstice. This arc turned out to be 1/50th of a circle. He concluded that the earth's circumference was fifty times 500 miles, or 25,000 miles, and thus he formed the basis for cartography based on surveying.

Globes

According to literary references, the first globes appear to have been made soon after the ideas of Aristotle and his followers became known. One early example, a large globe two meters in diameter supported on the shoulders of Atlas, is in the Museum of Naples. The globe probably dates from the fourth century B.C. and may have been made by or for the astronomer and philosopher Eudoxus (d. 386 B.C.). The philosopher Crates of Mallus is known to have made a globe in about 150 B.C. that reflected the Greek preoccupation with abstract philosophy. Since

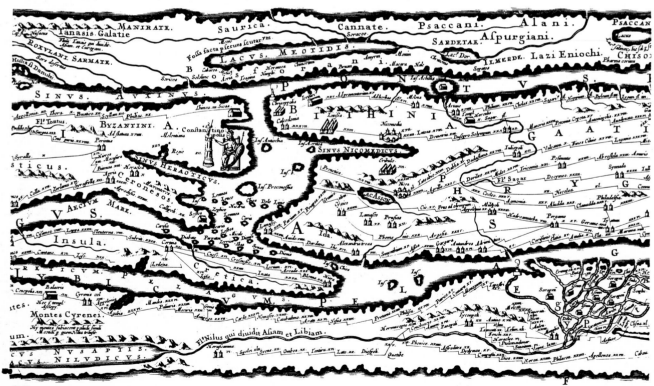

2.7
Tabula Peutingeriana,
A Roman Road Map
The imperial highways of Rome, from Britain to the Ganges, are shown on this 1-by-21-foot parchment cartogram or strip map, probably copied during the Middle Ages from an original dating from A.D. 250-500. Although geographic relationships are inaccurate, the map includes 5,000 place-names and gives distances between points. *Lloyd A. Brown,* The Story of Maps *(Boston: Little, Brown and Co., 1949). From the Peabody Collection, Enoch Pratt Free Library, Baltimore.*

the known world was such a small part of the globe's surface, Crates added three more imaginary continents for the sake of balance and symmetry, thus anticipating—unwittingly—the discovery of the Americas, Australia, and Antarctica.

Route Maps

Few maps of the Roman Empire exist, but medieval copies and text descriptions suggest an egocentric world view, similar to early Babylonian and Oriental examples and prompted, perhaps, by Rome's sense of its political importance. Rome and the Mediterranean appear in the center, surrounded by a ring composed of Europe on the left, Asia—the east—on the top, and Africa on the right. The Roman Empire occupies four-fifths of the area, while India, Scythia, and Sarmatia (Russia) are disproportionately small (2.6). A map like this was carved in marble under the direction of Marcus Agrippa (63-12 B.C.) and was placed near the Roman Forum as a symbol of Rome's power.

At the same time, in contrast to the Greek theoretical approach to mapping, Roman cartography was generally practical and suited to business and military applications. Although filled with fairly accurate and plentiful detail, the maps were rather weak in overall structure. The outstanding surviving Roman map and one of the chief sources of knowledge of Roman cartography is the Tabula Peutingeriana, developed between A.D. 250 and 500 (2.7). The map is named after its sixteenth-century collector-owner Konrad Peutinger of Augsburg and is probably a medieval copy of the original. A cartogram, or strip map, on parchment, one foot wide by twenty-one feet long, it shows the imperial highways from Britain to the Ganges River and gives distances between points, along with five thousand place-names. Greek latitude and longitude are ignored and land and road patterns bear little graphic relation to the actual distances given.

2.8
Ptolemy's World
This sixteenth-century woodcut is a copy of a map in *Geographica* by Claudius Ptolemy, keeper of the library at Alexandria in the second century A.D. Ptolemy's atlas was influential for over fifteen hundred years, despite some basic geographic errors. This edition of the atlas, edited by Michael Servetus and published in Lyon in 1535, was so objectionable to John Calvin that he ordered many copies burned. Early editions contained the heretical statement that the Holy Land, according to travelers, was not as fertile as generally believed. *Courtesy of the Trustees of the Boston Public Library.*

Scientific Mapping

Claudius Ptolemy, an Alexandrian astronomer and keeper of the library, made one of the great contributions to cartography with his *Geographica* in the second century A.D. (2.8). Following Hipparchus, Ptolemy used a regular placement of latitude and longitude and a systemic map projection, and located several places through astronomical observation. Although an original manuscript has not been found, several copies or amplified editions exit. Books II to VIII contain over eight thousand place-names with latitudes and longitudes, but few of these locations were mapped according to scientific observation. Book VIII presents principles of cartography, projections, and astronomical observation, and describes two conic projections. Most editions of *Geographica* contain a world map plus twenty-six detailed maps. *Geographica* was the most complete and accurate world atlas for over fifteen hundred years, but two major errors ran through Ptolemy's work, causing problems for the next several centuries. First, he believed the universe was earth-centered—that the sun literally "rose" and "set," as we still unthinkingly say. Second, he rejected Eratosthenes' measurement of the earth, accepting instead that of Strabo and the Greek astronomer Poseidonius and thus underestimating its size by 25 percent.

Theological Views of the World Map

During the Middle Ages Christian theology dominated cartography. The advanced Greek theories of the earth's shape and mapping were forgotten, along with Ptolemy's atlas. Not unlike Roman maps, medieval maps were often in the "T-in-O" or "T-O" form. "T-O" stands for *orbis terrarum,* or "circle of the earth," from "It is he that sitteth upon the circle of the earth . . ." (Isaiah 40:22). The form is also referred to as "wheel" or "Noachid"—the latter named for the biblical division of the world into three parts, one for each son of Noah. In these maps the earth appears as a circle divided by a T (2.9). East and Asia or the Orient are usually at the top, with Paradise sometimes at the top center. Europe is on the lower left, with Africa on the lower right, divided by the Mediterranean Sea. The Don and Nile rivers form the top of the T. Jerusalem and the Holy Land appear in the center in

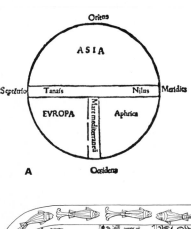

A

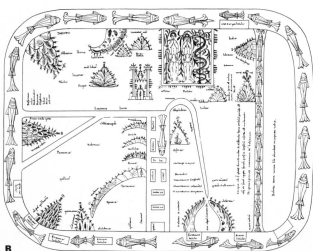

B

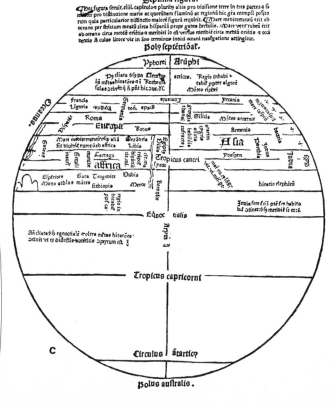

C

2.9
T-in-O and Zone Maps

Christian theology dominated cartography during the Middle Ages. In the T-in-O maps, east was at the top with Paradise in the top center. Europe was on the lower left and Africa on the lower right, separated by the Mediterranean. The Don and Nile rivers formed the top of the

T. Zone maps followed the Greek precedent of dividing the world according to *klimata*, or climate zones.

A
Zacharias, Orbis breviarium, *Florence, 1493 (Leo Bagrow, R. A. Skelton,* Meister der Kartographie)

B
A rectangular version of the T-in-O map by Beatus, a Benedictine monk, A.D. 787 (Lloyd A. Brown, The Story of Maps)

C
This zone map appeared in Ymago mundi *of Pierre d'Ailly,*

Louvain, c. 1483 (Leo Bagrow, R. A. Skelton, Meister der Kartographie)

D
Rudimentum novitiorium, *Lübeck, 1475 (Leo Bagrow, R. A. Skelton,* Meister der Kartographie)

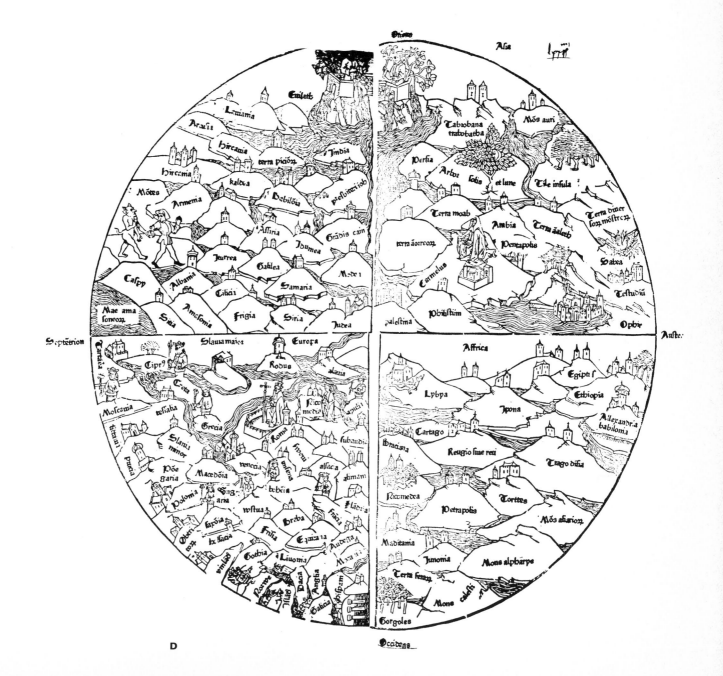

D

accordance with the Bible: "This is Jerusalem: I have set it in the midst of the nations and countries that are round about her" (Ezekiel 5:5). Such maps were largely of symbolic, theological, and ornamental value and would be useless for travel or geographic study.

Zone maps, another medieval map form, follow a Greek precedent. The earth is roughly divided into parallel zones, *klimata,* according to climate (2.9).

One of the finest medieval maps, the Hereford Map, was made about 1275 by Richard of Haldingham in Lincolnshire. Done in colors and gold on parchment, four by five feet, it decorated the altar of Hereford Cathedral, where it remains today (2.10). The map is in modified T-in-O form with east at the top and Jerusalem in the center. It contains some information from the writings of early geographers, along with Christian iconography, pictures, and descriptions of monsters and marvels. Gog and Magog, the biblical giants and personifications of evil, find a place in many of these medieval maps. Scale and lines of latitude and longitude are absent. A similiar but later map, the Ebstorf map of 1484, incorporates the world in the body of Christ.

Among the most practical medieval maps were the guides to sacred shrines and historic sites of the Holy Land for religious pilgrims (2.11). These were frequently route maps, early precedents for modern strip maps, showing the route, landmarks, and distances. Often, however, they were not in conventional map form but were simply lists of place-names and distances.

While Europe was preoccupied with religious maps, Arab cartographers carried on Greek traditions, making several refinements, and continued to study Ptolemy, which had been translated into Arabic. Perhaps the most important early Arabic map is a world map made in 1154 by the Arabic cartographer al-Idrisi for the court of Roger II, the Norman king of Sicily (2.12). As in most Islamic maps, south is at the top. Asia is shown in some detail, and the Caspian and Aral seas are correctly delineated.

2.10
Hereford Map
An elaborate T-in-O map, made about 1275 by Richard of Haldingham, decorated the altar of Hereford Cathedral. Actual geography is combined with legendary, historical, and religious elements. It includes only three continents and one ocean. The vivid pictorial presentation was well suited to the largely illiterate population of that time. The map is in gold and colors on parchment and measures 4 by 5 feet. *Photograph by kind permission of the Dean and Chapter of Hereford Cathedral.*

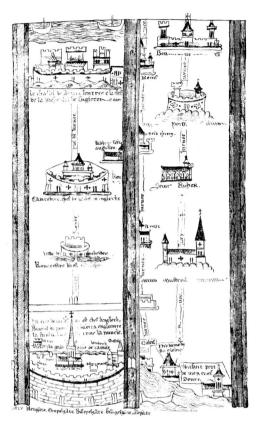

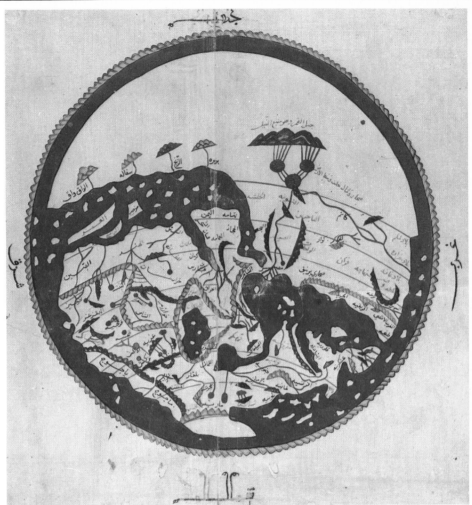

2.11
Medieval Road Map
Religious pilgrims in the Middle Ages used guides such as this strip map on journeys to the Holy Land. The route begins in London; Dover Castle is in the upper left and the English Channel is in the lower right. *Lloyd A. Brown,* The Story of Maps. *From the Peabody Collection, Enoch Pratt Free Library, Baltimore.*

2.12
Map of al-Idrisi
The Arab cartographer al-Idrisi made this world map for Roger II, the Norman king of Sicily, in 1154. The map served as a key to a large silver planisphere, also made by al-Idrisi. Zones are shown by curved parallels and south is at the top. This map is contained in a copy of al-Idrisi's geography dating from 1533. The manuscript was brought from Syria to England by the orientalist Edward Pococke (1604-1691). *Bodleian Library, Oxford University (MS. Pococke 375, folio 3v-4r).*

Seafaring: Portolani and Peripli

In contrast to the inventive maps of the Middle Ages were the *portolani* or "harbor-finding" charts, probably first developed by Genoese sailors during the second half of the thirteenth century (2.13). Made with the help of the magnetic compass, which came into general use at that time, the charts were far more accurate than earlier sailing maps based only on experience and measurement. On portolan charts north was usually at the top, one influence of the magnetic compass. They are characterized by myriad radiating and intersecting lines—rhumb lines or compass roses—which were used in establishing the course of a route from port to port. The "carte Pisani," or Pisan chart (c. 1300), is the oldest surviving example of such a map. Although inaccurate, it was the best navigating map available for more than three hundred years. Portolan charts were supplemented by *peripli,* or "coast pilots"—books of descriptions of directions, landmarks, danger points, tides, winds, distances between ports, routes, and other orientation features to aid sailors. This tradition continues today in the *Coast Pilots* of the United States National Ocean Survey.

The World Map Expands

Geographic Discovery, the Magnetic Compass, and Printing

Perhaps the most significant change in man's conception of the earth occurred in the fifteenth century. Growing knowledge of the earth through exploration upset the logic of old maps and theories of the flat earth. Three major events stimulated new approaches to cartography. First, Ptolemy's *Geographica* was rediscovered, translated from Greek into Latin in 1410 by Jacobus Angelus de Scarparia, and printed in 1475 in Vicenza, causing a sensation in Italy. Second, the invention of printing and engraving made possible distribution of exact copies of maps. For the first time maps could be standardized and studied in a comparative manner. Before printing, maps were duplicated by copyists who introduced considerable variation and invention into each copy. No two maps were identical even if made by the

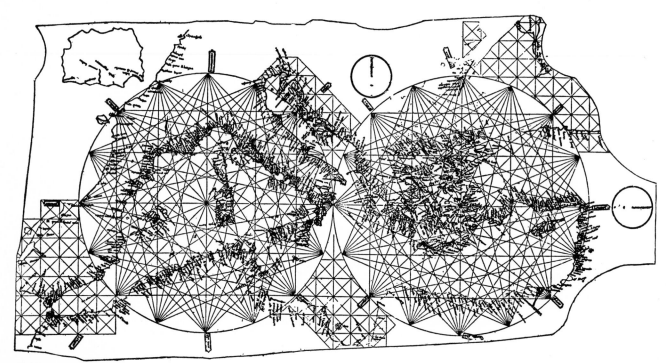

2.13
Portolan Chart
Genoese sailors probably developed the most accurate maps of the Middle Ages, the *portolani,* or sailing charts. The intersecting and radiating lines are rhumb lines, or courses, that connect various ports. *Erwin Raisz*, General Cartography.

same author or copyist. The third great contribution to fifteenth-century cartography was geographic discovery, which provided new data about the oceans, the continents, and the size and shape of the earth. Exploration was in turn made possible by the use of the compass and the development of new ships that could travel in the open sea for extended periods; previously, ships had been forced to follow coastlines. Particularly important were the Flemish karak and the Portuguese caravel—three-masted, decked ships, capable of holding provisions for several months, with rigging that allowed sailing in unfavorable winds and in open seas.

Discoveries about the earth have always found their best expression in map form. Of course, the spectacular event of the fifteenth century that changed the conception of the world, and hence the world map, was Columbus's discovery of America while he was searching for a western passage to the Indies (2.14). Erroneous geographic conceptions have sometimes led to new discoveries, as was Columbus's good fortune. Interestingly, it was probably just such an erroneous map that convinced Columbus there might be a western route to the Indies that would be shorter than going around Africa. Christopher and Bartolomeo Columbus, both chartmakers,

possessed a map by Paolo dal Pozzo Toscanelli (1397 -1482), a Florentine scholar, cosmographer, and physician. In 1474 King Alfonso V of Portugal had asked Toscanelli about the shortest sea route to India. Toscanelli provided the king with a map made in 1457, now called the Genoese map, accompanied by a letter in which he wrote:

> *I am sending His Majesty a map I have drawn, showing your coasts and islands, from which the way lies to the west, and the places one must come to. . . . Do not be surprised because I call the region of spices "western," whereas it is usually named "eastern"; for these regions can be reached by sailing due west. Therefore the straight lines drawn across the map show the distance from east to west. . . . (Leo Bagrow,* History of Cartography)

No one realized the extent of the Atlantic Ocean or that an entire continent might lie in the path to the west. The voyages of the Norsemen to North America in the eleventh century had either been forgotten or were unknown in southern Europe. If Ptolemy had not made a serious error in underestimating the size of the earth thirteen hundred years earlier, Columbus might not have believed in the western route to Asia.

2.14
Sketch Map by
Christopher Columbus
Columbus sketched this map of the northwest coast of Hispaniola in December 1492 on his first voyage to America. The only surviving map by him, it is in the collection of the Duke of Alba. *Leo Bagrow, R. A. Skelton,* Meister der Kartographie.

Vasco da Gama's discovery of a sea route to India around the Cape of Good Hope in 1498 and Balboa's discovery of the Pacific in 1513 added more new data to the world map. Ferdinand Magellan conceived of sailing around the world after studying charts that showed a strait between the southern tip of South America and Terra Australis. Had he known the size of the Pacific and how far south lay the strait, he might have been discouraged. With the completion of Magellan's three-year voyage around the world on September 8, 1522, the size of the oceans and the placement of the Americas were finally established and the useful life of Ptolemy's maps had come to an end.

Flattening the Spherical Earth: Mercator's Projection

As discoveries about the earth's geography accumulated, the need for a better way of representing the earth in two dimensions was urgent. Gerardus Mercator, born Gerhard Krämer in 1512 near Antwerp, developed the basis for modern, scientific cartography. A maker of maps, globes, astrolabes, and other instruments, he wished to produce a map that was more than artistic, one that was as accurate as possible and that gave a feeling of the earth's roundness. He was particularly interested in making a sailing chart where any straight line on the map would provide the sailor with a true course following compass directions. Mercator's solution to this mapping problem is now known as the "Mercator projection" and is still widely used in mapping today. Instead of relying on the antiquated maps of Ptolemy, he incorporated the new geographic data into a map of Europe in 1554 and a world map in 1569, both engraved on copper (2.15). When he died in 1594 he had begun work on a collection of maps that he called an "Atlas" —the first use of that term.

Measuring Longitude

A general concept of the earth's shape and size had been established, but it remained to develop accurate means for surveying and mapping whole countries, coastlines, and seas. The key would be to discover a means of determining longitude, which had been sought for two thousand years. For centuries sailors had sailed with uncertain knowledge of their east-west location, often causing great delay and sometimes casualty. Although latitude could be found by measuring the altitude of the sun and stars, determination of east-west postion required not only astronomical observation but an accurate clock. The method would be to compare local time, as determined by the position of sun and stars, with the time at the prime meridian, provided by the clock.

The need for measurement of longitude became urgent in 1493, when Pope Alexander VI issued the Bull of Demarcation to settle a conflict between Spain and Portugal. In this measure the Pope divided the "Western Ocean" with a meridian running from the North to the South Pole one hundred leagues from the Azores. The problem was that no one knew where the line was or how to establish it. At the end of the sixteenth century the question still had not been answered when Philip III of Spain offered a perpetual pension of six thousand ducats, a life pension of two thousand ducats, and a gratuity of a thousand more to the discoverer of longitude. The promise of this great reward produced many fantastic proposals but no solutions.

The key to solving the problem came in seventeenth-century France during the reign of Louis XIV (1638-1715) with scientific advances in time-keeping and astronomy. Louis XIV, who was an enthusiastic supporter of science through the encouragement of his adviser Jean Baptiste Colbert, built an observatory at Faubourg St. Jacques outside Paris. He also had two large elaborate globes, ten to fifteen feet in diameter—one of the earth, the other of the heavens—made by Père Vincenzo Coronelli (1650-1718), one of the great cartographers of the later Renaissance. In 1669 Jean Dominique Cassini, an Italian astronomer, came to work at the observatory (2.16). Through astronomical observation and use of a pendulum clock he and his associates were able for the first time to plot accurately the location of several French cities. In 1679 triangulation, or surveying of land along a meridian (Picard's meridian), was completed in France, providing an accurate baseline for measurement of the rest of the country (2.17). César François Cassini, grandson of Jean Dominique, completed the first scientific survey of France in 1744.

But the method of measuring longitude on land failed at sea, for the motion of pendulum clocks was upset by the ship's movement. It was not until 1773 that John Harrison, an English clockmaker, perfected after years of work a timepiece that functioned at sea. The ideal of Hipparchus and later of Ptolemy to locate accurately any place on earth—land or sea— was now realizable.

Mapping the Whole Earth

Beginning with Britain's Ordnance Survey in 1791, the rest of Europe followed France's lead and produced national surveys in the late eighteenth and early nineteenth centuries. During the second half of the nineteenth century Germany was the leader in scientific cartography. By the end of the nineteenth century all of Europe except for Russia was surveyed. Most of these surveys were administered by the armies, since accurate, large-scale maps were essential to the expanded military operations of the period. Still, it is estimated that even by 1885 less than one-ninth of the earth's surface had been surveyed. Only by the mid-twentieth century was the systematic mapping of Africa in progress. International mapping was difficult, not only because of the vast scale and cost of such an enterprise, but because it had political and defense implications. In fact, most accurate topographic maps were kept secret.

Aerial photography introduced yet another dimension to mapping, offering a maplike view of terrain without cumbersome surveying. Beginning with the first aerial balloon surveys by Aimé Laussedat in 1858 down to the airplane and satellite surveys of the twentieth century, new data became available to mapmakers and world mapping was easier to accomplish.

Remote sensing with radar or seismic and depth soundings has provided new geographic data of the ocean floor, impenetrable jungles, and the ice caps.

With each successive development in mapping techniques the earth has become less mysterious, more finite. Yet looking at a satellite view of the earth, small and fragile, floating in a dark void, we may feel much as ancient man must have felt, looking at his vaguely sketched map of the world—a small disk of land, surrounded by strange places and creatures, floating in a seemingly endless, unexplored sea. The frontiers of mapping have now moved from the earth to the moon, the planets, the universe. Despite the battery of techniques available, the mapmaker of today, as in times past, must have the wisdom to select the best methods for his purposes to make a map that is accurate and that speaks to its users.

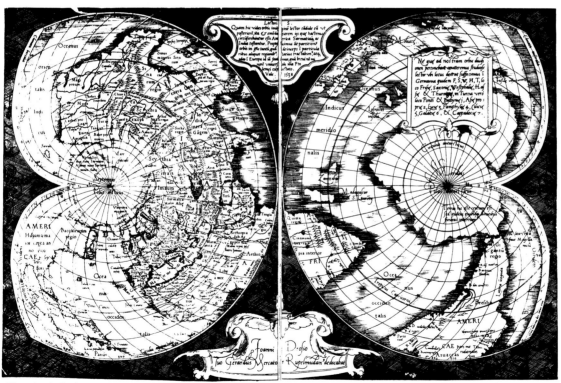

Mercator's Projection, 1538

Gerardus Mercator

2.15
Gerardus Mercator
Mercator, born in 1512 near Antwerp, developed a map projection still in use today. It was of particular value in sailing because a straight line on the map indicates a true course that can be followed without changing directions. Mercator's maps were more accurate than Pto-

lemy's and were based on the scientific and geographic knowledge of his era. The map shown here was done in 1538 and named the Americas for the first time. *Lloyd A. Brown*, The Story of Maps. *From the Peabody Collection, Enoch Pratt Free Library, Baltimore.*

2.16
Jean Dominique Cassini
Cassini, an Italian astronomer, worked at the Observatory of Paris during the reign of Louis XIV. Using his knowledge of astronomy, he accurately mapped the locations of several cities in France. *Lloyd A. Brown,* The Story of Maps. *From the Peabody Collection, Enoch Pratt Free Library, Baltimore.*

The Observatory of Paris

Jean Dominique Cassini

2.17
Triangulation of France
The triangulation, or surveying, of France along Picard's meridian in 1679 established an accurate baseline for scientific mapping of the rest of the country. France was the first country to complete a national survey. *Lloyd A. Brown,* The Story of Maps. *From the Peabody Collection, Enoch Pratt Free Library, Baltimore.*

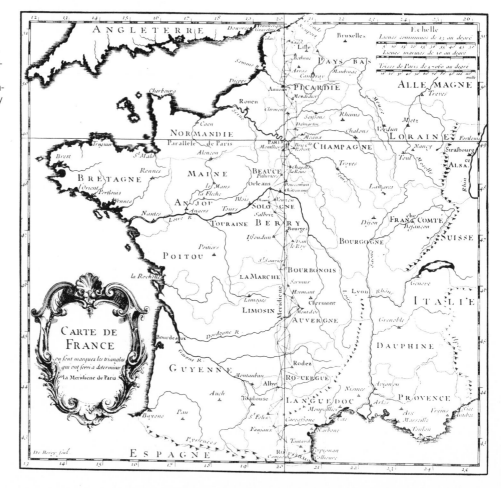

Part II
Mapping Techniques

3.1
Computer-Generated
Topographic Map
In this example of computer
mapping, a line grid has been
superimposed on a topographic
map. Elevation data at each intersection point were fed into
the computer. The resulting
map depicts topography by
means of a warped grid. In this
case the vertical dimension appears to have been exaggerated. Maps such as this are not
limited to topography but could
show spatial distribution and intensity of any variable, for example, population or productivity.
Experimental Map Program,
U.S. Army Engineer Topo-
graphic Laboratories, Fort
Belvoir, VA.

3 Land Form

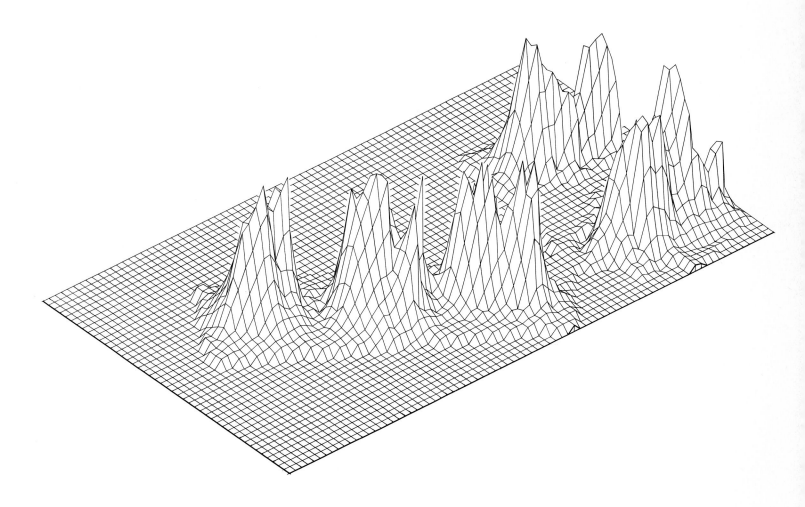

A major problem in the development of mapping has been that of representing the three-dimensional earth in two dimensions. Of course, the problem can be avoided by mapping on a globe—the only format in which distance, area, and shape can be accurate to scale—but a globe has disadvantages, too. It can usefully show only one half of the earth at a time from one vantage point, and it is difficult to store and transport unless it is inflatable. Areas cannot be represented at a large enough scale to show detail without making an impossibly large globe. Consequently, numerous ingenious projection schemes have been devised for flattening the skin of the peeled earth-orange (3.2). Some projections attempt to maintain the shapes or areas of land masses, some present ocean and seas accurately, some retain accuracy only in east-west distances.

All projections are compromises. Mapmakers and users should take care to use that projection which best suits their needs and makes the compromises with as few errors as possible. The wrong projection can be misleading, causing users to make serious mistakes in interpretation and mental image. The common Mercator projection, for example, has left countless students with the impression that Greenland is as large as South America.

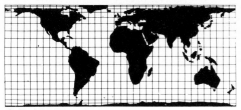
Cylindrical equal-area projection

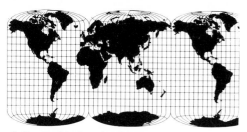
Gall cylindrical projection

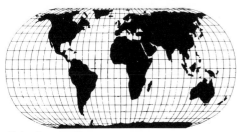
Eckert projection

Guillaume Postel projection

Sinusoidal equal-area projection

3.2
A Variety of Map Projections
Two-dimensional mapmaking inevitably involves distortion and error since the three-dimensional volume of the earth must be converted to a plane. Numerous techniques have evolved for compromising the errors that result from this transformation. Some systems attempt to represent area or shape as accurately as possible to the detriment of other features, while other projections are more concerned with direction or distance. Several projections are illustrated here. *Jacques Bertin, Sémiologie Graphique (Paris: Éditions Gauthier-Villars; Paris, New York, The Hague: Mouton Publishers; Paris: École des Hautes Études en Sciences Sociales, 1967).*

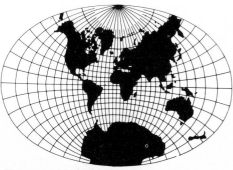
Stereographic projection

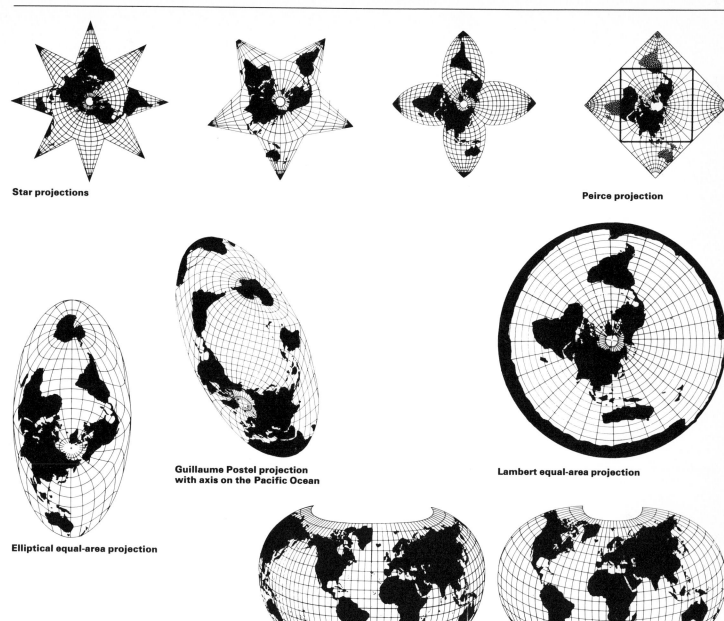

Star projections

Peirce projection

Elliptical equal-area projection

**Guillaume Postel projection
with axis on the Pacific Ocean**

Lambert equal-area projection

**Elongated "orange-peel" projection with
Pacific Ocean defined by land (Jacques Berti**

"Orange-peel" projection (Jacques Bertin)

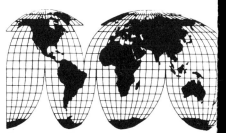

Goode's interrupted homolographic projecti

Maps of topography and natural features have the widest applicability of any map type. They are used extensively for scientific, sport, travel, and military purposes, as well as for research and planning in many fields. Representations of topography have tended to be at a small scale in contrast to most maps of man-made forms, since the perceived complexities of the man-made environment usually require maps of larger scale with more detail. Most maps of natural forms view the earth from above, rarely portraying land forms as they might be seen by the ground-level observer. On the other hand, the technology of the computer age has simplified the making of maps that encompass the ground observer's and the airplane pilot's points of view (10.2).

In representing topographic features, once again the problem of translating three dimensions into two occurs—in this case, it is not the sphere that must be flattened, but rather the form of hills and mountains. Terrain has been indicated with shade and shadow, topographic sections or slices laid flat on the map, "hachures" or short scratches, to show steepness of grade. Contour lines (isopleths), warped grids, land-form symbols, color coding of altitudes, and stereoscopic aerial photographs are other techniques for solving the problem. Sometimes two or more techniques are combined: for example, a contour map may be overlaid with a color or shadow-enhanced aerial photograph. One interesting aspect of the translation from three to two dimensions is found in mapping the oceans of the planet, where not only the topography of the ocean floor must be represented but also the various ocean currents above it.

Other layers of information are often superimposed on topographic maps: highways, vegetation, and place-names, for instance. Military maps often include evaluative information, such as the degree of visibility or concealment of a site, whether its soil permits mortarpit construction, or whether it is suitable for helicopter landings.

The computer storage of topographic information has made possible new applications for terrain maps. Geologists can study and predict earthquakes and volcanic eruptions, using three-dimensional views of each phase of the transformation. Developers and civil engineers can see the impact of large-scale earth-moving on water systems and terrain. Airplane pilots can examine the visibility of landings or defense installations from different points of view. Travelers and hikers can familiarize themselves with new terrain as seen from ground level before making the actual trip.

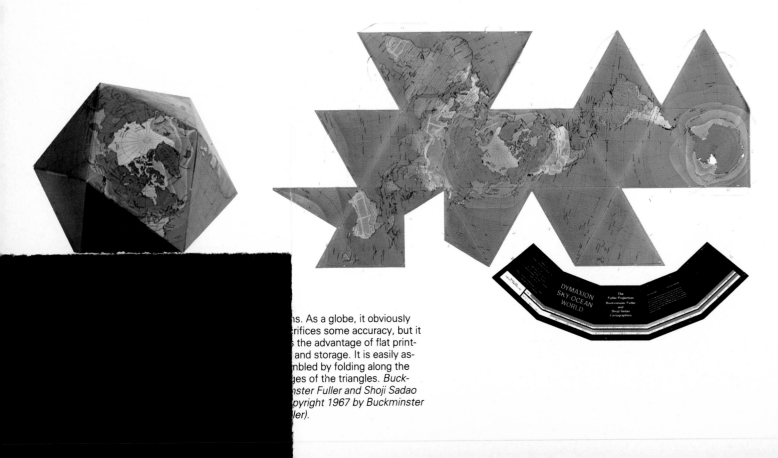

ns. As a globe, it obviously
rifices some accuracy, but it
s the advantage of flat print-
and storage. It is easily as-
mbled by folding along the
ges of the triangles. *Buck-
nster Fuller and Shoji Sadao
oyright 1967 by Buckminster
ler).*

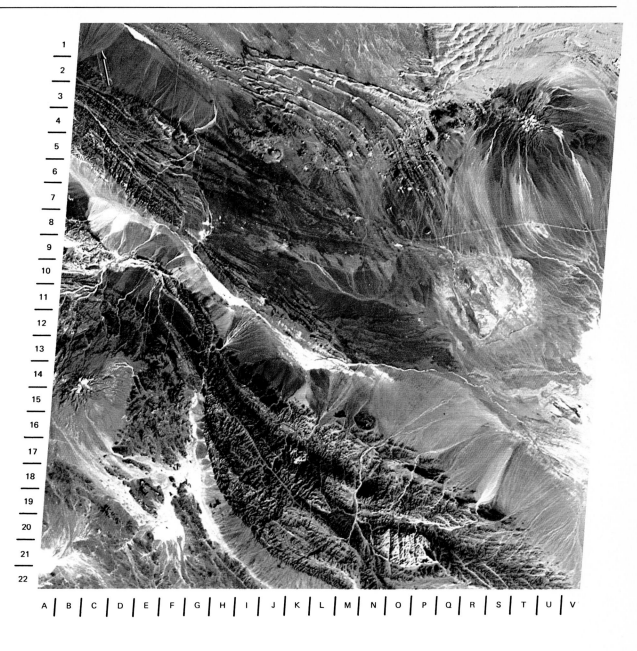

3.4
Landsat View:
The Baluchistan Desert

This Landsat view is not taken by a camera but is made by a "multi-spectral scanner" in a satellite orbiting 570 miles above the earth. Every 25 seconds an area 115 miles square is recorded. An oscillating mirror focuses visible and near-infrared light waves reflected from the earth into radiation detectors that measure the light intensities of each 1.1-acre unit. The values are converted to digital form and sent back to earth, where they are turned into images on film by an electron-beam recorder. Colors are not natural, but give better discrimination of elements than a conventional aerial photograph. Vegetation appears in reds, rocks and soil are bluish through yellow and brown, water is blue to black, and towns and roads are bluish black. New uses are still being found for Landsat maps, but they have been especially useful in geology, hydrology, agriculture, oceanography, and planning. *Nicholas M. Short, Paul D. Lowman, Jr., Stanley C. Freden, William A. Finch, Jr.,* Mission to Earth; Landsat Views the World *(Washington, DC: National Aeronautics and Space Administration, 1976).*

3.5
Computer-Generated Concealment and Topography Maps

Example **A** communicates topography by widely spaced parallel lines. The same site is shown from four points of view, demonstrating how a location — a military installation, for example — is concealed from view in one approach. North is shown by the arrow, and the box shape indicates the military installation. This technique is also useful in site planning, landscape architecture, and land development. Although manual construction would be tedious, computer storage of topographic data makes simulations and analyses such as these routine.

The second example (**B**) also uses parallel lines, here closely spaced, that wave up and down to show changes in contours. *Experimental Map Program, U.S. Army Engineer Topographic Laboratories, Fort Belvoir, VA.*

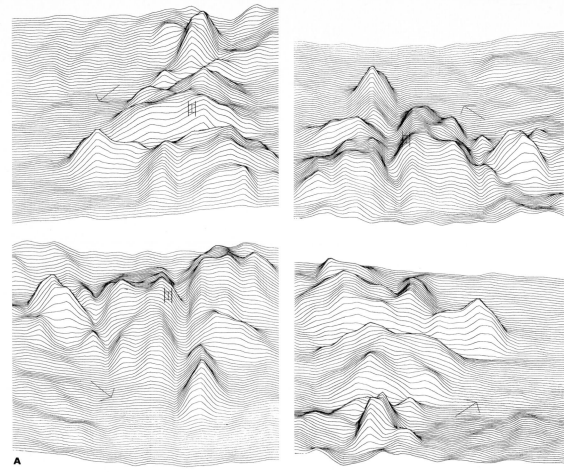

A

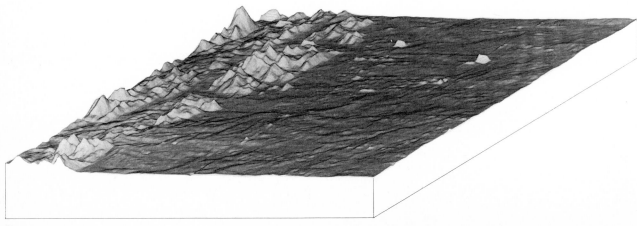

B

3.6
Digitized Topographic Map of Mount St. Helens

Here we see topography represented by means of a warped grid similar to that in 3.1. The grid, however, is much finer grain so that subtle changes in contour are more apparent. Straight baselines on each side of the quadrant help one judge changes of elevation. The two views show Mount St. Helens before (**A**) and after (**B**) the eruption of 1980. The U.S. Geological Survey is converting topographic data for the entire country to digital form for use in computer-aided mapping. *U.S. Geological Survey, National Mapping Division.*

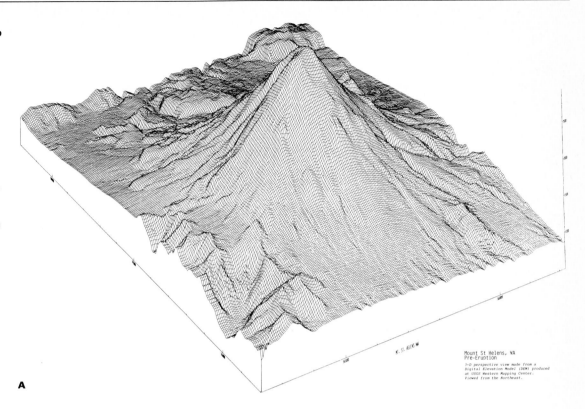

Mount St Helens, WA
Pre-Eruption
3-D perspective view made from a Digital Elevation Model (DEM) produced at USGS Western Mapping Center. Viewed from the Northeast.

A

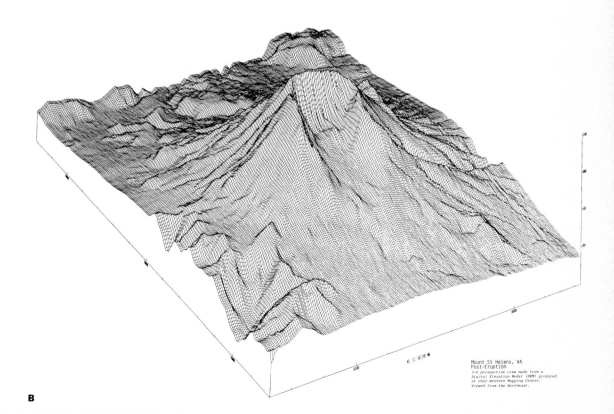

Mount St Helens, WA
Post-Eruption
3-D perspective view made from a Digital Elevation Model (DEM) produced at USGS Western Mapping Center. Viewed from the Northeast.

B

3.7
Bryson: Air Landing Graphic

An aerial photograph is the base for this experimental military map. Color is overlaid to indicate ground cover. The third layer of information relates to helicopter landing zones. Potential sites are outlined in heavy lines and are described by letter codes; detail photographs and descriptions of each site appear on the reverse side. Inappropriate landing sites are hatched over with widely spaced diagonal lines. *Defense Mapping Agency Topographic Center and U.S. Army Engineer Topographic Laboratories, Fort Belvoir, VA.*

Note: *The information portrayed on maps 3.7 and 3.8 is not to be construed as an official Department of the Army position unless so designated by other authorized documents.*

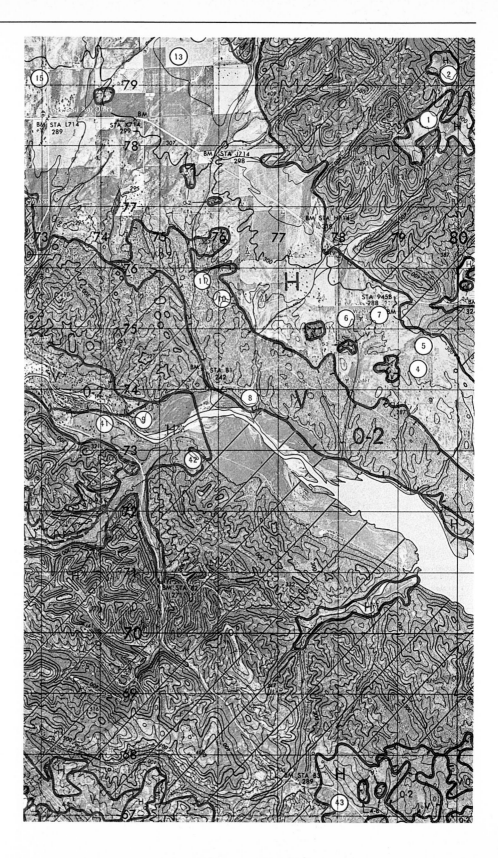

3.8
Bryson: Topography and Vegetation

Here shadows are used to enhance topographic contours. Color indicates the extent of canopy closure in forested areas; the darkest colors correlate with 75 to 100 percent canopy closure. Small, highly simplified maps in the margin aid understanding of the detail map; these summarize boundaries, soils, elevation, and ease of cross-country movement. *Defense Mapping Agency Topographic Center and U.S. Army Engineer Topographic Laboratories, Fort Belvoir, VA.*

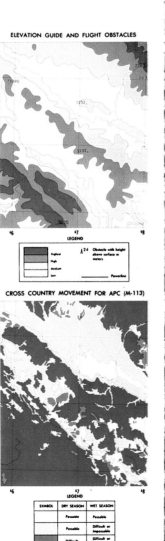

ELEVATION GUIDE AND FLIGHT OBSTACLES

LEGEND

CROSS COUNTRY MOVEMENT FOR APC (M-113)

LEGEND

SYMBOL	DRY SEASON	WET SEASON
	Passable	Passable
	Passable	Difficult or impassable
	Difficult	Difficult or impassable
	Impassable	Impassable

INDEX TO BOUNDARIES
AND RELIABILITY

SAN ANTONIO RESERVOIR
Maximum elevation 780 feet
Minimum elevation 662 feet

3.9
Raised Relief Topographic Maps

Terrain is presented in three-dimensional model form on molded plastic sheets. Vertical dimensions are exaggerated. Standard map information—roads, rivers, place-names, boundaries—is printed on the map. While the technique is effective in illustrating mountainous areas, it produces an ordinary flat map in areas of level terrain. Maps like these are useful for display and teaching and require less interpretation of terrain symbologies than do flat maps, but they are somewhat difficult to store and can be awkward to handle. *Defense Mapping Agency Topographic Center, Washington, DC; produced by Hubbard, Northbrook, IL.*

3.10
Stereo Map: Lycoming and Clinton Counties, Pennsylvania

Aerial photographs become more meaningful and realistic when made in stereo pairs (**A**). The three-dimensional effect is created by taking two separate photographs from the point of rotation of each eye and then viewing the photographs in a stereoscope so that each eye sees only one picture. When each eye transmits its own picture to the brain, the perception of depth is created. Compare the aerial photographs with the U.S. Geological Survey Quadrangle of the same area (**B**). *U.S. Geological Survey.*

  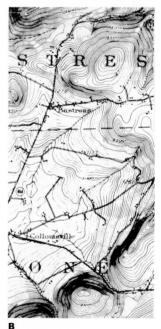

A

B

3.11
Topographic Map of
Switzerland
(Topographische Karte der
Schweiz)

Artful shading gives this elegant nineteenth-century engraving of the Swiss Alps a very three-dimensional feeling, although it is simply a plan. Topography is shown by "hachuring," first used by F. Delapointe in 1671 and further developed by Johann George Lehmann in the late eighteenth century. Short lines (hachures) indicate slopes, with thicker lines for steeper slopes. In addition, light and shadow enhance the mountain forms. The technique depicts topography well, but it is difficult to obtain the precise topographic data of a contour map.

General Guillaume Henri Dufour (1787-1875) began the surveys for this map in 1830, finishing the map thirty-four years later. The first sheets were published in Bern in 1842, but this example dates from 1889. The original maps were cut into pocket-sized cards and mounted on cloth backing. Thus, they were very durable and could be easily folded without fear of tearing along the creases. (Original scale 1:100,000.)

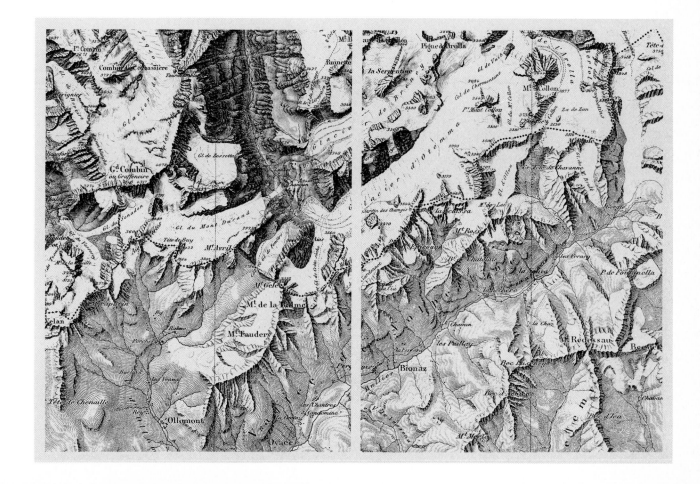

3.12
Military Maps: Columbus

A complex system of color, outline, shading, and numbers forms the language of these interpretative maps. The relative suitability of the soil for construction of foxholes and mortarpits is shown in map **A** by using symbolic ovals of various colors and textures that suggest foxholes. Areas of a given construction class are outlined in black lines with hatched edges to indicate construction time in man-hours. A clear white foxhole with a single hatch outline is best for construction, while a gray foxhole with a red *x* in an area outlined with no hatch mark is unsuited to foxhole or mortarpit construction because of rocky, shallow soil, or high water table. Colored areas communicate airburst effectiveness: pink areas offer the least protection (less than 25 percent) from a burst 20 meters above ground; speckled green areas offer the best protection (more than 75 percent).

Map **B** shows the probability of aerial detection within the same area. Color indicates chance of detection: green represents less than a 25 percent chance, and yellow, a 50 to 75 percent chance. Within these areas, red numbers show horizontal visibility (in meters) and black numbers show fields of fire (in meters) as limited by terrain. *Experimental Map Program, U.S. Army Engineer Topographic Laboratories, Fort Belvoir, VA.*

Topographic base

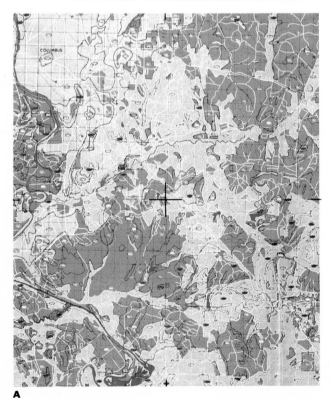

A

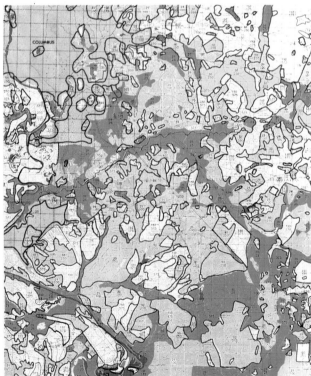

B

3.13
Ground Tactical Data:
Manatí, Puerto Rico

Color and texture differentiate areas on this military map of ground tactical data. Color identifies soil type and texture classifies vegetation. Widely spaced lines show percent of slope; for example, horizontal lines mean 3 to 10 percent slope (relatively flat) and vertical lines, 45 to 100 percent slope (very steep). Various patterns of dotted and dashed lines show stream width and depth. The colors and textures of this map have been well chosen to create a highly legible result. *U.S. Army Engineer Topographic Laboratories, Fort Belvoir, VA.*

Note: *The information portrayed on maps 3.12 and 3.13 is not to be construed as an official Department of the Army position unless so designated by other authorized documents.*

3.14
Pictorial Map Graph: Eight Landscape Types

Eight typical landscape types on Martha's Vineyard are depicted in chart form in terms of six policy variables critical to development. The combination of illustrative landscape segments and verbal information makes for easy comparison and understanding of both landscape and policy questions. One can read the charts either vertically, cutting across various landscapes by focusing on a single aspect, or horizontally, following a single landscape type through a number of aspects. *Kevin Lynch and Sasaki, Dawson, and Demay Associates, Inc.,* Looking at the Vineyard *(West Tisbury, MA: Vineyard Open Land Foundation, copyright 1973).*

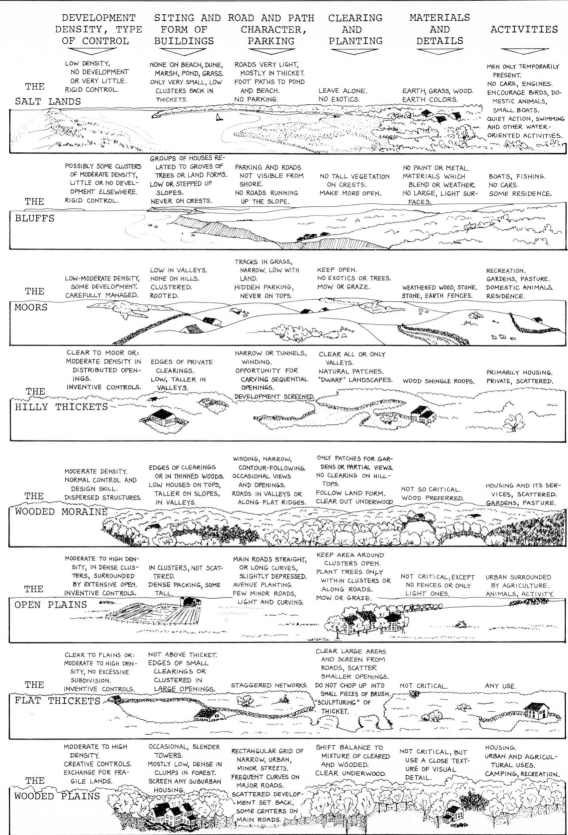

3.15
Eskimo Coastline Relief Carvings

Although these wood carvings might appear to be abstract sculpture, they are in fact highly detailed and accurate coastline maps carved by Eskimos. Portable and durable, they were ideal guides for hunting and fishing. Eskimos were unusual among primitive people in their skills in depicting topography. This is surprising, since cultures whose art is highly stylized, such as the Eskimo, usually produce stylized and therefore inaccurate maps. Eskimo mapping skills included maps drawn freehand, which often covered several hundred miles and were accurate enough to be usable. Compare these carvings with the Marshall Islands stick charts in 5.6. *Leo Bagrow, R. A. Skelton,* Meister der Kartographie *(Berlin: © 1973 Safari Verlag).*

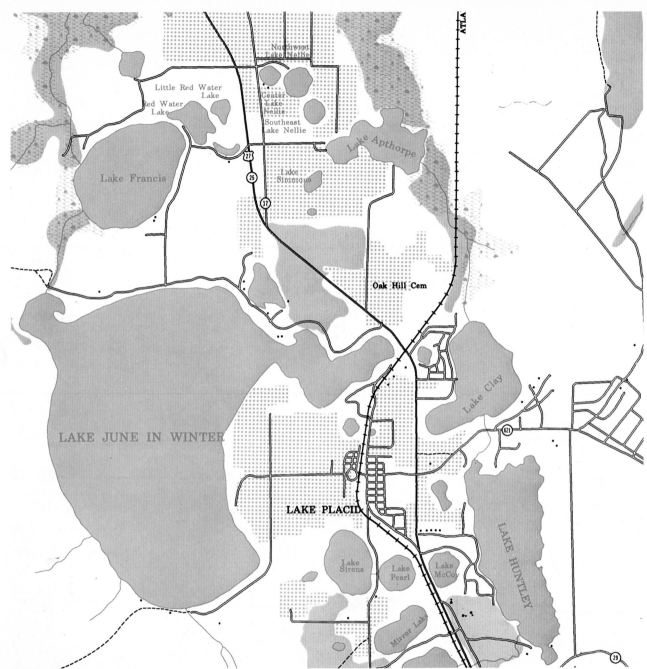

3.16
Computer-Generated Map:
Lake Istokpoga, Florida

The Lake Istokpoga map was printed from computer-stored data. The result is a very legible map, but in this case, one that is not graphically innovative. Map data were organized in eleven hand-drafted manuscripts, each representing a separate class of information. Computer processing was per- formed separately for each data set to convert it to digital form. Computer storage of map data allows the cartographer to select those classes of data he is interested in and to then have the map printed in far less time than a hand-drawn map would require. *U.S. Army Engineer Topographic Laboratories, Fort Belvoir, VA, 1976.*

3.17
Geological Map: Soviet Union

Diverse patterns and colors are used to map the stratigraphy of the Lake Balkash - Alma-Ata region in Kazakhstan in the central Soviet Union. Various patterns of dots, geometric forms, and line segments as well as color intensities illustrate surface structure, zone boundaries, and geological strata. The lengthy and complex legend (*Obozna-cheniya*), almost as large as the map itself, sets out the symbols in great detail. The map has much artistic appeal as well as considerable practical and scientific value. *Designed and printed at the Leningrad Mapworks, 1972. Editors: cartographer, N. V. Klyushnika; geologist, N. P. Pezhemskaya; technical editor, L. A. Solovyova. The map was approved by the Scientific Publishing Union on December 26, 1963, and supplementally reviewed on June 22, 1972.*

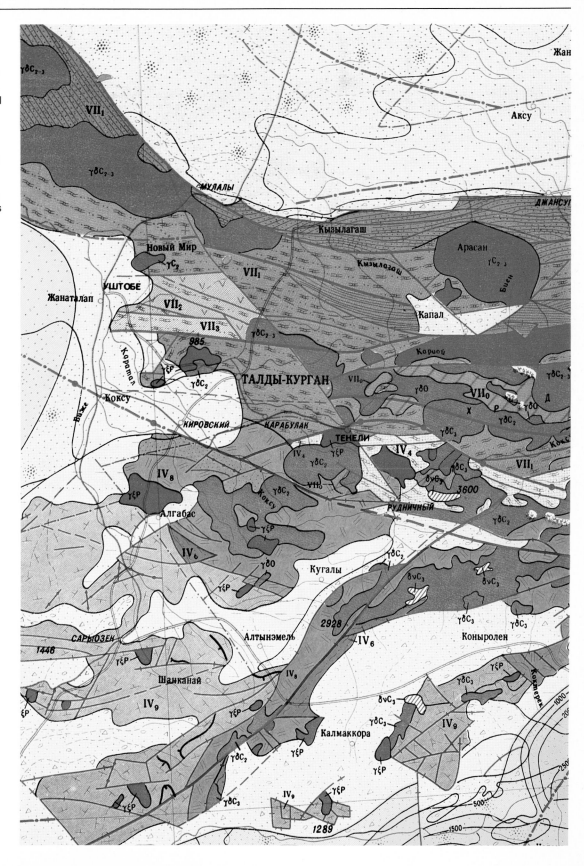

3.18
Nighttime Satellite
Photograph

From a weather satellite at night the United States looks like a galaxy of stars viewed through a telescope. Innumerable lights communicate settlement patterns and the great urban concentrations of the Northeast. Nighttime brightness is probably proportional to the energy consumption of various regions, but may not be proportional to per capita consumption. Satellite images have also been made of heat loss and dramatically point out energy waste. At a much larger scale, where individual buildings may be identified, such photographs have great value in energy conservation programs. *Official U.S. Air Force Photo.*

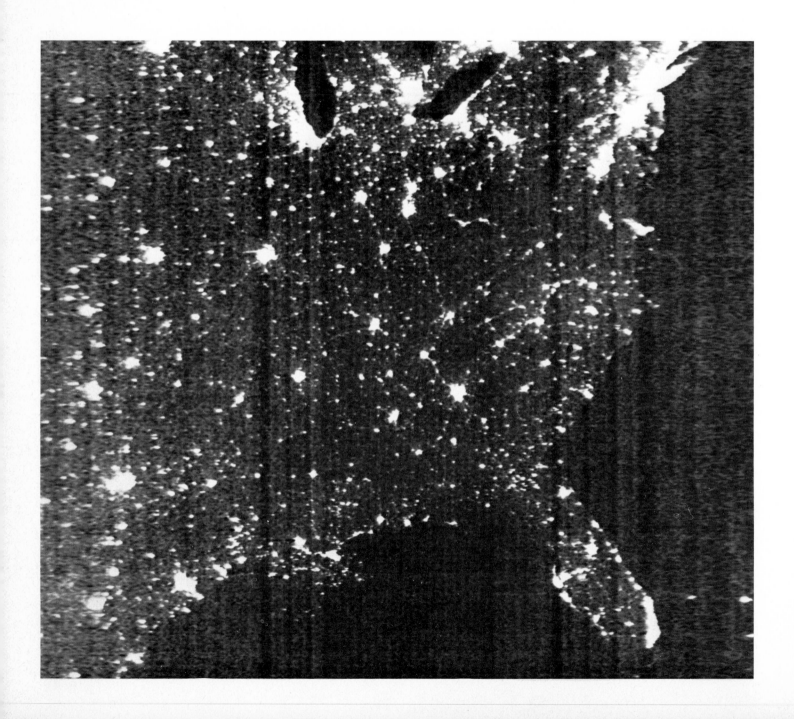

3.19
Satellite Photograph with
Graphic Overlay

This satellite photograph of part of the Western Hemisphere is made more intelligible by a graphic overlay. Geographic coordinates, outlines of land masses, and political bounda- ries are delineated in dotted lines. Use of dotted rather than solid lines reduces interference with the photo base. *National Weather Service, Washington, DC.*

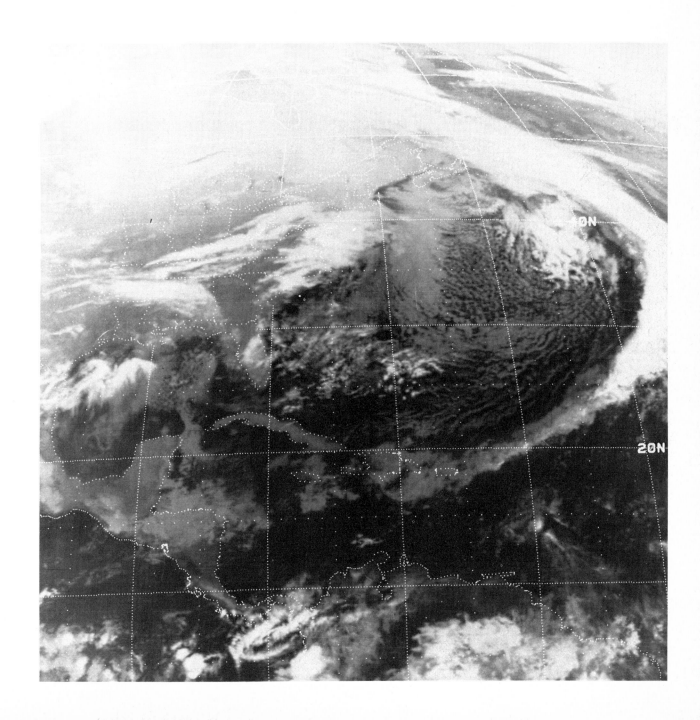

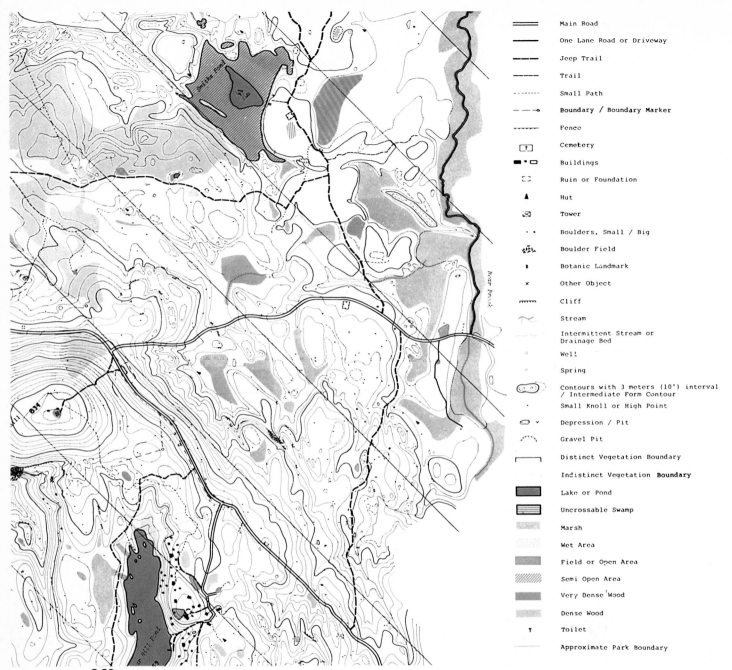

═══════	Main Road
───────	One Lane Road or Driveway
─ ─ ─ ─	Jeep Trail
────────	Trail
··········	Small Path
─ ─ ─o	Boundary / Boundary Marker
⌄⌄⌄⌄⌄⌄	Fence
[↑]	Cemetery
■ • ▫	Buildings
⊏ ⊐	Ruin or Foundation
▲	Hut
⊠	Tower
· •	Boulders, Small / Big
⁂	Boulder Field
▪	Botanic Landmark
×	Other Object
⌂⌂⌂⌂	Cliff
∿	Stream
	Intermittent Stream or Drainage Bed
○	Well
⌣	Spring
⬭	Contours with 3 meters (10') interval / Intermediate Form Contour
·	Small Knoll or High Point
⬭ ⌄	Depression / Pit
⌢⌢⌢	Gravel Pit
⌐ ¬	Distinct Vegetation Boundary
	Indistinct Vegetation **Boundary**
▓	Lake or Pond
▤	Uncrossable Swamp
░	Marsh
░	Wet Area
▒	Field or Open Area
▨	Semi Open Area
▓	Very Dense Wood
▒	Dense Wood
⊤	Toilet
───────	Approximate Park Boundary

3.20
Orienteering Map:
Bear Brook State Park

Orienteering is one of the newer competitive sports. Those taking part navigate from point to point with the aid of a special map, as quickly and efficiently as possible, by whatever route they interpret as best for them. The sport is well established in Scandinavia and is now spreading. The orienteering course is set with a series of check points between start and finish lines. It takes intelligence to "read" and to understand the terrain, and stamina to cover the course in the most efficient manner. An orienteering map is based on the topographical map of an area, but refined to include many details of the terrain that most cartographers would ignore. Cliffs, large and small boulders, intermittent streambeds, man-made structures, ruins, fences, and small footpaths are added, giving the orienteer full data by which to navigate. In addition, contour lines are drawn in precisely, and the types of ground cover are added to indicate the degree of difficulty in traversing each area, all to aid the orienteer in route selection. In order to include such details, the scale of orienteering maps typically varies from 1:10,000 to 1:20,000. The idea behind a complete and accurate orienteering map is to eliminate luck as a factor that may aid or hinder any competitor. *New England Orienteering Club, Inc., Sudbury, MA.*

3.21
Red Sea Diver's Guide

This handsomely presented diver's guide provides site information from various perspectives for a number of diving sites. Each site is clearly and elegantly presented in a double-page spread. Starting at the regional scale, sites are identified on a topographic map, followed by an eye-level photograph of the view one has in approaching the site. An aerial photograph of the site and its context has clear route and terrain information superimposed on a transparent overlay. A sectional drawing of the site is keyed into the aerial photograph. A final photo, showing the diver's view of the underwater site, helps the diver decide whether to choose this site or another in the book. This excellent visual material is supported by well-organized and brief verbal material giving location, route, site descriptions, and special conditions. *Shlomo Cohen,* Red Sea Diver's Guide *(Tel Aviv, Israel: Red Sea Divers, Ltd., copyright 1975).*

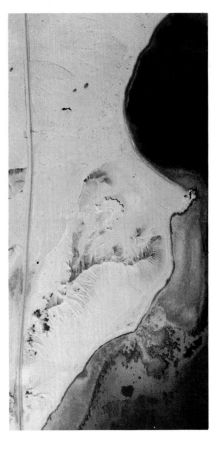

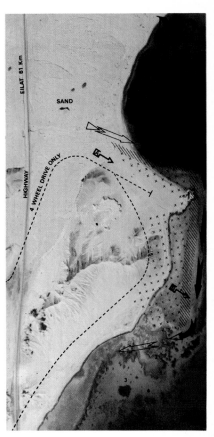

DEVIL'S HEAD

Route No. 8*
Ref: 11888378 34"41'00"E 29"07'30"N
Departure: Aqua Sport – 61 km. (38.4 mi.)
Road Condition & Route: South on the road to Ophira with good asphalt followed by 400 m. (1,320 ft.) with Four wheel drive.

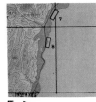

This is a prominent solitary rock on the water's edge sculptured by wind erosion and it can be easily seen from the main highway (A). Both beach roads on each side of the head leading from the highway are extremely difficult and should not be attempted without four wheel drive.

A vertical reef of 15 m. (50 ft.) depth begins due north of the head and then curves around it to the south. With deep water nearby and the absence of reef patches, one may find large fish along this stretch of coral: schools of *Caranx* and even the occasional shark exploring the reef. The best entry for a dive is on the northern side of Devil's Head where there is sandy bottom and no reef. The rough beach road leading to this point can be easily seen from the highway. If you have an extra driver, dive along the entire reef and finish on the southern side of the head where your vehicle can be waiting.

3.22
Seattle: Shadow Patterns

Delineation of shadow patterns is another way of indicating topography. In this map, the light gray tone indicates a mid-morning shadow·and a dark gray tone indicates a late afternoon shadow on December 22. Black areas are dark in both the morning and the afternoon. The technique is valuable in site planning. *Urban Design Section,* Seattle Urban Design Report *(Seattle: Department of Community Development, 1971).*

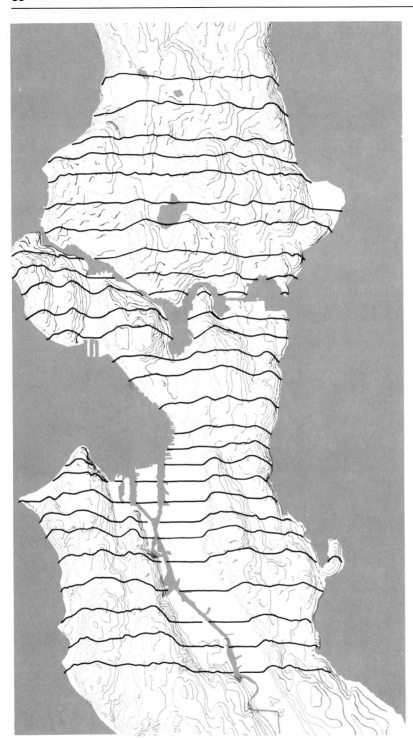

3.23
Seattle: Sequential Sections

Sequential sections offer an interesting alternative means of displaying topographical information by showing the cross-section of topography for one direction only. The technique gives a better sense than conventional methods of travel conditions over the land in the same direction as the contour lines. The selection of the intervals and direction of slicing are obviously crucial. *Urban Design Section,* Seattle Urban Design Report *(Seattle: Department of Community Development, 1971).*

3.24
Weather Charts

A computer printout is combined with human analysis in the typical weather "surface chart" (**A**). Weather observations are entered into the nationwide weather information system once each hour by weather stations across the country. Every three hours a national surface chart is printed out at each station. The array of numbers is coded to represent various weather factors: cloud cover, direction and speed of wind, pressure, dewpoint, and precipitation. A meteorologist interprets the chart to create a weather forecast. *National Weather Service, Washington, DC.*

Compact weather reporting systems such as the Alden Marinefax IV Recorder (**B**) can be used on board ship. Forty-five weather stations around the world transmit marine weather data and forecasts via radio using an international symbol system. Maps show highs, lows, wind direction and speed, wave height and patterns, sea ice, water temperature, cloud patterns, and storms. *Courtesy Alden Electronic and Impulse Recording Equipment Co., Inc., Westborough, MA.*

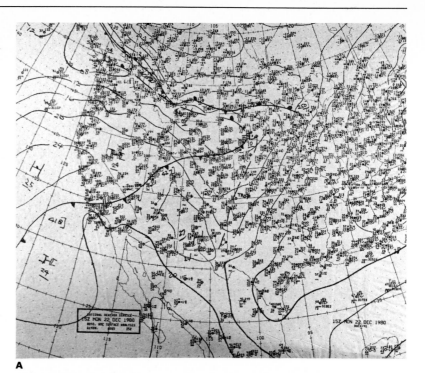

A

B

3.25
Infrared Reflectance

Infrared reflectance of land and water surfaces is shown in this map of a region in the Middle East. The data were obtained by means of a high-resolution scanning infrared radiometer on board the unmanned satellite *Nimbus 3*. The information was recorded cell by cell and then portrayed in a format in which the color of each square stands for a range of relative reflectance. The colors were chosen to stay close to "natural" colors; hence, the areas of lowest reflectance, which correspond to water, are pictured in blue. The highly reflective desert areas are in beige. The large blue area at the lower right of the map is the Red Sea. *Norman H. McLeod (NASA) in A. H. Oort, "The Energy Cycle of the Earth,"* Scientific American, *September 1970.*

4.1
Panorama: Florence
This beautiful old engraving of
Florence's skyline shows the
city's major architectural landmarks, which are numbered
and keyed into the legend at
the bottom. Panoramic views
such as this obviously are not
adequate for finding one's way
within the city, since no streets
are shown. However, skyline
views can aid general orientation and trip planning by showing detailed views of landmarks
and cityscape relationships.
Shoreline elevations were often
used in this way in early sea
charts (4.5). *F. B. Werner, Cartographer.*

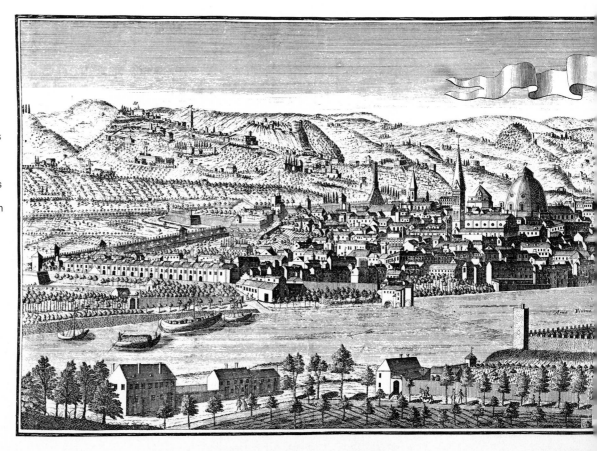

4   Built Form

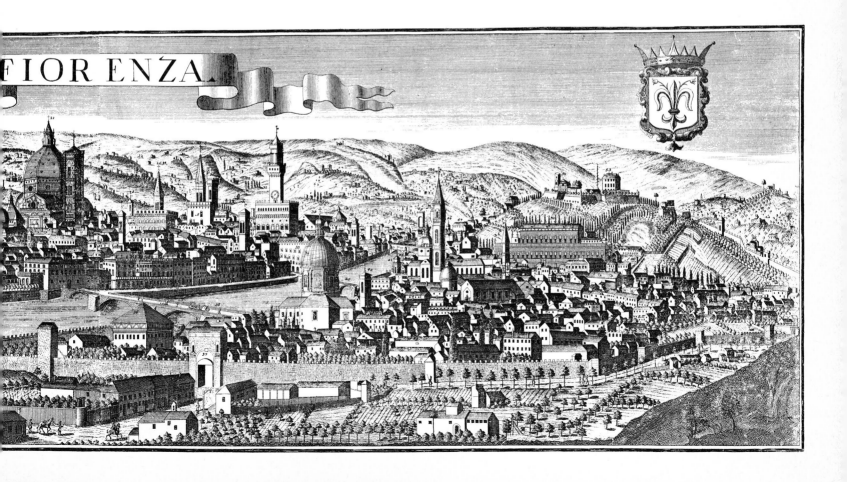

FIORENZA.

From early times man has attempted to simplify or make more understandable his surroundings. "Built form" includes all the constructions of man, from buildings to cities. The problem of representing in two dimensions a man-made environment such as a city that is three-dimensional, large-scale, multisensory, and absorbed over time—not in an instant—is difficult, probably impossible. No map can totally represent the experience of being surrounded by and moving through a construction as enormous and complex as a city, and perhaps no map needs to do so.

Early attempts at mapping built form were often naive, but also very direct. Plan views, eye-level facades, and perspectives were frequently combined in the same map (4.14). Another approach was the panoramic skyline view (4.1). Although such maps cannot be considered accurate or objective, they may convey the way people thought about the place.

Today, plan views of streets and structures can be technically correct, but they are usually too abstract and bear little relation to the way the place looks and feels (4.12, 4.41). One may walk down a street every day for years and still not be able to recognize it in plan form. Plan views are the most removed from reality because they exclude the major ingredient of the ordinary street image, namely, vertical surfaces. This is not to say that plan views are never recognizable or useful. They portray fascinating "footprints" of buildings and have special value in the mapping of distinctive monuments or ancient archaeological sites, such as Delos and Miletus (4.16, 4.17). Plan maps also can give a sense of the private city, the character of spaces hidden from view and access.

In designing a map of built form, the choice of point of view is important. Will one look straight down on the place from a lofty vantage point as in a plan, or will one see it from a bird's-eye perspective? Will it be a skyline view, a street-level view or elevation, a cut-away section, or some combination of these? Will the mapmaker use measured facade drawings, cartoons, or photographs? Will he use verbal descriptions or a three-dimensional model? Then there is the important question of selection and emphasis. Will one attempt to picture all structures, as in the Paris Plan Turgot (4.15) or the Manhattan Axonometric map (4.20), or will the mapmaker select only a few significant landmarks, as in the map of Florence (4.8)? The challenge of mapping selected aspects of built form has led to an astonishing variety of mapping techniques, as we shall see in this chapter and those that follow.

4.2
Panoramic Perspective: Penn Mutual's Philadelphia

Views seen in four directions from the top of the Penn Mutual Tower are shown as aerial perspectives, joined to make one map. The technique is useful as a view guide, but has many limitations. The diagonal intersections of the four perspectives create confusing, discontinuous street patterns. Street names and site identifications face four different directions, making use clumsy. The map is dominated by the vantage point, Penn Mutual Tower. The technique avoids some of the problems of the "fish-eye" view (which also provides a panorama with central focus; compare 4.21), but it creates other problems. *Courtesy of and copyrighted © by The Penn Mutual Life Insurance Company, 1976.*

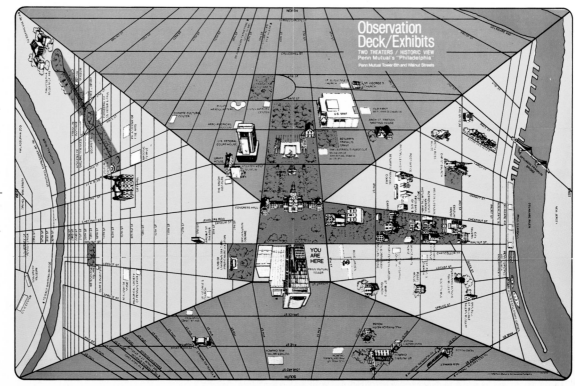

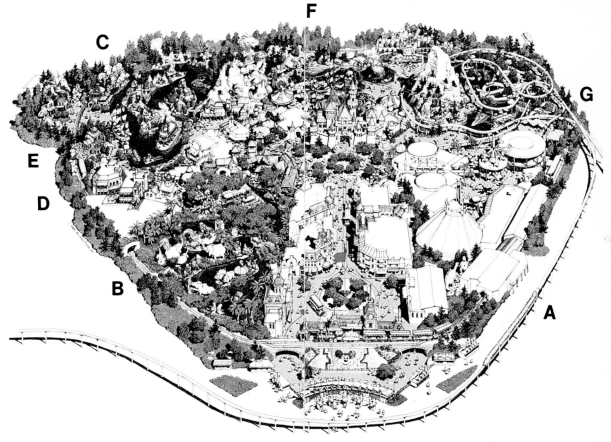

4.3
Aerial Perspective Drawing: Disneyland

A drawing, unlike an aerial photograph, allows one to focus on important features and to eliminate unnecessary detail. Furthermore, a perspective sketch is far more evocative of what Disneyland is like than a flat map would be. The letters around the map relate to text descriptions of the various districts. *Drawing by Charles Pigg, in Richard Saul Wurman, LA/Access (Los Angeles: Access Press, Inc., © 1980).*

4.4
Distorted Bird's-Eye Perspective View: New Orleans

Distortion of the earth's curvature in this aerial view allows the mapmaker to focus on the area that interests him while showing its relation to the larger region. As one moves away from the central area, less and less information is given. The city curves over the horizon, suggesting that it is far more vast than it actually is. The band of sky at the top is a useful terminating device and balances the blue Mississippi River at the bottom right. Within the focus area, selected landmark buildings in three-dimensional aerial views are identified verbally. Since the map is designed for motorists, street patterns, names, and directions are shown clearly, along with major orientation features and freeway access ramps. *Copyright © Perspecto Map Co., Inc., Richmond IL 60071. Map artist, Eugene Derdeyn.*

4.5
Sailing Chart and Coast-line Views: Annapolis

This mid-nineteenth-century map aids sailors by supplementing the conventional depth map with four shoreline views illustrating buildings and land forms as they would be seen from water approaches. The shoreline views are largely self-explanatory but have brief verbal identifications of landmarks and sometimes include harbor entrance depths in fathoms. *U.S. Department of Commerce, National Oceanic and Atmospheric Administration, National Ocean Survey.*

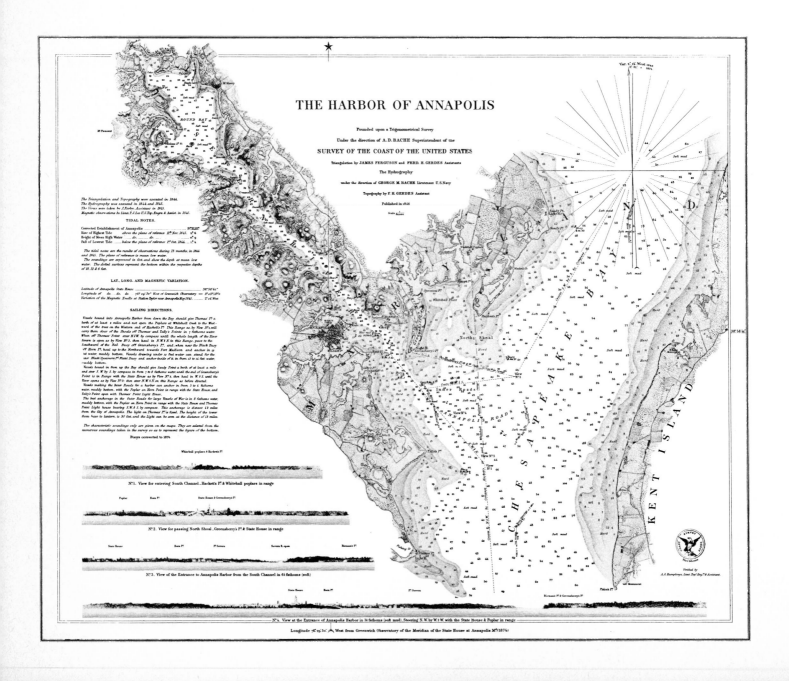

4.6
Photographic Panoramas: Monument Valley and New York City

Monument Valley, Arizona, and New York City are show in panoramas taken with the Cirkut camera. The view in Monument Valley encompasses 240 degrees; New York is viewed from Brooklyn in a 330-degree panorama. A comprehensive sense of environment is created in these views, although some distortion — as the bridge reveals — is inevitable. Panoramas can be useful in identifying landmarks that are seen from one vantage point, but they are not practical route guides because street patterns and most terrain details are absent. In these examples, the panoramas would function better as maps if landmarks were named. *Photographs by Jerry Dantzic. Monument Valley: © Jerry Dantzic 1978. New York City: © Jerry Dantzic 1975, courtesy of the Museum of Modern Art.*

4.7
Baedeker's Genoa

This elegant map of central Genoa uses intersecting concentric line patterns flowing out from the land to create a striking pattern in the harbor. Hill forms are drafted with similar elegance. Parks, piazzas, and built-up areas are identified, as well as churches and major public buildings of interest to a tourist. Everything is handled in plan form with no indication of three-dimensional qualities except for selected hills. Hills occurring under built-up blocks are not indicated. Notable buildings are shaded darker than the surrounding blocks but in the same color, making them somewhat difficult to identify. *Karl Baedeker,* Italy: Handbook for Travellers, Part I, *12th ed. (New York: Charles Scribner's Sons, 1903).*

4.8
Florence: Plan of the City
Major landmarks are carefully delineated in three dimensions with correct orientation and scale against the background of a simple but correct street map (compare 4.1). Because only a few buildings were chosen for illustration there was no need for other distortions, such as widening of the streets (compare 4.20). Blocks are shaded, leaving the streets white and more legible. The map is attractive and easy for strangers to use. *Reproduced from the plan of Florence by Litografia Artistica Cartografica, Florence, Italy.*

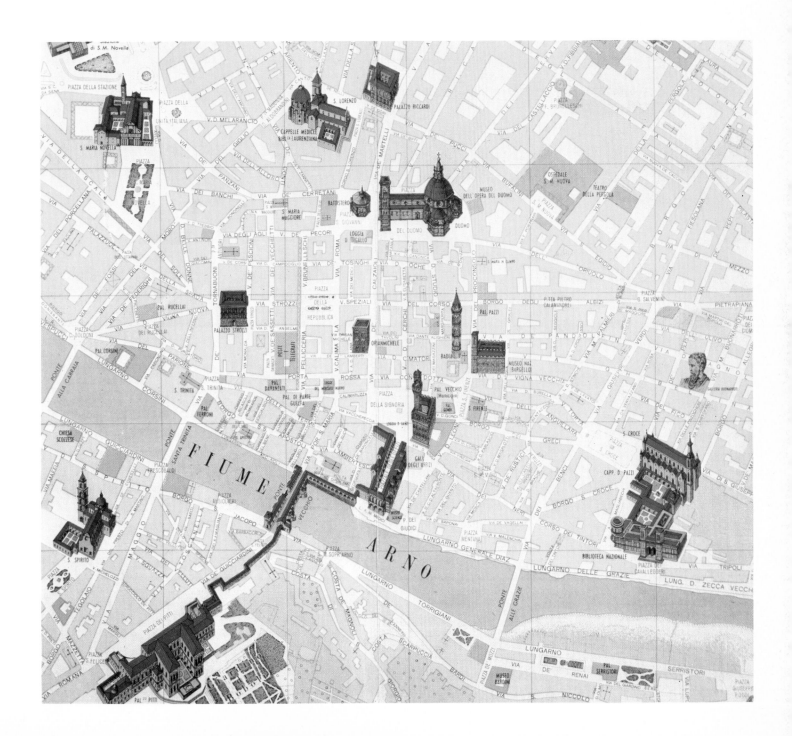

4.9
Plan-Perspective: La Terra de Hochelaga nella Nova Francia

Based on the description of Jacques Cartier, this drawing of the fabled Indian city on the site of Montreal originally appeared in Giambattista Ramusio's *Delle navigationi e viaggi,* published in Venice in 1556. The village is shown in plan with elements keyed to the legend at the side.

The stockade is shown in aerial perspective around the plan. The town is superimposed on a perspective view of the region that includes terrain, vegetation, Indians, and Europeans. *Courtesy Cornell University Libraries and Historic Urban Plans, Ithaca, NY.*

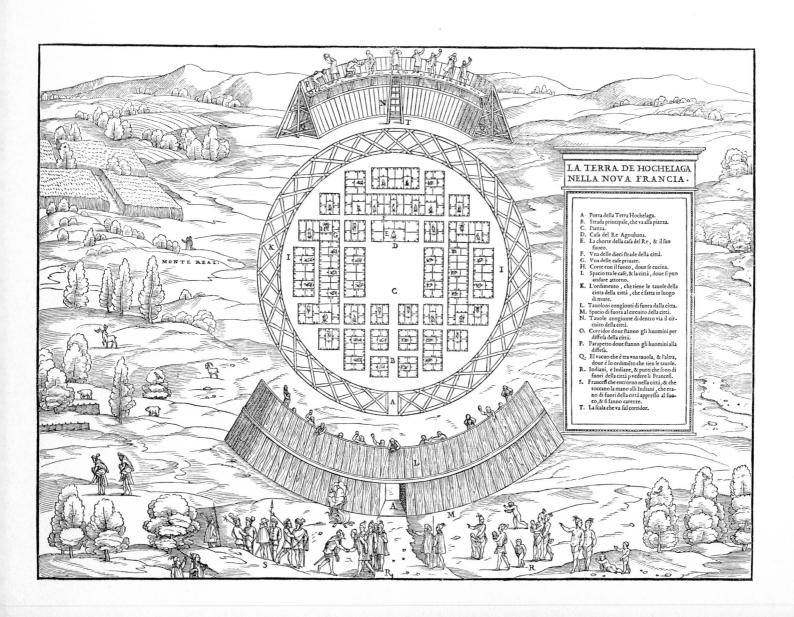

4.10
Plan-Panorama: Mexico-Tenochtitlán

This fascinating Spanish map, attributed to Hernando Cortes and first published in Nuremberg in 1523, combines several mapping techniques: plan, elevation, and 360-degree panorama. The central area shows a plan of the city with elevations of buildings laid flat on it. Around this a panoramic view radiates from the center. Interestingly, some of the boats in the water do not follow the radiating principle and are upside down with respect to everything else. *Courtesy of the American Museum of Natural History.*

4.11
Plan-Perspective: Mexico-Tenochtitlán

In this 1556 map the old Aztec city is shown shortly after its conquest by the Spanish. Elevations and axonometric views of buildings and mountains are superimposed on a plan view of the region. South is at the top, as in 4.10, but in contrast to 4.10, this map maintains a consistent orientation. *Courtesy Cornell University Libraries and Historic Urban Plans, Ithaca, NY.*

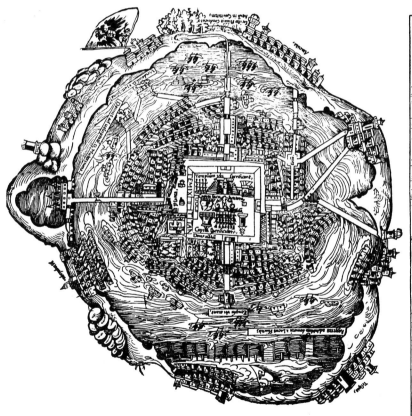

4.12
Brussels
Legible but rather conventional, this street map uses a simple and effective device to give blocks a three-dimensional sense. Two sides of each block are rendered in thicker lines, which give a feeling of bulk that in turn strengthens the street system. Streets are clearly labeled and major avenues are differentiated from minor streets by use of uppercase letters.

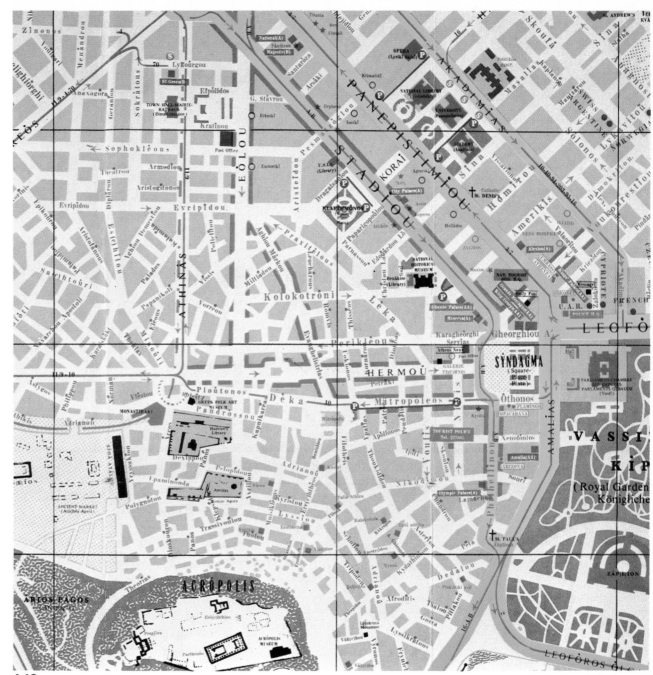

4.13
Athens

This attractive map has a unique sense of style and unusually good balance between importance of the information and its graphic strength. Plans of major historic sites are shown in some detail. This is useful in many cases, such as the temples, where the plan bears a close resemblance to what one sees; for many modern buildings plans would be less informative. Blocks are simple colored shapes with no outline, making street patterns and names quite easy to read. In general, this approach is far better for showing street patterns than an outline method, which complicates the appearance of a map and can make it more difficult to use. The street trolley network is identified without detracting from other information by an overlay tone of light yellow. Principal shopping streets are clearly shown by red bands on the edges of the blocks. *Copyright J. Sakellaridis, Interpress, Athens.*

4.14
Pictorial-Elevation Map: Jerusalem, 1584

Elevations, aerial perspectives, and plans are combined in this sixteenth-century map of Jerusalem. Important biblical events are illustrated around the perimeter of the wall. Note the hills shown in perspective in the foreground and background. Details make this a fascinating historical view into the past life of the city. Because of the naive, nontechnical presentation, all of the information is accessible to laymen. Compare this with the contemporary pictorial map of Jerusalem (4.34). *Adrichomio,* Theatrum Terrae Sanctae, *1584; courtesy Cornell University Libraries and Historic Urban Plans, Ithaca, NY.*

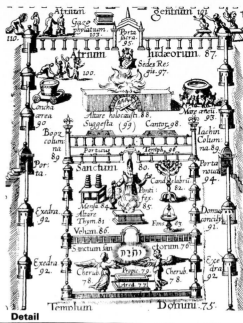

Detail

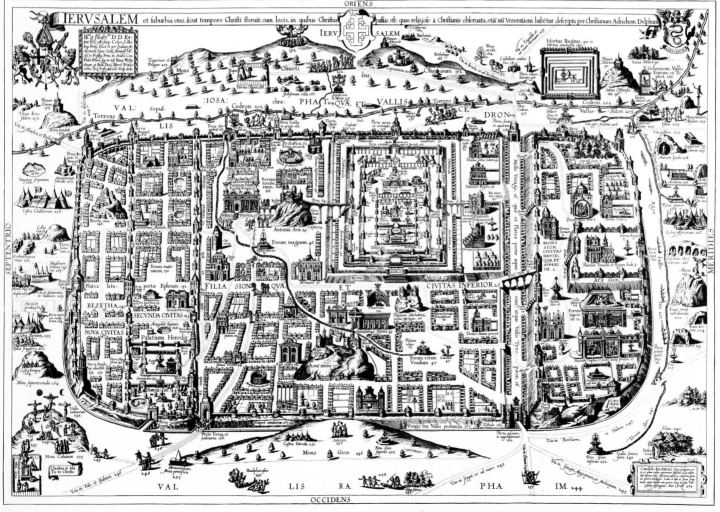

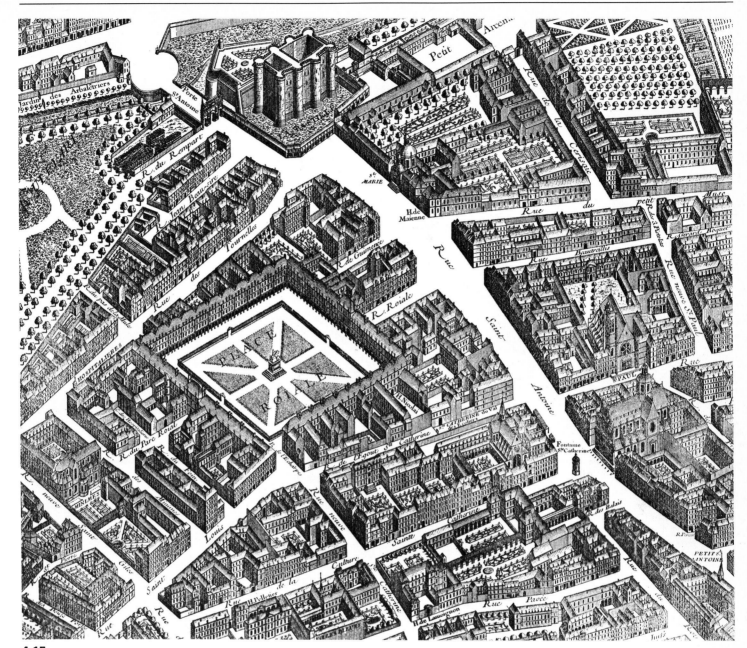

4.15
Paris: Plan Turgot, 1734

Elegance and detail are the outstanding qualities of this eighteenth-century engraved map. Buildings are shown in axonometric projections, with correct detail and orientation. Streets, however, are widened so that they don't disappear behind buildings. The map allows study and armchair travel in depth, but it could also be used for real travel. Because of its detail, this technique is eminently well suited to the foot traveler. *From* Paris au XVIII Siècle; Plan de Paris en 20 Planches; Dessiné et gravé sous les ordres de Michel Étienne TURGOT, Prévôt des marchands; Commencé en 1734—Achevé de graver en 1739; Levé et dessiné par Louis Bretez *(Paris: A. Taride, 1908). Photo courtesy of Harvard College Library.*

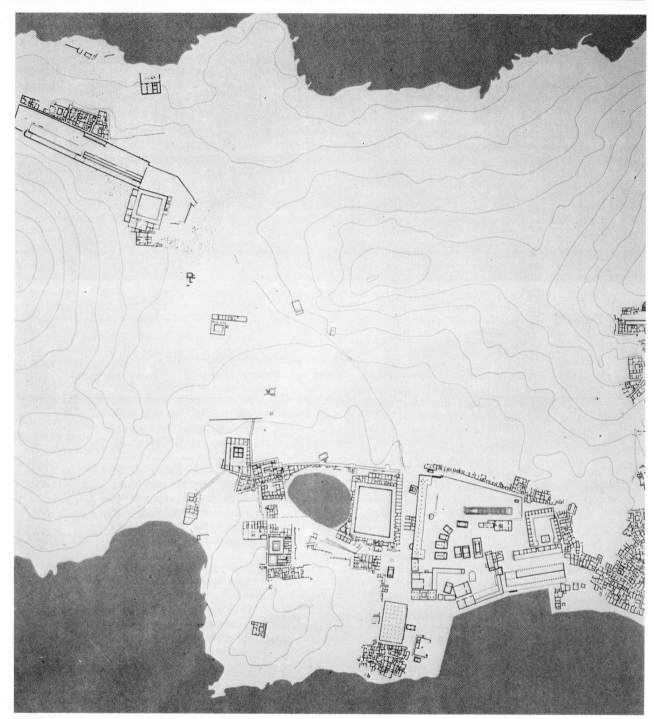

4.16
Archaeological Map:
Delos

The ancient Greek city of Delos
is shown in plan on topographic
contour lines of the site. By
combining architectural plans
with topography at a large
scale, a compelling archaeological plan is created. The map can
also be used for travel, but
might be confusing to the layman unless labels and other orientation aids were added.
Edmund N. Bacon, Design of
Cities *(New York: Viking Press,
copyright 1967, revised 1974).*

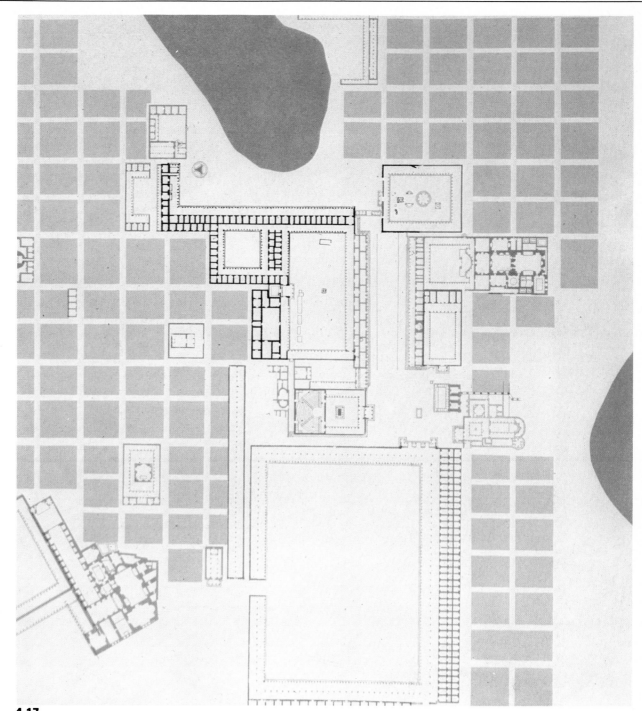

4.17
Development of Miletus
Historical development of the
ancient Greek town of Miletus
is expressed by means of color
in this sharply delineated
ground plan. Black lines represent Greek construction at the
end of the fourth century B.C.
Hellenistic additions in the mid-
second century B.C. are shown
in blue, and Roman work from
the second century A.D. is
shown in yellow. The flow of
public and semipublic spaces at
the ground level is beautifully
expressed. *Edmund N. Bacon,*
Design of Cities *(New York:
Viking Press, copyright 1967,
revised 1974).*

4.18
Aerial Photograph:
Manhattan
Aerial photographs provide a
wealth of information and are
highly useful for many tasks in-
volving strategy, evaluation, or
description. For some uses, the
detail is overwhelming, making
interpretation difficult. Shadow
patterns can block out large
areas of information or some elements may be difficult to interpret through lack of definition. In general, aerial photos
are not suitable tools for navigation or fast action because they
contain too much redundant information. Moreover, the verbal
and numerical identification, important in such tasks, is lacking.
*New York City Planning Com-
mission,* Plan for New York
City: Manhattan *(Cambridge,
MA: MIT Press, 1969); copyright © 1969, Department of
City Planning, City of New York.*

4.19
Lower Manhattan Plan
Shadows highlight building
forms to create a very comprehensible but detailed plan
view of Lower Manhattan.
Every building is shown. It
closely resembles the aerial
photograph but simplifies and
adds emphasis, eliminating
nonessential details, such as
rooftop equipment or vehicles.
Such maps can be useful for
planning or local travel but are
too detailed for quick reference
or regional travel. *New York
City Planning Commission,* Plan
for New York City: Manhattan
*(Cambridge, MA: MIT Press,
1969); copyright © 1969, Department of City Planning, City
of New York.*

4.20
Axonometric Pictorial Map: Manhattan
Buildings are shown with detail and accuracy in this map of central Manhattan. Vertical dimensions are somewhat exaggerated and streets are widened to allow more space for tall buildings. Nevertheless, many street segments are obliterated by skyscrapers. The map is a tour de force in detailed cartography. Enormous amounts of data were collected in the field through photographs and sketches; aerial photos were also essential. Maps such as these are fascinating for study purposes and are useful for small-area travel; for larger trips the detail is an impediment to rapid use. © *1968 and 1975, Anderson Isometric Maps, New York City.*

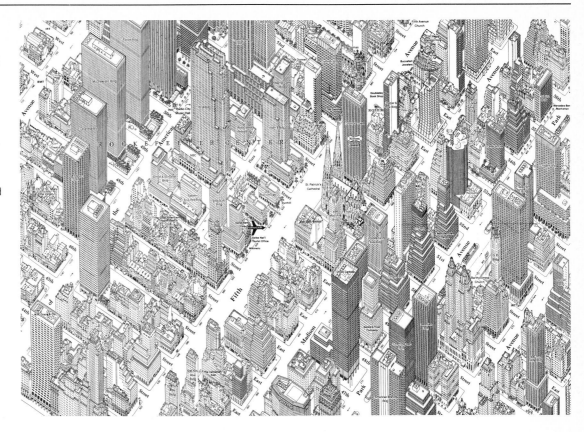

4.21
Fish-Eye Aerial Photo of Manhattan
The "fish-eye" lens, by means of distortion, allows the camera to take in a much wider field of vision than would normally be possible. Information is clearest and most useful in the center; extensive surroundings are visible but recede rapidly, giving only impressionistic information (compare 4.4, 4.32). Such photographs are useful in giving a specific place a sense of context or in focusing attention, but their application is limited. With added labels or a graphic overlay to identify buildings, streets, or districts, this photograph would begin to function as a map. *David Langley, photographer; for McCaffrey and McCall, New York; copyright 1978 by Hiram Walker Importers, Inc., Detroit.*

4.22
Symbolic Map:
Philadelphia

The street grid of downtown Philadelphia is replaced by strings of symbols—buses, baseballs, circus tents, houses. Although the symbols seen here don't appear to relate directly to Philadelphia's activity patterns but rather to activities associated with Philadelphia in general, the technique could be useful. The dominant activities of major streets could be portrayed by a similar symbolic code: major bus-line streets by elongated buses, a street with open-air markets by food carts, or streets with movie theaters by film reels. It is an imaginative scheme deserving further exploration. *Richard Saul Wurman, 1976 AIA National Convention, Philadelphia.*

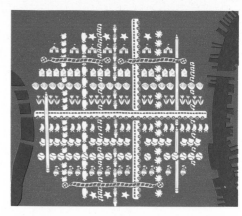

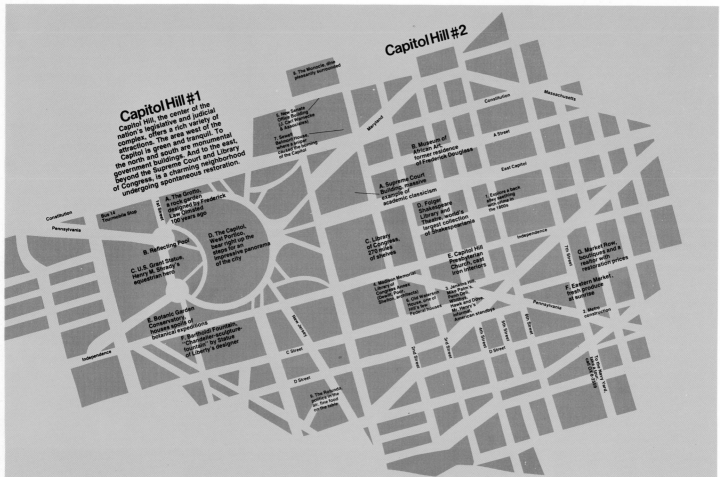

4.23
Annotated Schematic
Map: Washington, DC,
Capitol Hill

Simplification of reality is essential in making a good map. This map has been reduced to a schematic block pattern shown in solid color. Points of interest and major streets are indicated verbally. Such maps are inexpensively and quickly produced and are suitable for single-purpose use. This one is meant to tell visitors about the highlights of Capitol Hill; it is one of a set of maps treating several districts of Washington, DC.

Richard Saul Wurman, Peter Bradford, Jane Clark, Kay Layne, James Bailey, et al., for the American Institute of Architects, Washington, DC.

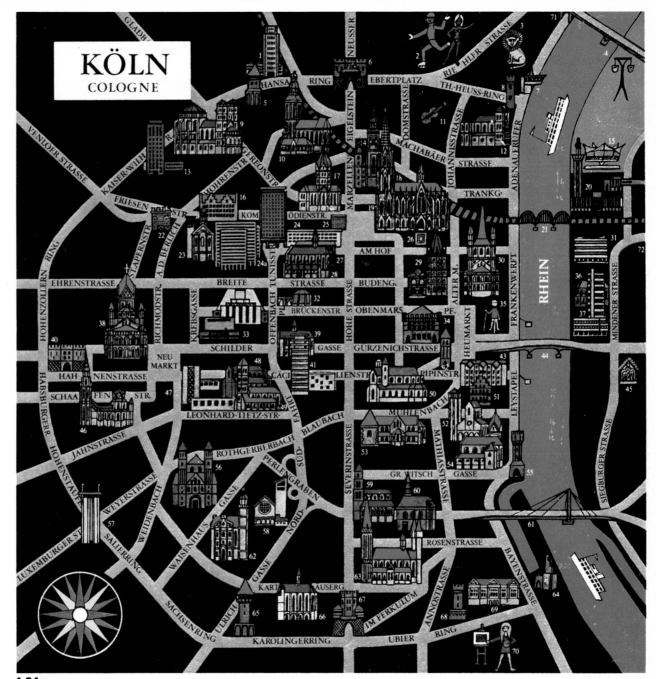

4.24
Tourist Map: Cologne
Color, typography, and stylized delineation combine to make this a handsome tourist map. Major sites are drawn as simple elevations that lie flat on the plan and are keyed by number to an index. Minor streets appear to have been eliminated. Like many tourist maps, this one is probably more successful in arousing interest than in actually guiding tourists through the city. However, the technique could produce a completely useful map. *By Herbert Lemkes for Verkehrsamt der Stadt Köln, Germany.*

4.25
Cross-Section Map:
New York Underground

In this novel map Manhattan appears to be carved out of its surroundings to expose the underground network of utility, automobile, and transit tunnels. Aerial cross-sections are useful for explaining relations between the visible surface and the hidden underground; the technique is not particularly effective as a travel aid. *Jerome Kuhl in* AIA Guide to New York City, *by Norval White and Elliot Willensky (1967, 1978).*

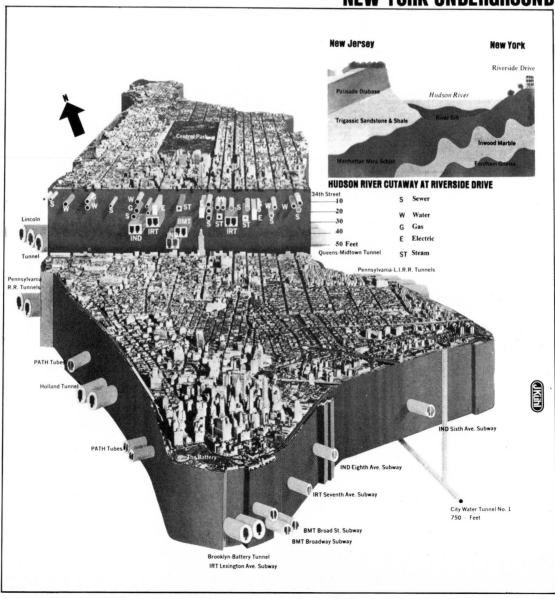

NEW YORK UNDERGROUND

4.26
Section-Plan Map:
Novanoah II

Two different plan levels are shown in cross-section along with a vertical section of this giant futuristic city. The Empire State Building provides scale. Multiple views are often helpful in conceptualizing the form and organization of a complex and vast environment such as this. In this case the dissimilarity be- tween the different levels sug- gests that many more plans would be necessary for actual travel in "Novanoah." *Reprinted from Paolo Soleri,* Arcology: The City in the Image of Man, *by permission of the MIT Press (Cambridge, MA: copyright © 1969 by the Massachusetts Institute of Technology).*

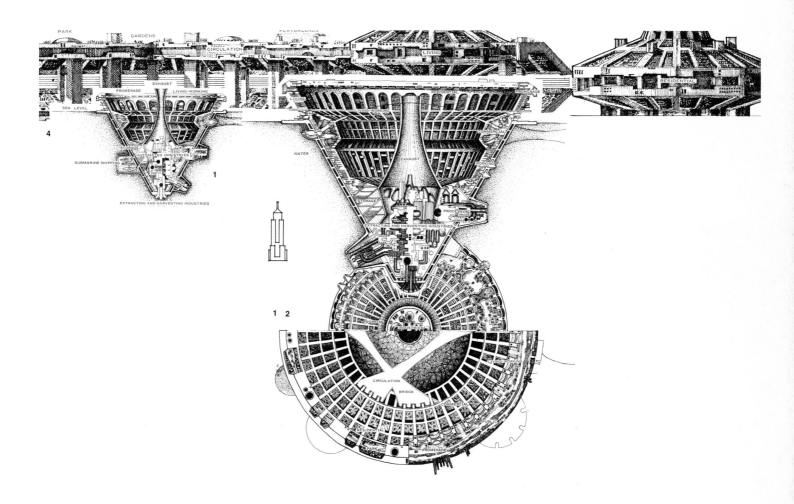

4.27
Pictorial Map: Dry Dock Country

Cartoon techniques are used in this pictorial map. Streets are very legible, but the block pattern is distorted to suit the format. Facades, landmarks, signs, symbols, and activity are suggested for each block, but one senses from the graphic style that many liberties have been taken by the designer. The map is fun to look at but would not be the best travel guide. Note that the facades shown are mainly those facing south. *By Geer, Dubois, Inc., for Dry Dock Savings Bank, New York City.*

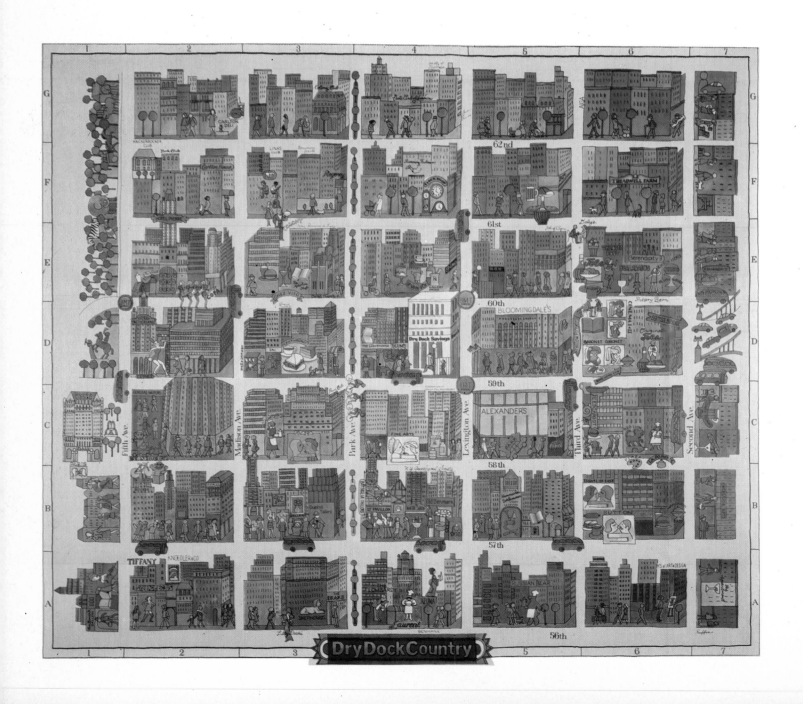

4.28
Pictorial Landmark Map:
Boston Discovery Map
Major historical sites and visitor
services are depicted in three
dimensions and annotated with
cartoon-style balloons. Thus,
symbol-learning and index-
checking are not required, making the map suitable for inexpe-
rienced map users. The map is
designed to guide the typical
visitor along a network of
pedestrian trails in Central Boston. Landmark buildings are accurately located and oriented,
but are somewhat enlarged.
Sketches were developed from
field photographs and drawings.
The map is part of a larger orientation system found in the
city itself, consisting of trail
blazers, site markers, and
kiosks with pictorial district
maps. The authors first used
this mapping technique in the
late 1960s to illustrate their
Urban National Park plan for
Lowell, Massachusetts. That
map, which had a lower density
of information, effectively communicated with a variety of
community groups and government agencies and was an important factor in the implemen-
tation of the park. The mapping
technique is useful for communicating with a general audience, but extensive field work
and testing are normally required to produce such maps.
(Compare 4.8, 4.20, 4.34.) *De-*
sign and graphics by Michael
and Susan Southworth, Boston;
© *1979 by Michael & Susan*
Southworth.

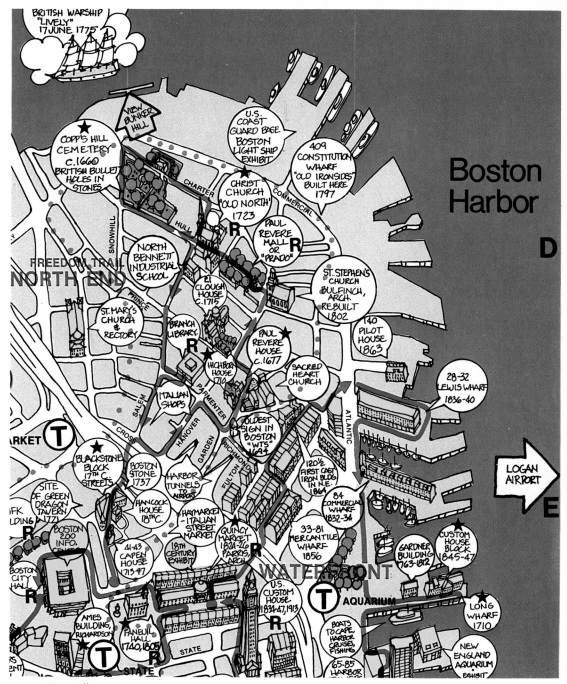

walking trail
★   registered landmark
🔔   major exhibits and info. centers
····· 18th century water edge
Ⓣ   public transit
R   restroom
H   hotel

4.29
Elevation-Plan Map: Park Mall, Detroit

To solve the problem of giving detailed architectural and landscaping information on one drawing, building facades were laid flat on both sides of the street plan. The original plan was sixteen feet long, but was reduced to several smaller sizes for a variety of uses. The technique is most appropriate to linear systems, such as streets, rivers, or railways; networks or overall areas would be difficult to represent in this way. *Plan and graphics by Michael and Susan Southworth, Boston, MA.*

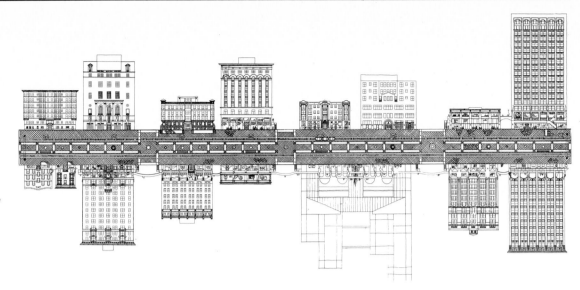

4.30
Pictorial Map: Nagasaki Harbor

This multi-oriented woodcut map of Nagasaki Harbor, printed between 1661 and 1672, has not settled on any one viewpoint. It illustrates international trade, with Dutch ships and Chinese junks in the harbor and pictures of foreign merchants in the lower left (Arab, Dutch, and Chinese, from left to right) next to a chart of distances by sea from Nagasaki. Trees, ships, topography, and buildings are shown pictorially and the street pattern seems to be fairly detailed and accurate. It is possible that this map was a promotional piece to encourage foreign merchants to come to Nagasaki, since all other Japanese ports excluded foreign trade at that time. *Courtesy of the British Library.*

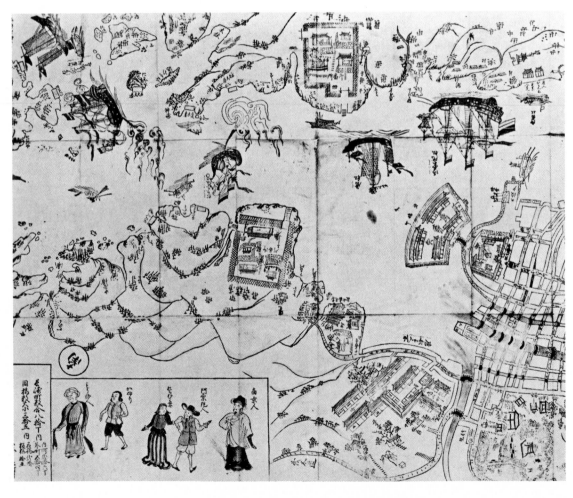

4.31
Historic Mantorville, Minnesota

A simple street map is made more imageable by surrounding it with sketches of several landmarks that are keyed back into the map. Although this technique requires the user to jump back and forth between the map and the sketches, the map is kept free of distracting information and is easy to use. For large areas with numerous sites, however, the technique becomes impractical. *By Ron Hunt for Mantorville Restoration Association, Mantorville, MN.*

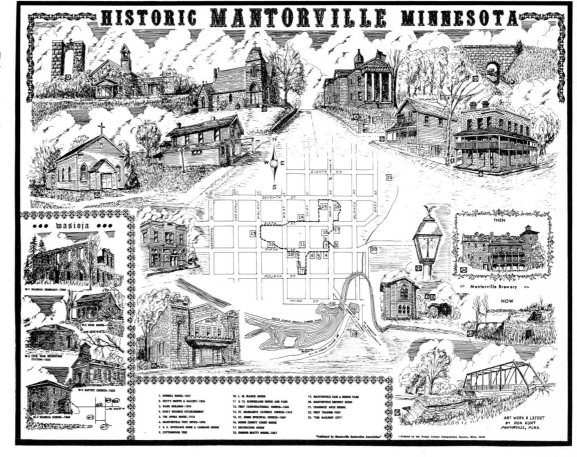

4.32
Zoom Map: Yeshiva University

A school with a regionally dispersed campus had the difficult problem of showing the location and transportation connections between the several campuses, as well as the appearance and layout of each campus. This was accomplished on one map by means of an unusual zoom technique. The pieces of land seem to pop out of the distance and float like magic carpets close to our view. *Copyright © Perspecto Map Co., Inc., Richmond, IL 60071. Map artist, Eugene Derdeyn.*

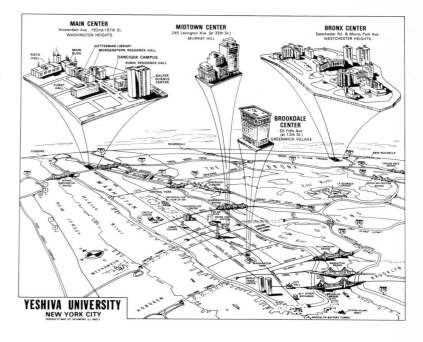

4.33
Floating Landmark Map: Cambridge

The "floating landmark" style is popular for tourist and poster maps, which are essentially montages of key images. Precise information is unnecessary and distortion is a crucial part of the style. Landmarks are drawn at an enlarged scale and face in any direction without regard for reality. As a result, buildings that are actually quite remote from one another appear to be next-door neighbors. Because of the distortions, omissions, incorrect orientation, and misleading juxtapositions, it is not possible to use this type of map for navigation. Rather, it serves as a poster, souvenir, or advertisement. People like the rough, unpretentious, and personal quality that results. It is nonthreatening and invites visual exploration.
Archar Inc., 1200 Aerowood Drive, Unit 29, Mississauga, Ontario, L4W 2S7. Copyright 1980

4.34
Floating Landmark Map:
Jerusalem
Another example of the "float-ing landmark" approach, this map shows many landmarks pictorially but takes great liber-ties in orientation and scale. Landmarks often face in the wrong direction with respect to the street base and are out of proportion to the streets and blocks. As a result, it is difficult to use the map for precise travel, although it is useful for obtaining a sense of the loca-tion and general character of sites (compare 4.14). *Design by I. Blaushild, artwork by R. Vero (Tel Aviv: Amir Publishing Ltd., copyright 1976).*

4.35
Soft Manhattan #1:
Postal Zones
Amusingly interpreted by an artist, here Manhattan's zip-code zones become soft sculpture. Land areas are formed of kapok-stuffed canvas bags. *By Claes Oldenburg, 1966; stenciled canvas, kapok, 80 by 30 inches. Courtesy Albright-Knox Art Gallery, Buffalo, NY; gift of Seymour H. Knox, 1966.*

4.36
Relief Maps: Peking and Rome
In this technique, outstanding features of several cities were modeled in clay relief panels. Models were made of fifty cities, all at the same scale, thus facilitating comparative study. Sizes ranged from one to twelve 8-by-8-inch modules. The models were then photographed, using a textured screen overlay to create more graphic consistency in the final product. The technique is simple and provides an easily understood and appealing representation of a place. *Richard Saul Wurman and students,* Cities: Comparisons of Form and Scale *(Raleigh, NC, 1974; distributed by MIT Press).*

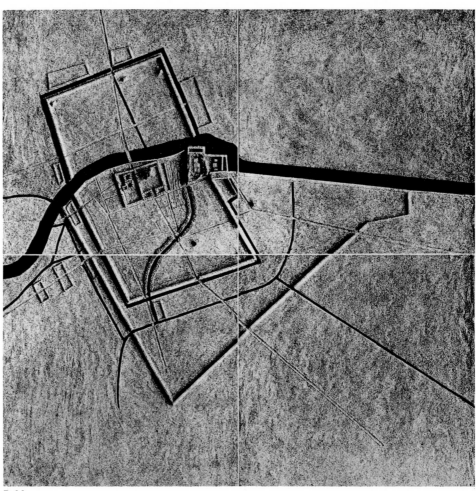

Peking

Rome

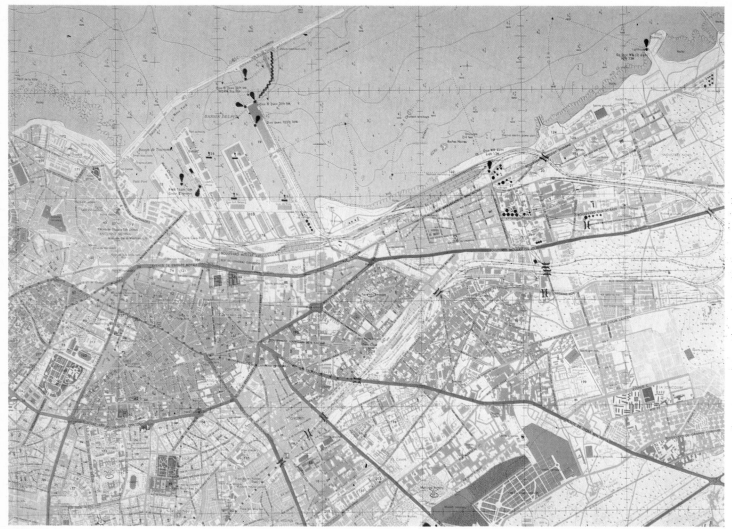

4.37
Casablanca: Building Type

Useful for engineering and military purposes, this map shows building height and construction type. The plan shape of buildings or groups of buildings is shown. Color hue indicates construction type; for example, steel-frame buildings are yellow, concrete are red, wood are brown, and "shacks" are orange. In addition, color value indicates building height. Three values are used — light (one to three stories); medium-cross-hatched (four to six stories); and dark (over six stories). *U.S. Army Engineer Topographic Laboratories, Fort Belvoir, VA, 1974.*

4.38
Casablanca: City
Perspective
Generalized heights and shapes of buildings are shown in this map. Building heights are not to scale, but are shown in three height categories. This map technique is useful in giving a rough idea of the form of urban areas but would be inappropriate when detailed information is needed. *U.S. Army Engineer Topographic Laboratories, Fort Belvoir, VA, 1974.*

4.39
Address Finder:
Répertoire des Rues

Another type of map is a city street directory. In this excellent guide, all the streets in Paris are listed alphabetically down the far-left column. The number of the district in which the street occurs is in the second column, followed by the letter and number of the corresponding quadrant on the accompanying map. The last three columns list the intersecting streets at the beginning and end, and the closest Métro station. The comprehensive nature of the list makes it a valuable tool for a visitor, particularly one using public transit. However, it cannot answer visitors' questions, such as, "Where is this place in relation to X?" "Where are the theaters?" "What does the place look like?" and so on. *Raymond Denaés,* L'indispensable Paris par arrondissement, *(Paris: Éditions L'indispensable).*

Rues	A	Plan	Commençant	Finissant	Métro
Jos.-Sansbœuf...	8	I 12	Pépinière, 6...	Rocher, 9...	Saint-Lazare
Joséphine...	18	D 15	Damrémont, 117	en impasse...	Jules-Joffrin
Josseaume (pass.).	20	N 25	Haies, 67...	Vignoles, 72...	Buzenoal
Josset (pass.)...	11	N 21	Charonne, 38...	av. Led.-Rol.101	Ledru-Rollin
Joubert...	9	I 13	Ch.-d'Antin, 35.	Caumartin, 58...	Ch.-d'Antin
Joudrier (imp.)...	11	N 24	bd Charonne, 85	...	Bagnolet
Jouffroy (pass.)...	9	I 15	bd Montmart.10	Gr.-Batelière, 9	Rich.-Drouot
Jouffroy (rue)...	17	G 10	bd Péreire, 2...	av. Wagram, 80.	Wagram
Jour (du)...	1	L 16	Coquillère, 2...	Montmartre, 9..	Les Halles
Jourdain (du)...	20	D 5	Pyrénées, 65...	Belleville, 154 ..	Jourdain
Jourdan (bd)...	14	M 15	Am.-Mouch.100	a. Gl-Leclerc129	Pte d'Orléans
Jouvence (imp. de)	18	S 10	Alésia, 245,...	...	Plaisance
Jouvenet (sq.)...	16	Q 3	Jouvenet, 16 ...	...	Chardon-Lag.
Jouvenet (rue)...	16	Q 3	av. de Vers., 152	Boileau, 51...	Chardon-Lag.
Jouy (de)...	4	N 18	N.-d'Hyères, 37.	Fran.-Miron, 58	Saint-Paul
Jouye-Rouve ...	20	I 22	Belleville, 60...	J.-Lacroix, 66 ..	Belleville
Joyeux (cité)...	17	D 12	Epinettes, 53 ...	en impasse...	Pte St-Ouen
Juge (rue)...	15	O 7	Viala, 9...	Violet, 6,...	Duplex
Juge (villa)...	15	O 7	Juge, 22...	en impasse...	Duplex
Juges-Consuls (d)	4	M 17	Verrerie, 68 ...	Cl.-St-Merri, 1.	Hôtel-de-Ville
Juillet...	20	K 23	Bidassoa, 44...	Bidassoa, 54....	Martin-Nad.
Juin (cour)...	11	N 20	p. Cheval-Blanc.	...	Bastille
Jules-Bourdais ...	17	F 8	bd Berthier, 134.	a. Brunetière, 31	Champerret
Jules-Breton...	13	R 18	J.-d'Arc, 172 ..	bd St-Marcel,37	Saint-Marcel
Jules-César...	12	O 19	bd Bastille, 22..	Lyon, 43...	Arsenal
Jules-Chaplain...	6	Q 13	N.-D.d.-Ch., 60.	Bréa, 21...	Vavin
Jules-Cheret...	20	N 26	Mendelssohn, 10	Dr-Déjerine, 9...	Pte Montreuil
Jules-Cherete...	16	L 5	bd E.-Augier, 36	Pompe,...	La Muette
Jules-Cloquet...	18	D 14	a. Ch.-Alb., 20	Pte St-Ouen, 11	Pte St-Ouen
Jules-Cousin...	4	O 19	bd Henri-IV, 17.	Petit-Musc., 12.	Sully-Morl.
Jules-David...	20	I 26	Paul-Meurice,41	Hors Paris...	Pte des Lilas
Jules-Dumien...	20	J 25	Pelleport 108...	H.-Poincaré, 3	Pelleport
Jules-Dupré...	15	T 8	Périchaux, 2...	bd Lefebvre, 95.	Pte Versailles
Jules-Ferry (bd)...	11	K 19	a. République,13	Fg-Temple, 28 ..	République
Jules-Guesde...	14	R 12	Vercingétorix,17	R.-Losserand, 18	Gaîté
Jul.-Hénaffe (pl.).	14	U 13	Besunier, 1...	Verrells, 40 ...	Pte d'Orléans
Jules-Janin (av.)...	16	M 5	Pompe, 12...	Pompe, 32...	La Muette
Jules-Joffrin (pl.).	18	E 16	Ordener, 82...	Mont-Cenis, 77.	Jules-Joffrin
Jules-Jouy...	18	F 15	Francœur, 12...	Cyr.-Bergerac, 3	Lamarck-Cau
Jules-Lefebvre ...	9	H 13	Clichy, 49...	Amsterdam, 68...	Liège
Jules-Lemaître...	12	Q 26	bd Soult, 62...	V.-d'Indy, 1...	Bel-Air
Jules-Pichard...	12	S 24	Jardiniers, 13...	Meuniers, 35...	Pte Charenton
Jul.-Renard (pl.).	17	G 7	Claude-Debussy	Gouvion-St-Cyr	Champerret
Jul.-Sandeau (b.).	16	L 4	Oct.-Feuillet, 2	a. H.-Martin,101	La Muette
Jules-Siegfried...	20	K 26	Irénée-Blanc ...	Paul-Strauss, 32	Gambetta
Jules-Simon...	15	Q 7	Croix-Nivert141	Cournot, 2....	Félix-Faure
Jules-Vallès...	11	N 22	Chanzy, 23...	Charonne, 102..	Charonne
Jules-Verne...	11	IJ 20	Orillon, 21...	Fg-d-Temple,98	Belleville
Julia-Bartet...	14	U 9	pl. Pte Vanves...	bd Ad.-Pinard...	Porte Vanves
Jul.-Lacroix (p.)...	20	J 22	Couronnes, 41..	Couronnes, 49..	Couronnes
Julien-Lacroix...	20	I 22	Ménilmont., 33	Belleville, 56...	Couronnes
Julienne (de)...	13	S 16	Pascal 62...	bd Arago, 45...	Glacière
Juliette-Dodu...	10	I 20	Cl.-Vellefaux, 3	Gge-a.-Belles, 20	Col.-Fabien
Juliette-Lambert...	17	F 9	bd Péreire, 36 ..	b. Malesh., 190.	Wagram
Jumeau (imp.)...	19	F 20	Tanger, 45...	...	Riquet
Junot (av.)...	18	F 14	Girardon, 3...	pl. C.Pecqueur,1	Lamarck
Junot (imp.)...	20	I 25	Haxo, 101 bis...	...	Télégraphe
Jura (du)...	13	R 17	bd St-Marcel, 49	Oudry, 10,....	Campo-Formio
Jussienne (de la)	2	K 16	Et.-Marcel, 40..	Montmartre, 41.	Les Halles
Jussieu (place)...	5	P 17	Linné, 24 ...	Jussieu, 19...	Jussieu
Jussieu...	5	P 17	Cuvier, 10...	Car.-Lemoine 35	Jussieu
Juste-Métivier...	18	F 14	av. Junot, 27...	Caulaincourt, 56	Lamarck
Justice (de la)...	20	K 26	Surmelin, 70 ...	bd Mortier, 61..	Pelleport
K					
Kabylie (de)...	19	G 19	bd Villette, 216.	Tanger, 12,....	Stalingrad
Keller...	11	N 21	Charonne, 41...	Roquette, 72 ...	Ledru-Rollin
Kellermann (bd)...	13	V 17	av. d'Italie, 192.	M.-Mouchez, 99.	Porte d'Italie
Kellermann (v.)...	13	V 18	b. Kellermann22	...	Porte d'Italie
Keppler...	16	J 8	Bassano, 21 ...	Galilée, 40 ...	George-V
Keufer...	13	V 17	Kellermann, 31.	Max-Jacob...	Porte d'Italie
Kléber (av.)...	16	J 7	pl. Etoile...	pl. Trocadéro, 4.	Etoile
(No 39 à 90)...		K 7	...	...	Kléber
(No 91 à fin)...		L 7	...	...	Trocadéro
Kléber (imp.)...	11	J 24	av. Kléber, 62 ..	en impasse...	Boissière
Kossuth (place)...	9	I 15	Chateaudun, 12.	Fg Montmart 58	N.-D.-Lorette
Kracher (pass.)...	18	E 16	Clignancourt 137	Neuve-I-Ch., 8.	Simplon
Kuss...	13	V 17	Peupliers, 39...	Bril.-Savarin, 16.	Maison-Blanc
Kuszner (pass.)...	19	J 21	Belleville, 17...	Rébeval, 26 ...	Belleville
L					
Labat...	18	F 16	Poissonniers, 61.	Bachelet, 12....	Marcad.-Pois.
La Baume (de)...	8	I 10	Courcelles, 20..	av. Percier, 11..	Miromesnil
Labie...	17	H 7	av. Ternes, 79...	Brunel, 46 ...	Porte-Maillot
La Boétie...	8	I 11	pl. St-August., 3	av. Ch.-Elys., 60	Miromesnil
(No 52 à fin)...		J 10	...	...	St-Ph.-Roule
Labois-Rouillon...	19	E 20	Curial, 29...	Aubervilliers 164	Crimée
Labor (cité)...	19	E 22	Couronnes, 55..	...	Couronnes
Laborde (de)...	8	I 12	Rocher, 11...	Miromesnil, 58	St-Augustin
La Bourdonnais...	7	M 8	quai Branly, 61..	pl. Ecole-Milit.4	Ecole Militaire
La Bourdon. (pt.)...	7	I 7	pt de l'Alma...	pont d'Iéna ...	Alma-Marc.

4.40
Environmental Control Map: Management of Main Street

This map is not concerned with topographic form per se but with who controls and manages elements of the built environment. It points out that although a street appears simple, a maze of agencies, individuals, and organizations is involved in making it what it is. The technique is most relevant to planning and administration. *Michael Southworth and Kevin Lynch,* Designing and Managing the Strip, *Joint Center for Urban Studies of MIT and Harvard, Working Paper No. 29, 1974.*

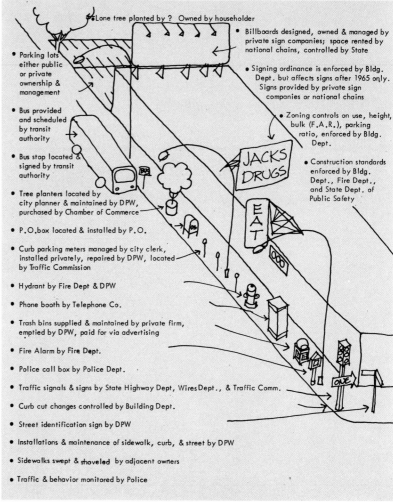

4.41
Sanborn Insurance Map: Spokane, Washington

Developed for insurance purposes, the Sanborn maps are the only readily available source of detailed building information in the United States. Building shapes, construction types, addresses, property lines, streets, underground utilities, and land-use information are given. The maps are periodically updated. They are useful in planning and construction but are too detailed for general use. *Sanborn Map Company, Inc., Pelham, NY.*

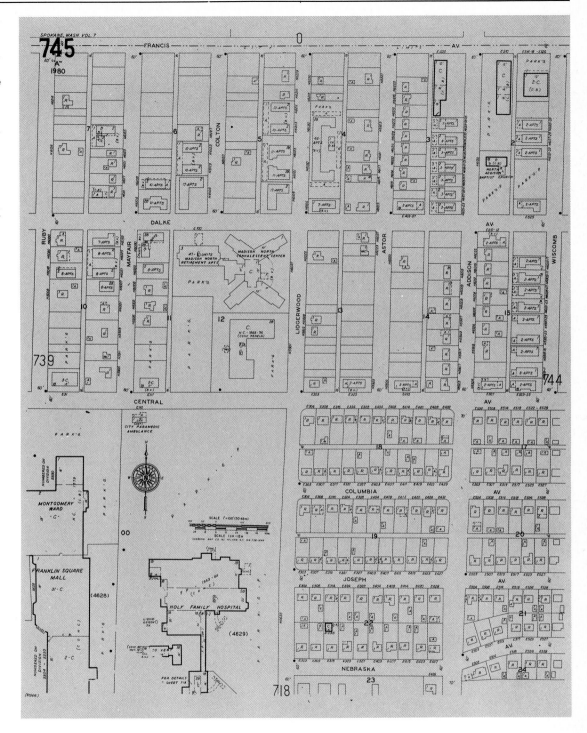

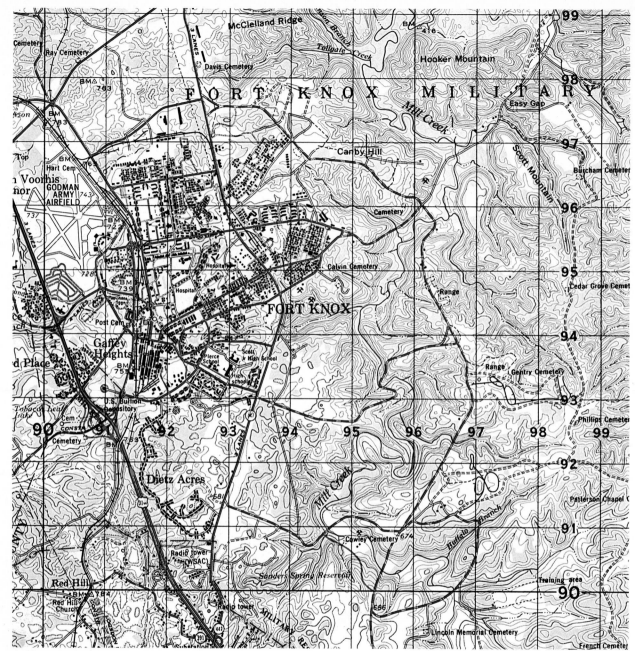

4.42
Vine Grove, Kentucky
Without sacrificing legibility, this military map conveys large amounts of information. Locations of individual buildings are shown, along with topography and ground cover. Roads and railroads are clearly described in terms of type, capacity, and condition. Finally, political boundaries and compass coordinates are indicated. Such maps are well suited to activities requiring detailed planning and action but are less useful in travel or tasks requiring broad analysis and generalization. *Defense Mapping Agency Topographic Center, Washington, DC.*

4.43
Stuttgart and Environs

This map provides a good sense of the texture and density of built-up sections and their relation to natural areas. Buildings are simplified into block patterns, leaving fine-grained patterns of streets. Major highways are clearly differentiated from other routes by line treatment. The map can be used for travel on the highway network but not for local travel; it is more useful as a reference or planning map to make one familiar with the region than as a guide map.

4.44
Model: Detroit

Three-dimensional models can provide convincing and easy-to-understand information about environments. They are one of the ideal techniques for representing the actual experience of a place, especially when used in conjunction with optical devices that simulate being in and moving about the environment. Models are useful for a variety of training, strategy, and planning purposes. For those who cannot read two-dimensional maps, they are invaluable, but have the obvious disadvantages of being cumbersome and expensive to make (compare 4.51). *Detroit City Plan Commission, 1964.*

4.45
Tactile Model for the
Blind: Philadelphia,
Independence Hall Block
This model was developed to
communicate the form and
pathways of the Independence
Hall area to the blind. Surface
textures are emphasized in the
model and are keyed in the legend. Braille information is included on the model. The
model was developed in clay
and cast in fiberglass. It is per-
manently located outdoors in
front of Independence Hall.
Richard Saul Wurman; photo-
graph by Joel Katz.

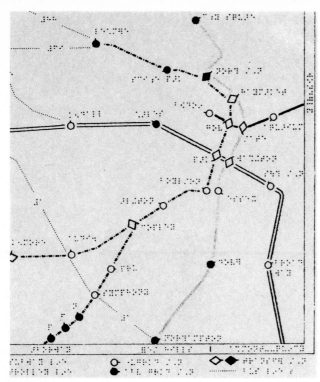

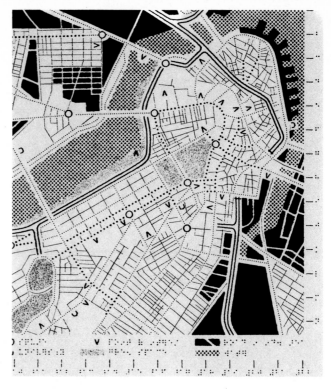

4.46
Braille-Tactile Map:
Boston and Cambridge

Maps for the blind, a fascinating branch of cartography, also have implications for the sighted. Buildings and pathways are embossed in low relief, creating a map that is in many ways more concrete and intelligible than most printed maps. For the blind, special attention is given to navigation aids and problems; for example, curbs and other barriers or hazards are tactually emphasized, as are guidance cues such as paving texture, fences, or walls. Place names are usually embossed on the maps in Braille. (For more information see Ann Middleton Kidwell and Peter Swartz Greer, *Sites, Perception, and the Non-Visual Experience*, American Foundation for the Blind, 1973.) *Prepared by MIT Planning Office, manufactured by Ithamai Kutai, distributed by Howe Press of the Perkins School for the Blind, Watertown, MA; copyright 1973 by the Massachusetts Institute of Technology.*

4.47
Braille Map: MBTA System
Tactile Route Map

The Braille map of the Boston subway system presents the route diagram with raised ridges defining the lines, station names in Braille, and a raised dot on the line for each station location. The routes are also printed in color and station names are printed in letters, allowing for interaction with the sighted. Additional information, including instructions and information about each station, is keyed into the map from several attached sheets in Braille. Relative distances between stations are distorted in the diagram, which may present planning problems for the blind just as it would for the sighted. *Robert Amendola and Gilligan Tactiles, Inc., for Massachusetts Commission for the Blind and Massachusetts Bay Transportation Authority, Boston, MA; copyright 1974.*

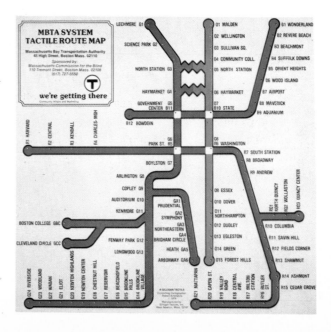

4.48
Compact Map: London

Through a clever trick of folding and cutting, one can view consecutive sections of this London map without ever opening more than one fold. The map first opens like a conventional book, allowing one to turn to the general area of interest within London, for example, Kentish Town or Camden Town. One then flips down the flaps to reveal the partially hidden sections. Strangely, all areas of the map are thus made accessible, unlike conventional folded maps, which leave most of the map "inside" and inaccessible. As long as one wants to proceed section by section, the system works well. However, if an overall view is needed there are problems. Because of the cuts and unusual folding, the map is difficult to open fully and once it is spread out, it tears easily along the slits. Thus, it is best used as a handbook in its compact state. British army road maps are made in a similar fashion. *Falk-Verlag GmbH, Hamburg, Den Haag; copyright by Falk-Verlag, Hamburg.*

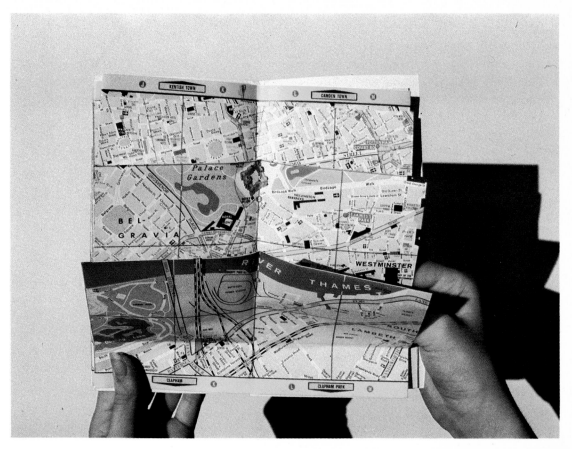

4.49
Pop-Out Map: Yellowbird Migration Guide

Storing the bulk of a paper map can be a problem—complicated folds leave one wondering how to open or refold it. Although this design prototype is schematic, it addresses itself to the folding problem by using a pop-out technique. Ingenious folding allows one to open or close the map in one motion. The technique is appropriate only for small maps such as this (8¼ by 10 inches), which folds down to 3½ by 5 inches. *Courtesy of Delta Air Lines.*

the regional center

A Comprehensive Plan for Downtown Buffalo, New York

4.50
Embossed Map: Buffalo

A low-relief representation of Buffalo is achieved by embossing a map pattern on heavy paper. In this case the relief is not high enough to be of much use to the blind; the map is intended for the sighted. The technique is attractive but not entirely practical. The embossing process is expensive and paper is of course subject to damage; plastic or metal would be durable substitutes. The advantage is that such maps can communicate the three-dimensional form of buildings and topography more directly than drawings (compare 3.9).
Wallace, McHarg, Roberts & Todd, The Regional Center: A Comprehensive Plan for Downtown Buffalo *(New York, 1971).*

4.51
Relief Map: Washington Mall

The Washington Mall and its associated landmark sites and institutions are attractively modeled in high-relief white plastic. Trees and streets are differentiated from grassy lawns through various relief patterns. Pictograms provide information about the institutions and introduce verbal descriptions of adjacent sites. The map is mounted in enclosed kiosks at several points along the Mall. The map is not designed for use by the blind, but the technique could be adapted to include Braille and other tactile information (compare 4.44, 4.45). *Wyman and Cannan Co. (New York) for Smithsonian Institution, National Park Service, the Capitol, National Gallery of Art, and the National Archives. Susan Hamilton, Project Director.*

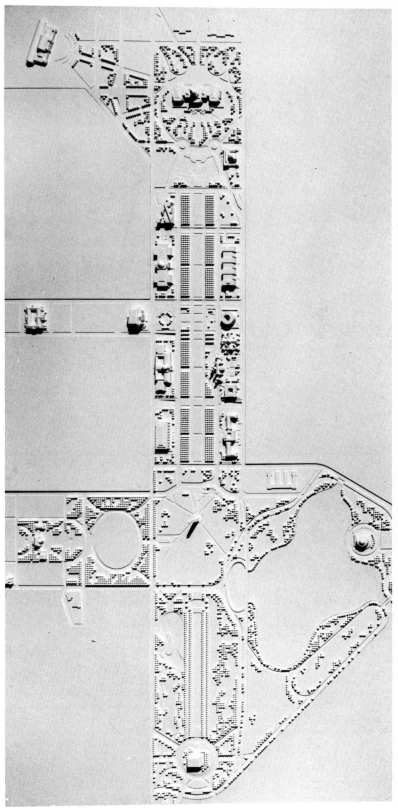

5.1
Pictorial Subway Guide for Children

The Boston subway system is represented pictorially to meet the special needs of children. Destinations of particular interest are shown in sketches colored to match the lines on which they occur. Boston has four color-coded lines—the Blue Line, Red Line, Orange Line, and Green Line. Each subway line is shown as a separate strip map to focus on its individual character and to simplify use. Pictures are stylized typical views or symbols associated with locations, such as a diver and fish for the Aquarium, an elephant for the Zoo, a swan boat for the Public Garden. Relations between lines are indicated by intersecting arrows in the appropriate color for each line, as well as by small "spider" diagrams that show the overall system with station names and line colors.

Such pictorial representations of prominent destinations enable users to form a quick image of the character of each subway line and to recall the stations. The designers felt this approach would help children to discover the city. A child can travel through the pictures, select a place that is appealing, note the name of the station and its relation to other stations on the line, and then figure out how to get there. The map stands in sharp contrast to the common "spider" diagram transportation maps, which intentionally exclude all contextual character for the sake of diagrammatic simplicity. It was considered important to reduce the amount of sophistication and knowledge children must possess to use this map. *Copyright © Boston Children's Museum 1980. Jim Zien, DETOURS Project Director; map graphics by Michael and Susan Southworth. Supported in part by a Youth Project Grant from the National Endowment for the Humanities.*

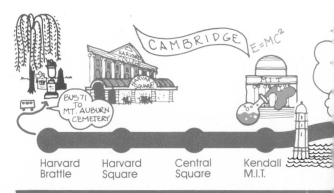

red line

Beacon Hill/PARK STREET
Boston Common/PARK STREET
Boston Tea Party Ship/SOUTH STATION
Charles River/Esplanade/CHARLES-MGH
Children's Museum/SOUTH STATION
Department Store/WASHINGTON

Freedo
Hart N
Harvar
JFK Libr
Informo

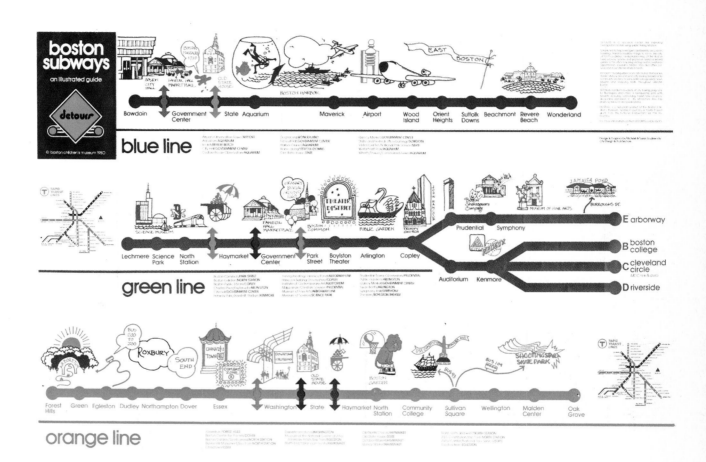

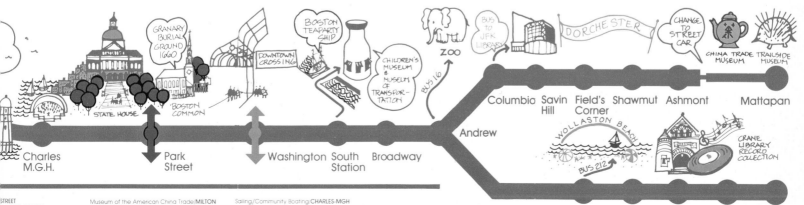

Land form and built form together make up the environment with which most of us are familiar. If we did no more than look at it, we might need only pictures or maps that are no more practical than that of the seventeenth-century Dutch cartographers (2.2). But we do not just contemplate our surroundings; we function within them, usually by going from one place to another. The problem of "How do I get from here to there?" is a fundamental one. Thus, route maps are among the most necessary of map types.

Strip maps are one of the earliest attempts to solve the problem. By focusing on the best route from one place to another, they are simple to construct, require a much smaller data base than area maps, and permit considerable flexibility in presentation. Early examples are the Roman road map, Tabula Peutingeriana (2.7), the medieval guide for religious pilgrims from London to Jerusalem (2.11), and the seventeenth-century English map of the road from York to West Chester (5.28). The technique is just as useful today, as the Triptik of the American Automobile Association shows (5.15).

The problem becomes more complicated, of course, when many routes and alternative forms of travel converge in an area. Then routes cease to be simple and become networks. Network maps are useful in presenting whole systems, such as subway or bus routes, or regional highway or airway complexes. In system maps, ease and speed of comprehension are often important, since masses of people rushing to and from urban destinations—subway users, for example—need quick information. Route and network maps also have many specialized applications as in hiking, walking, and bicycle guides.

Networks of whatever sort demand their own mapping techniques. Several maps in this chapter have pared down the basic information to a bare minimum, becoming elegant diagrams that simply identify decision points and lines, helping the map user understand where he is in relation to where he wants to go with minimum distraction. Other examples attempt to solve the problem of relating the network to the larger environment—a problem that can be distressing to the traveler who is lost or who wants to venture outside the system. Such maps try to provide connections to the real world in more naturalistic portrayals than schemata can give.

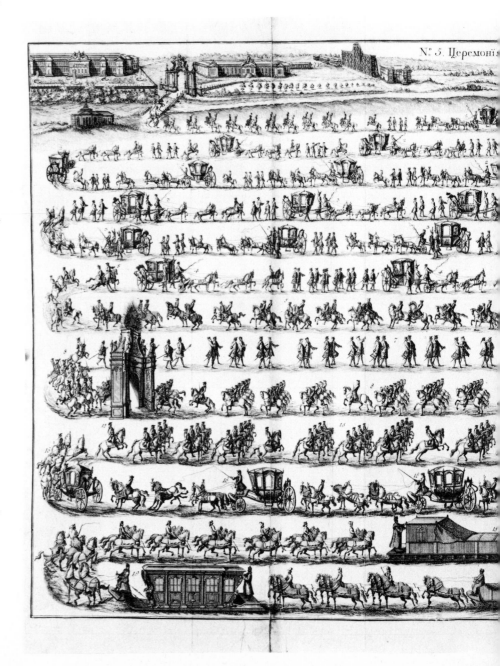

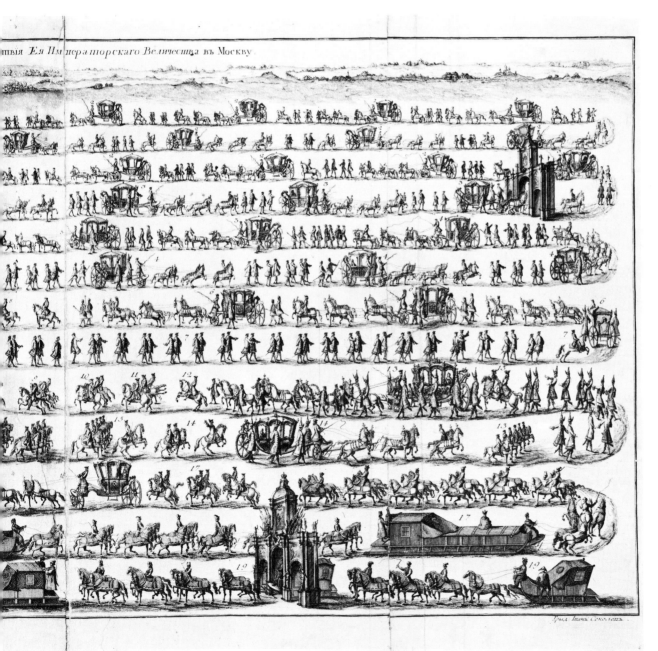

ствія *Ея Императорскаго Величества* въ Москву.

5.2
Route Map: Ceremony of the Procession of Her Imperial Highness, the Empress Elizabeth, from the Kremlin Winter House to the Annenhoff Winter House, 1742

This engraving is primarily an event map, depicting a journey by horse, carriage, and sleigh from St. Petersburg to Moscow. Members of the royal entourage are shown in great detail along with several landmarks denoting milestones of the trip. No attempt is made to indicate proper direction from landmark to landmark, but distance is suggested by the length of the neatly alternating line of participants. The primary intention was probably to express the grandeur of the procession and to identify the participants. The engraving was probably made in St. Petersburg, Russia, in 1744. *Photograph courtesy of The Metropolitan Museum of Art, Harris Brisbane Dick Fund, 1944.*

5.3
Pictorial Route Map:
The Nile

This charming map of the Nile portrays the archaeological sites and modern settlements in evocative sketches in ink and soft washes of color. More detailed information appears in the margins in sketches and text. Handsome and enticing, the map is a delight to the armchair or actual traveler in Egypt and enhances a boat trip on the Nile by identifying and visually organizing in sequence all the sites. *Copyright and published by Lehnert & Landrock, K. Lambelet & Co., Cairo.*

Top half

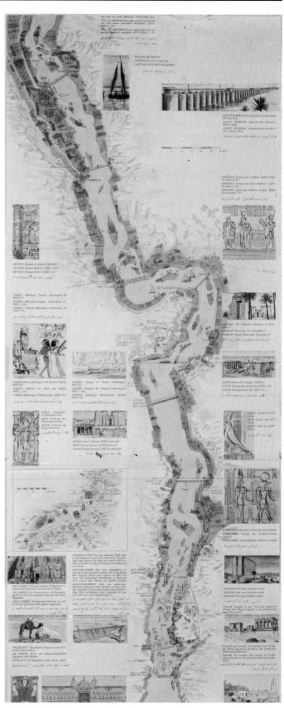

Bottom half

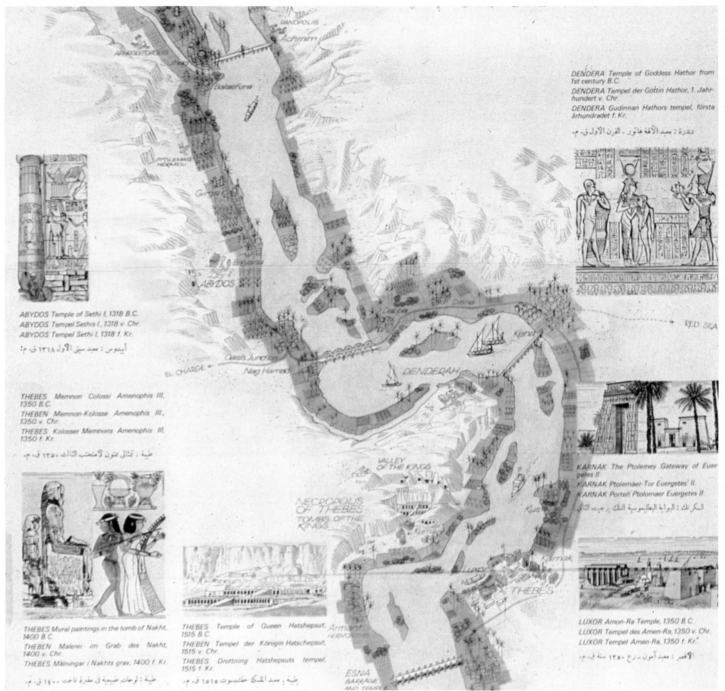

DENDERA Temple of Goddess Hathor from
1st century B.C.
DENDERA Tempel der Göttin Hathor, 1. Jahr-
hundert v. Chr.
DENDERA Gudinnan Hathors tempel, första
århundradet f. Kr.

دندرة : معبد الآلهة هاتور ـ القرن الأول ق. م.

ABYDOS Temple of Sethi I, 1318 B.C.
ABYDOS Tempel Sethis I, 1318 v. Chr.
ABYDOS Tempel Sethi I, 1318 f. Kr.

أبيدوس : معبد سيتي الأول ١٣١٨ ق. م.

THEBES Memnon Colossi Amenophis III,
1350 B.C.
THEBEN Memnon-Kolosse Amenophis III,
1350 v. Chr.
THEBES Kolosser Memnons Amenophis III,
1350 f. Kr.

طيبة : تماثيل ممنون لأمنحب الثالث ١٣٥٠ ق. م.

THEBES Mural paintings in the tomb of Nakht,
1400 B.C.
THEBEN Malerei im Grab des Nakht,
1400 v. Chr.
THEBES Målningar i Nakhts grav, 1400 f. Kr.

طيبة : لوحات ضيعية فى مقبرة ناخت ١٤٠٠ ق. م.

THEBES Temple of Queen Hatshepsut,
1515 B.C.
THEBEN Tempel der Königin Hatschepsut,
1515 v. Chr.
THEBES Drottning Hatshepsuts tempel,
1515 f. Kr.

طيبة : معبد الملكة حتشبسوت ١٥١٥ ق. م.

KARNAK The Ptolemey Gateway of Euer-
getes II.
KARNAK Ptolemäer-Tor Euergetes' II.
KARNAK Porten Ptolomaer Euergetes II.

الكرنك : البوابة البطلمية للملك برجيت الثانى

LUXOR Amon-Ra Temple, 1350 B.C.
LUXOR Tempel des Amen-Ra, 1350 v. Chr.
LUXOR Tempel Amen-Ra, 1350 f. Kr.

الأقصر : معبد آمون ـ رع ١٣٥٠ سنة ق. م.

Detail

5.4
Verbal Strip Map: A Trip down the Grand Canal, Venice

A trip down the Grand Canal is presented verbally in a double-column format with the sequential views on the left and right differentiated. Although this is constructed with one direction in mind and is easiest to use that way, the agile reader can take the route backward. Either forward or backward, the problem in this kind of mapping of very similar undifferentiated events is that one might mis-identify just one site and from then on be completely incorrect without knowing it. Use of reference addresses, unique and identifiable passing events, or pictures of landmarks would help keep one on the track. The system is suited to any pathway, from hiking trail to train route or highway. *Karl Baedeker,* Italy: Handbook for Travellers, Part I, 12th ed. *(New York: Charles Scribner's Sons, 1903).*

5.5
Verbal Route Program: Angers-Gien or Gien-Angers

The text sets forth the route program with related map segments. As the margin arrows indicate, the program is designed to work either forward or in reverse, although it is more laborious to read upward, skipping one paragraph at a time. This is a good example of the possibilities of verbal mapping at the re-gional scale. Orientation directions are not generally given, however. The map segments support the verbal mapping, helping people to organize the itinerary visually and stay on the route. *Michelin,* Châteaux of the Loire, *6th ed. (© Michelin et Cie, Propriétaires-éditeurs, 1977).*

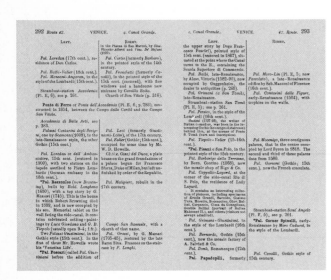

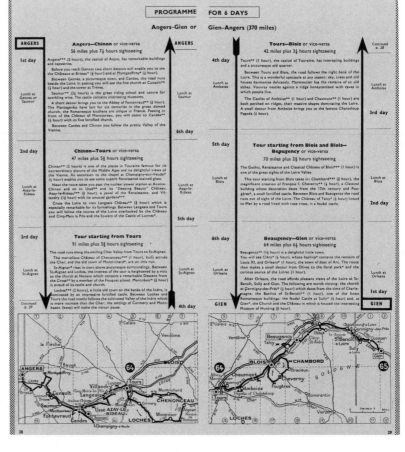

5.6
Navigational Stick Chart: Marshall Islands

The stick charts of the Marshall Islanders combined primitive and sophisticated abstract qualities. The mapping technique was fully developed before the Islanders had any written language. A grid of palm sticks, tied together with coconut fiber, indicates open sea over a territory of several hundred miles, while curved sticks show prevailing wave fronts. Shells show the relative location of islands and threads show where islands come into view. The charts were used on canoes during journeys. Use of the stick charts ended in the nineteenth century with the introduction of conventional maps by Europeans. *Reproduced by courtesy of the Trustees of the British Museum.*

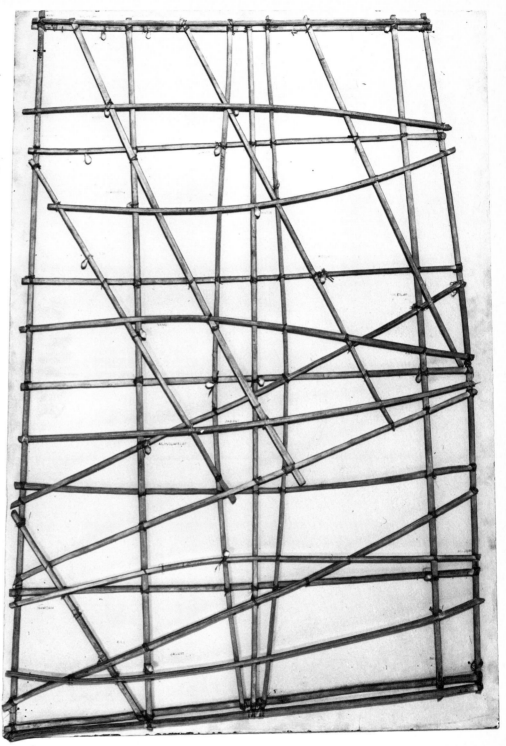

5.7
**Diagrammatic Strip Map:
Los Angeles**

The fashionable Beverly Hills shopping street of Rodeo Drive is reduced to simple yellow blocks and white bands for streets. Shop names are listed in the correct locations and a few addresses are given for ref-

erence. No irrelevant information is allowed to clutter the map. The map is graphically appealing, easy to make, and simple to use. *Richard Saul Wurman, LA/Access (Los Angeles: Access Press, Inc., © 1980).*

RODEO DRIVE   6

		Santa Monica Boulevard	
P		P	
Boulmiche		Nili Design Jewelry	
		Little Santa Monica Boulevard	
Hunter's Books	463	466 Carroll And Co. Men	
Lina Lee		Carroll And Co. Women	
Bottega Veneta		Eres	
Theodore		Cafe Swiss	
Theodore Man		P	
Saeeda		Williams Sonoma	
Courreges		Pierre Deux	
La Bagagerie		Elizabeth Arden / Delman Shoe Salon	
		Bijan	
Rodeo Collection		Amelia Gray	
		Edwards-Lowell	
Juschi		Johnson & Murphy	
Kurt Geiger of Bond Street		Jon Peters	
Vidal Sassoon		Eileen's Jewelry	
Fred Joaillier	401	400 Marie Augustine Cosmetic	
		Brighton Way	
Mr. Guy	369	372 Mr. G.	
P		Andrea Carrano	
		Glasner & Teba Jewelers	
P		Beverly Rodeo Hotel	
Gucci		Cafe Rodeo	
Hermes		Cecil Gee of London	
Wally Findlay Galleries		Gilda Antique Jewelry	
Omega		Bally of Switzerland	
Celine		Saint Laurent/rive gauche	
Ted Lapidus	329	Richard Bertine / Klein Art Galleries	
Knights Ltd.		332 Kazanjian Jewelers / Casserole Catering	
Jerry Magnin/Polo		Daisy	
Polo by Ralph Lauren		Mille Chemises	
Inamori		David Orgell	
Gunn Trigere Ltd.		Nazareno Gabrielli	
Right Bank Clothing & Tea Room		Georgette Klinger	
Matthews		Francis Klein Antique Jewelry	
Jax		Y. C. King & Sons / George Deming	
Jewels by Edwar		Battaglia	
Yves St. Tropez			
Alpha Cubic	301	300 Van Cleef & Arpels	
		Dayton Way	
Giorgio	273	272 Marion Wagoner	
		Petersen Galleries	
Frank Hoffer		P	
Brown Derby		American Savings	
9525	9537	9535	9475
		Wilshire Boulevard	
	9500		
Beverly Wilshire Hotel			

Rodeo Drive

Not to scale

RTD/LOCAL BUS LINES

76	Brentwood		UCLA	**Beverly Hills**
78	Silverlake	**ABC TV**		Silverlake
81	Woodland Hills	Sherman Oaks	Studio City	**Hollywood**
83	**Santa Monica**	**UCLA**	**Beverly Hills**	Downtown
86	Downtown	Burbank	**NBC Studios**	Van Nuys
87	USC Med Center			Boyle Heights
89	Mid-Wilshire			**Hollywood**
91	Downtown	**Hollywood**	**Beverly Hills**	**Century City**
92	Compton	Watts	Downtown	El Sereno
94	Downtown	**Hollywood**		West Hollywood
95	**Griffith Observatory**		**Exposition Park**	
96	Gardena	Hyde Park	Mid-Wilshire	**Hollywood**
114	Carson	Compton	Lynwood	
142	Athens	Watts	Huntington Park	Boyle Heights
151	Canoga Park	Woodland Hills		Chatsworth
152	Woodland Hills	Northridge	**Universal Studios**	
153	Chatsworth	Woodland Hills		Winnetka
154	Northridge	Tarzana	Van Nuys	Burbank
155	Tarzana	Northridge	Mission Hills	San Fernando
156	Mission Hills	Encino		Granada Hills
157	Sherman Oaks	**San Fernando Mission**		Sylmar
158	Chartsworth	Granada Hills	Panorama City	Sherman Oaks
159	Studio City	N Hollywood	Sun Valley	Studio City
160	Studio City	N Hollywood	Pacoima	San Fernando
161	Westlake Village		Agoura	Canoga Park
162	San Fernando	Sun Valley	Burbank	Sherman Oaks
163	Canoga Park	Reseda	Van Nuys	**Bur Airport**
164	Canoga Park	Reseda	Van Nuys	Burbank
165	Canoga Park	Reseda	Van Nuys	**Bur Airport**
166	Lakeview Terrace		Arleta	Northridge
168	Pacoima	Arleta		Northridge
169	Canoga Park	Panorama City	**Bur Airport**	Sunland
175	Trancas	**Point Dume**	**Malibu**	**Santa Monica**
202	**Downtown Minibus**			
206	**Airport Minibus Shuttle**			
210	**Hollywood**	Inglewood	Hawthorne	Torrance
212	Inglewood	**Hollywood**	Burbank Studio	**Bur Airport**
232	Long Beach	**Redondo Beach**		**LA Airport**
306	Compton			Watts
354	Hyde Park			South LA
356	Hyde Park	South LA		Huntington Park
359	Hawthorne	South LA	**Watts Towers**	Watts
420	Downtown	East LA	Monterey Park	Alhambra
422	Downtown	Monterey Park		El Monte
423	Long Beach	South Gate	Commerce	Altadena
424	Cal State LA	Rosemead	South LA	El Monte
425	East LA	Highland Park	Pasadena	Altadena
426	Downtown	Alhambra	Rosemead	El Monte
428	Downtown	Alhambra	Temple City	South Arcadia
430	Glassell Park	Highland Park	San Gabriel	El Monte
431	Rosemead	San Marino		Altadena

● Routes to Grand Tour Attractions

● Routes which stop Downtown

RTD/LOCAL BUS LINES

432	Downtown	San Marino		Arcadia
433	Altadena	Pasadena	Temple City	El Monte
434	Glendale	La Canada	Pasadena	Duarte
435	Altadena	Pasadena	Arcadia	El Monte
436	Pasadena	Eagle Rock	Glendale	**Hollywood**
438	Altadena	Pasadena	Arcadia	Duarte
440	Pasadena	Arcadia	Azusa	Pomona
441	La Puente	West Covina	Covina	Glendora
443	La Puente	West Covina	San Dimas	Glendora
445	Hacienda Heights		West Covina	Claremont
446	El Monte	Baldwin Park	West Covina	Walnut
451	Pomona			Claremont
452	Pomona			Pomona
453	Pomona			Claremont
454	Pomona			Pomona
821	Cerritos	La Mirada	Whittier	Pico Rivera
822	East LA	Pico Rivera	Whittier	La Mirada
825	Whittier	Norwalk		Artesia
826	Huntington Park	Maywood	Bell Gardens	Downey
827	Seal Beach	Norwalk	Whittier	El Monte
828	**Marina del Rey**	South LA	Downey	Whittier
829	Pasadena	Pico Rivera	Lakewood	Seal Beach
831	Lakewood	Paramount	Downey	Pico Rivera
832	Westchester	Inglewood	South Gate	Norwalk
834	**LA Airport**	Inglewood	South Gate	Lynwood
836	El Segundo	Hawthorne	Norwalk	Brea
838	El Segundo	Hawthorne		Lynwood
840	El Segundo	Gardena	Norwalk	La Mirada
841	San Pedro	Long Beach	Compton	Huntington Park
842	Dominguez Hills		Compton	Downey
844	Compton	Paramount	Bellflower	La Mirada
846	**Redondo Beach**		Bellflower	Buena Park
849	San Pedro			Harbor City
861	**Manhattan Beach**		Lawndale	Hawthorne
867	**Redondo Beach**		Hawthorne	Inglewood
869	**Marineland**	**Redondo Beach**		Inglewood
871	**Redondo Beach**		**LA Airport**	Downtown
872	(Sat., Sun. only) San Pedro			**Ports O'Call**
874	(Weekdays only)		San Pedro	**Ports O'Call**
877	**LA Airport**	**Marina del Rey**	Culver City	**Hollywood**

AIRPORT SERVICE BUS ROUTES

AS	**LA Airport**	Downtown Hotels
AS	**LA Airport**	Mid-Wilshire Hotels
AS	**LA Airport**	**Hollywood** Hotels
AS	**LA Airport**	**Beverly Hills** Hotels
AS	**LA Airport**	Pasadena Hotels
AS	**LA Airport**	San Gabriel Valley Hotels
AS	**LA Airport**	Long Beach Hotels
AS	**LA Airport**	Orange County Hotels

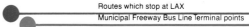

● Routes which stop at LAX

● Municipal Freeway Bus Line Terminal points

5.8
Bus Chart: Los Angeles
This chart is actually a series of diagrammatic strip maps of bus routes. Routes are listed in numerical order with end points and primary destinations listed verbally. The chart is attractive and easy to read, but no information is given about interconnecting bus routes or travel time. Route colors differentiate various types of buses: red lines go to major tourist attractions, orange lines begin or end downtown, green lines stop at the airport, and blue lines are part of the municipal freeway bus system. *Richard Saul Wurman and Michael Everitt, in Richard Saul Wurman,* LA/Access *(Los Angeles: Access Press, Inc., © 1980).*

5.9
Route Map: Place St. Michel to the Pont Sully, Paris

This map suggests a sight-seeing route (shown in red on the original) and indicates major landmarks in pictorial terms. Major vantage points are indicated by the fanlike symbol. The accompanying text provides a running verbal description of the sites in sequential order. *Michelin,* Paris and Principal Sights Near By *(Michelin copyright 1968, English ed.)*

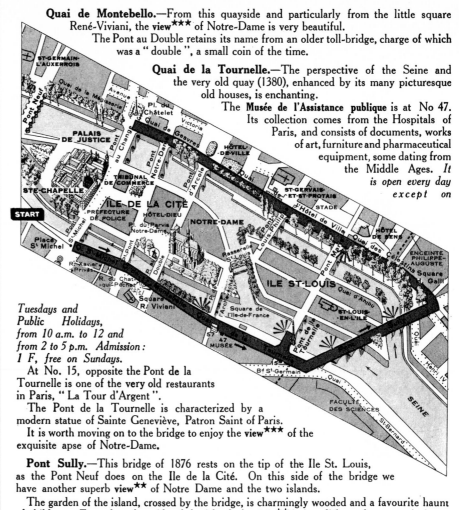

Quai de Montebello.—From this quayside and particularly from the little square René-Viviani, the **view**★★★ of Notre-Dame is very beautiful.

The Pont au Double retains its name from an older toll-bridge, charge of which was a " double ", a small coin of the time.

Quai de la Tournelle.—The perspective of the Seine and the very old quay (1380), enhanced by its many picturesque old houses, is enchanting.

The **Musée de l'Assistance publique** is at No 47. Its collection comes from the Hospitals of Paris, and consists of documents, works of art, furniture and pharmaceutical equipment, some dating from the Middle Ages. *It is open every day except on*

Tuesdays and Public Holidays, from 10 a.m. to 12 and from 2 to 5 p.m. Admission : 1 F, free on Sundays.

At No. 15, opposite the Pont de la Tournelle is one of the **very old** restaurants in Paris, " La Tour d'Argent ".

The Pont de la Tournelle is characterized by a modern statue of Sainte Geneviève, Patron Saint of Paris.

It is worth moving on to the bridge to enjoy the **view**★★★ of the exquisite apse of Notre-Dame.

Pont Sully.—This bridge of 1876 rests on the tip of the Ile St. Louis, as the Pont Neuf does on the Ile de la Cité. On this side of the bridge we have another superb **view**★★ of Notre Dame and the two islands.

The garden of the island, crossed by the bridge, is charmingly wooded and a favourite haunt of children. From the other side of the island, the **sight**★★ is in a different key, more intimate and perhaps more delightful.

5.10
Verbal Map: Guide to the Appalachian Trail in Maine

In this excellent verbal hiking guide, route directions are identified and arranged by distance from the starting point. This example presents a 12.5-mile segment of the trail. A pedometer is helpful to the hiker so that decision points can be anticipated. For hikers who want to travel in the opposite direction, a reverse set of instructions follows. Numerous landmarks and descriptions are given at each decision point. A simple topographic reference map accompanies each trail segment in the guide. *Maine Appalachian Trail Club, Inc.,* Guide to the Appalachian Trail in Maine, *Publication No. 1, 9th ed. (Augusta, ME, copyright 1978).*

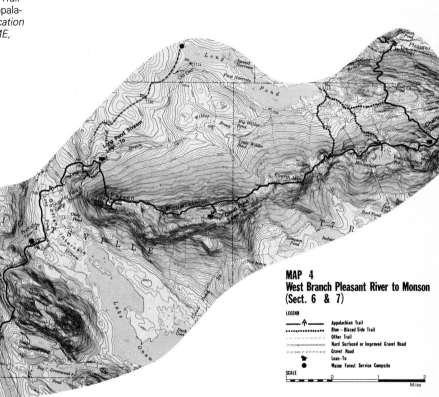

MAP 4
West Branch Pleasant River to Monson
(Sect. 6 & 7)

LEGEND

━━ⒶⒶ━━	Appalachian Trail
••••••••	Blue – Blazed Side Trail
————	Other Trail
═════	Hard Surfaced or Improved Gravel Road
────	Gravel Road
▄▀▄	Lean-To
●	Maine Forest Service Campsite

SCALE 0   1   2 Miles

SECTION 6
PLEASANT RIVER, WEST BRANCH TO BODFISH FARM
17.0 MILES

Direction N. to S.	**TRAIL DESCRIPTION**

Miles   **Trail Data** (see page 127 for opposite direction)

0.0 m. Section begins on south bank of West Branch Pleasant River. It is ¾ m. back across river and east along Pleasant River Road, to the end of car road from Katahdin Iron Works at Hay Brook. Trail south follows tote road upstream along bank of Pleasant River for 0.1 m. then turns SW away from River.

0.6 Cross gravel lumber road, follow branch road directly opposite for short distance then **turn left**, leaving branch road (ahead it continues 1½ m. to Long Pond) and begin steep ascent.

1.4 Reach top of ascent and proceed across more level section.

1.7 Reach worn tote road and continue ahead. To right, it is 1.7 m. to Chairback Mtn. Camps on east end of Long Pond (this was former A.T. route. On A.T. cross outlet of East Chairback Pond and skirt south shore.

2.3 Skirt west and south shore of small unnamed pond. Ascend steadily beyond.

3.3 Reach narrow col between Chairback and Columbus Mtns. At junction of trails in boggy area, A.T. **turns right**. To left is ½ m. blue-blazed side trail to summit of Chairback Mtn. (elev. 2,219 ft.) with good views into Pleasant River Valley and of White Cap. Ahead, in col, an obscure trail leads south off range 2 1/3 m. to Big Houston Pond Camps. A small spring may be found down this trail 30 yds. From this junction, it is 150 ft. along A.T. to **Chairback Gap Lean-to** on side of col. See section on **Lean-tos & Campsites** for description of lean-to and its accommodations. Beyond lean-to, Trail ascends steeply.

3.8 Reach ledge near summit of Columbus Mtn. (elev. 2,342 ft.).

4.0 10 yds. to left of Trail is cairn marking viewpoint to south. Beyond, descend steadily toward prominent West Chairback Pond, between Columbus and the next peak on the Range, Third Mtn.

SECTION 6

PLEASANT RIVER W. BR. TO BODFISH FARM

Direction N. to S.	

4.9 In sag, cross outlet of West Chairback Pond, then cross old tote road. To right, it is 2.2 m. to Chairback Mtn. Camps on Long Pond. To left, road leads 0.2 m. to shore of West Chairback Pond, a beautiful mountain tarn. A.T. continues ahead and soon begins to climb Third Mtn.

5.6 Reach Monument Cliff at summit of Third Mtn. (elev. 2,069 ft.).

5.7 Blue blazed side trail **to left** leads 100 yds. to ledge with views to south of Indian Pond and Benson Mtn. After short descent, pass bog in small sag. Beyond, descend steeply.

6.5 Reach junction of blue-blazed side trail to right, leading off ridge 2.1 m. to Chairback Mtn. Camps.
    A.T. beyond begins ascent of Fourth Mtn. It climbs over a number of "knobs" and a series of open ledges.

7.8 Reach wooded crest of Fourth Mtn. (elev. 2,425 ft.). Descend steeply beyond into sag between Fourth and Barren Mtns.

8.5 Reach bottom of sag. To right is rough trail, blue blazed, leading north off the range, 1¾ m. down to the shore fo Long Pond at the old "Seaboard" Campground now an old lumber camp clearing. A.T. swings left and crosses interesting bog. Beyond it begins ascent of Barren Mtn.

9.8 Side Trail on left leads 150 yds. to spring, and then to view point with view to the south.

10.1 Blue-blazed side trail on left, leads 0.2 m. to **Cloud Pond Lean-to** on shore of pond. See section on **Lean-tos & Campsites** for description of lean-to and its accommodations. A.T. gradually ascends along crest beyond.

11.1 Reach summit of Barren Mtn. (elev. 2,670 ft.) at abandon firetower. View here is excellent in all directions. Beyond, descend steeply to west.

12.8 Reach Barren Ledges.

12.9 Blue-blazed side trail leads 75 yds. to viewpoint at head of of slide on Barren.
    On A.T. begin very steep descent off Range.

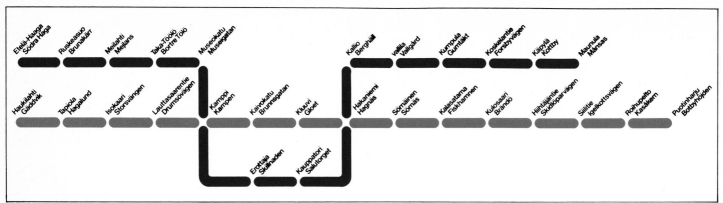

5.11
Line Diagram for Helsinki Subway

A graphic alternative to the London Underground approach (5.13), the Helsinki subway system looks like a string of sausages. Stations are emphasized by breaks in the route. Although graphically elegant, indicating stations as breaks rather than enclosed spaces or masses may confuse some users. *Ola Laiho, Esko Miettinen of G4, Designers, Helsinki; courtesy GRAPHIS Press Corp., Zurich, Switzerland.*

5.12
Pictorial Bus Route

Communicating route information without confusion is a problem because so much is available. This map eliminates all but the essential information. The route itself is given visual dominance by increasing its width and printing it in color. Intersecting bus and subway lines are indicated to aid trip planning. Bus schedules are printed on the reverse side of the folder. Major recognizable landmarks on or near the route are shown in pictorial terms. The pictorial technique was used to make the maps readily usable by the general public. More than 150 of Boston's bus routes have been mapped in this way (compare 5.1, 5.18). *By Michael & Susan Southworth, City Design & Architecture; copyright 1980 Massachusetts Bay Transportation Authority, Boston, MA.*

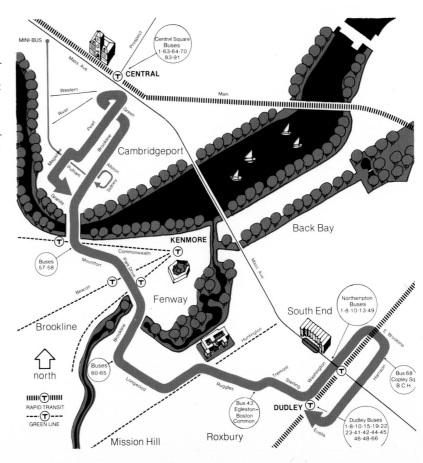

5.13
London Transport Underground System

The London Underground Map, considered a classic diagrammatic system map, has been the model for numerous maps in other cities. The system portrayed is extensive and complex so that focus on its key components—stations and routes—is helpful. The different lines are color-coded to make it easier to follow an individual line from beginning to end without getting tangled up in the other lines. Easily identifiable symbols are used for stations and interchanges. Unfortunately, light yellow was chosen for the Cir-

cle Line, making an outline necessary. As a result, graphic treatment of this line is inconsistent with the rest of the map.

Showing a system in a void does have its problems. Where am I? Where is the line going? To answer questions like these, references outside the system are needed. The only reference here—not a particularly useful one—is the Thames River. *Designed by Paul E. Garbutt and Harry C. Beck; by permission of London Transport Executive. Copyright London Transport Executive.*

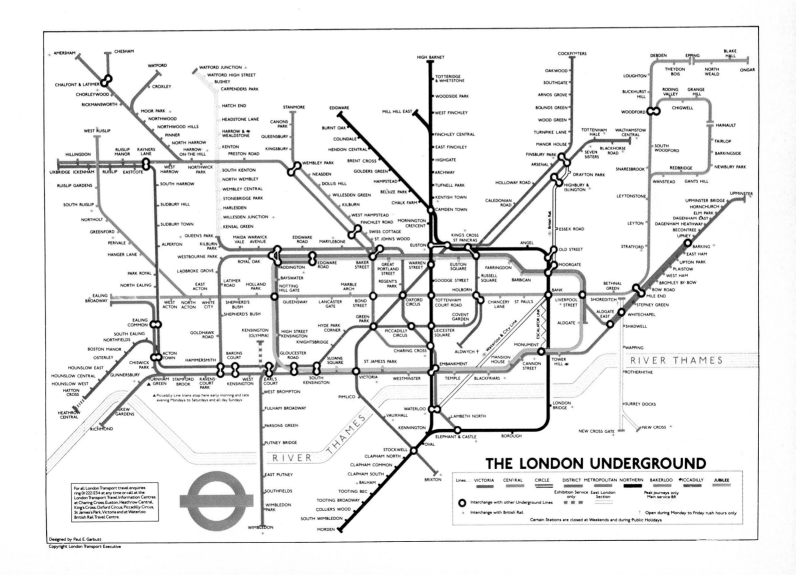

THE LONDON UNDERGROUND

5.14
Verbal Route Guide: Up the Coast to Malibu

Verbal maps, in addition to being understandable by those who have problems with conventional maps, can provide more information and a stronger environmental sense. This bicyclists' guide from Santa Monica to Malibu evokes in a few words strong pictures of the landscapes, people, and activities one can expect to find along this section of the Pacific Coast Highway. Each route begins with an abbreviated assessment in terms of length, terrain, traffic, and recommended season or time. Then comes a paragraph describing the whole experience in general terms. Next, points of interest are described with special attention to comforts and interests of the cyclist. These are keyed to a skeletal reference map. *Gershon Weltman and Elisha Dubin,* Bicycle Touring in Los Angeles *(Los Angeles: Ward Ritchie Press, copyright 1972 by the authors).*

IO   UP THE COAST TO MALIBU

LENGTH: *26 miles round trip*
TERRAIN: *Mainly flat*
TRAFFIC: *Medium to heavy*
BEST RIDDEN: *Any time of the year*

The ride from Santa Monica to Malibu on Pacific Coast Highway has a great sense of distance and place, despite its reasonable length. You leave the big city behind, pedal steadily on through vast, scenic spaces, and finally arrive at a quaint village with beautiful and distinctive inhabitants. It is sort of cross-country touring in miniature, a foreign experience in your own backyard. Pacific Coast Highway is a fast road, with a goodly amount of car and truck traffic, particularly in summer. But there are marked shoulder lanes on both sides, so that the cyclist is removed somewhat from the main stream. In addition, motorists are more used to seeing bicycle riders on this stretch of open road than elsewhere, and tend to give them wide berth. En route, we have plenty of time to take in the various features of the seaside environment: the eroded palisades, the mountain canyons running into the ocean, the shifting sands, the offshore reefs, and the way the coastline is formed into numerous small bays. The breeze usually blows directly offshore, cleaning the air without really slowing our progress in either direction. Each season has its own pleasures on the beach, from the refreshing swims of summer to the envigorating air and churning seas of winter. Having sampled one, the cyclist will want to explore them all.

65

Along the Way

1. Our sea ride begins on the Pacific Coast Highway at the mouth of Santa Monica Canyon, where Chautauqua Boulevard meets West Channel Road. Will Rogers Beach has ample parking; but on summer weekends, the lots fill up early, so an early start is best then. The cozy eateries and drinkeries in the Canyon offer a stirrup cup of various kinds to the dauntless rider.

2. Will Rogers Beach State Park stretches for over three miles of coastline to Castle Rock at the city limits. The large and good-looking apartments that have been built against the palisades are probably the wave of the future — a compromise between those who want to live at the beach and those who want to use it.

3. Around Topanga Canyon Boulevard we encounter the older type of oceanfront development: rows of shoulder-to-shoulder homes, cottages, apartments, and clubs, which barricade the beach quite effectively against the public. Access ways have now been opened by the County at several points, and cyclists will be pleased that the days of such completely selfserving land use are probably over.

4. The scalloped beaches just west of Topanga have close-in reefs which attract many fish, as well as the favorite game of skin divers — the California Spiny Lobster. We may meet some of the wet-suited hunters on shore, or see their red and white flag bobbing on the waves.

5. We approach Malibu along a continuous line of dwellings, punctuated by quick food stands, shops, gas stations, and whatall, most with giant overhead signs. Not a great deal of respect has been shown here to our splendid Riviera.

66

---

6. Malibu Pier is a properly salty collection of seafood restaurants and fishing supply shops. Locals drop their lines from pierside, while others take the sports fishing boats which leave from pier's end for cruises up the coast. A good place to relax for a while over a soft drink, a beer, or a hot cup of coffee, depending on you and the season.

7. Gidget is alive and well at Surf Riders State Beach, just west of the Malibu Pier. This portion of surf line has been reserved for the hot-doggers and hang-tenners, and one can see them hard at it whatever the weather or time of day.

8. We bear left onto Malibu Road, which carries us two-and-a-half miles further along the shoreline, beside some of Malibu Colony's finest and most interesting beach houses. Spare and simple Hunt house, at 24514 Malibu Road, has received special commendation; it was designed in 1955 by Craig Ellwood. The road runs into the Coast Highway near Solstice Beach, and here we turn around to retrace our route back to Santa Monica Canyon. Don't worry, the ocean views are never the same twice, and the way back proves just as intriguing as the way out.

Bike riding in the city—new wonders to see each block, plus exercise.

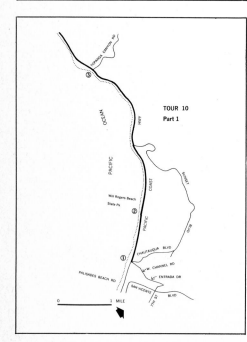

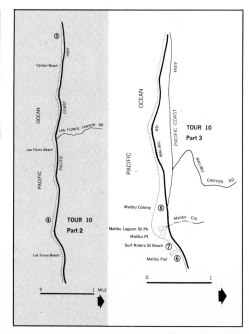

5.15
Triptik

Triptiks are personalized route maps prepared by the American Automobile Association. Given any origin and destination in North America, the AAA uses standardized maps of route segments to prepare a strip map of the entire itinerary. The recommended route is marked in felt marker; the route proceeds sequentially from front to back of the booklet. Detailed maps and verbal descriptions of metropolitan areas are included for each segment of the route. The system is valuable for the motorist and could be adapted to other forms of transportation. *Copyright © AAA. Reproduced by permission.*

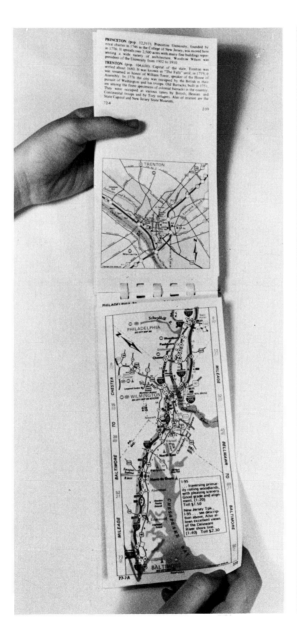

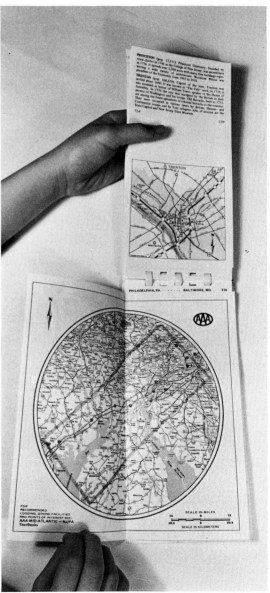

5.16
System Diagram with Landmarks: Washington, DC, Metro

The Washington, DC, Metro diagram is a variation on the subway "spider" diagrams of other major city subway systems and attempts to relate a rather abstract diagram to the real city by using common references. Several geographic landmarks are included—the Potomac and Anacostia rivers are in pale blue, district and county boundaries are in gray, and public lands are in light green, with several of the most prominent building facades in simplified form in white. Within the fat, colorful lines are two sizes of white dots for the stations and circled dots that represent stations serving as transfer points between lines. Whenever possible, the station names have been located in the horizontal position for ease of reading even when the lines are not vertical (compare 5.13). *Graphic design by Bill Cannan and Co., New York City, for Washington Metropolitan Area Transit Authority.*

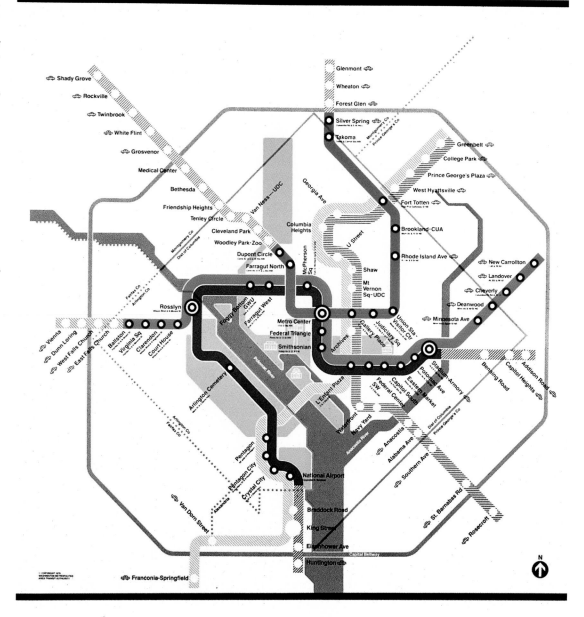

5.17
Bus Routes: Seattle-King County

One of the more successful solutions to the problem of bus-system mapping, this map of Seattle shows the entire geographic context and street system in pale background tones. To avoid information overload, only major streets are named. Routes are identified by frequently spaced large numbers. Unfortunately, there is occasional overprinting of route numbers and street names. Supplemental street maps are needed for detailed street finding, but transfer from this map to a street map is made relatively simple by the undistorted street grid used as a base.
Metro Transit, Seattle, 1975.

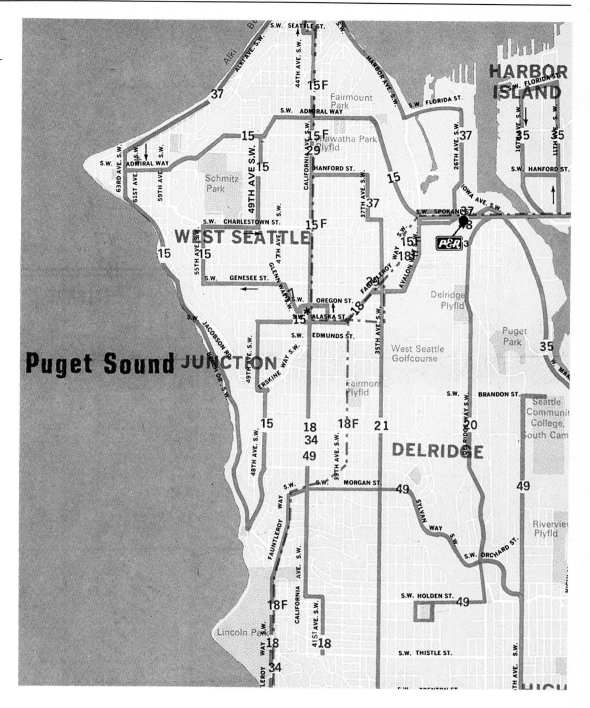

5.18
Strip Maps: Paris Buses
These bus route maps provide the names of major stops and Métro connections, as well as fare divisions for Paris bus lines. The routing directions, turns, and so on are approximately correct, but the user must know where he is going in terms of the major stop names in order to use the maps. No information about specific sites, intersecting streets, or notable buildings is included except indirectly, as in the use of the ''Hotel de Ville'' Métro station as a major stop.

Presenting the bus lines individually, as this collection does, makes them easier to follow than a single mapping of complex, interwoven bus lines, which requires difficult untangling. It is easy to comprehend the skeletal information, but one is left without much sense of the surroundings since the lines are shown virtually in a vacuum (compare 4.39). *Raymond Denaès,* Guide Général de Paris *(Paris, Éditions L'indispensable).*

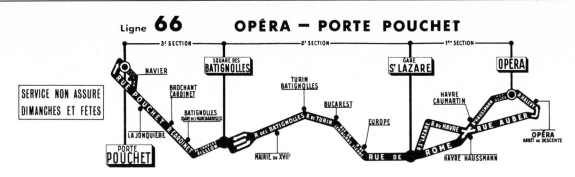

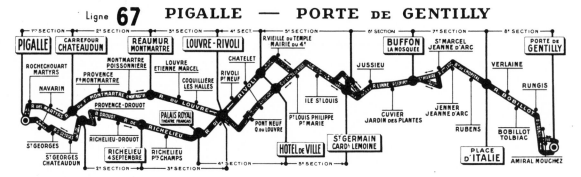

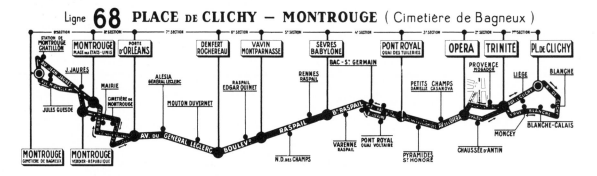

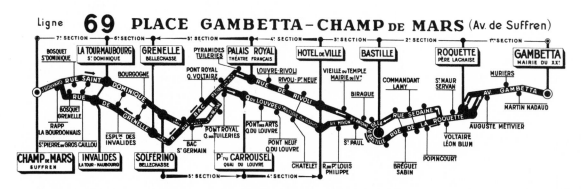

5.19
Highway Intersection Map: Detroit

The needs of highway drivers are the focus of this map. Each access and exit point in the system is detailed, but all other information outside the highway system is ignored. Sections of the highway that have no decision points are compressed to save space.

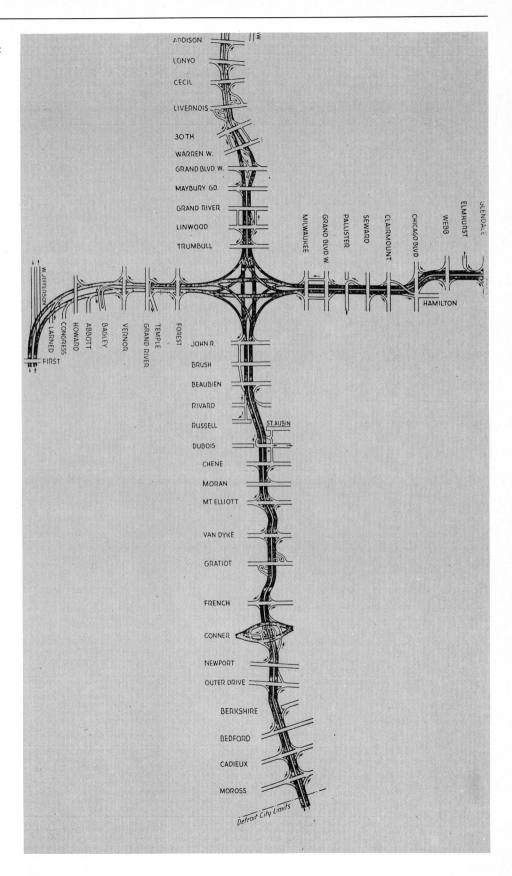

5.20
New York Subway Map

This map attempts to solve many of the functional problems of earlier New York subway maps. Care has been taken to give many geographic references, including streets, street names, and several landmarks and points of interest. The Manhattan street pattern has been distorted, however, to accommodate the complexity of the subway network. Instead of using the color-coding and rigid geometry of the elegant Vignelli map (5.22), only one color— red—is used for all subway lines; different lines are identified by numbers or letters at stations and along routes. This facilitates reproduction of the map in a variety of media and color formats and eliminates the need for color discrimination. The map was tested extensively before final delineation. Such testing is essential to the success of a complex public map. *New York City Transit Authority.*

5.21
Manhattan Bus Guide

This rather successful bus map uses four colors—red, orange, blue, and green—to distinguish northbound, southbound, westbound, and eastbound buses. Buses are identified by numbers inside circles along routes. The light gray street pattern helps make the map intelligible, but only streets traversed by buses are named. As with the New York subway guide (5.22), inclusion of district names and more landmarks would make the map more useful. *New York City Transit Authority; copyright 1974.*

5.22
New York Subway Guide

The complex New York subway system, a maze of intersecting and overlapping routes, is simplified in a handsome diagram of color-coded route lines in the manner of the London Underground map (5.13). Distances are distorted for the sake of clarifying the diagram. Streets and some landmarks are named to provide orientation, but more orientation cues, such as district names, would be helpful. Color-coding is useful when no more than a handful of readily distinguished colors is necessary. Testing has shown that color discrimination of the general public is not reliable for coding of more than five or six variables. *Massimo Vignelli, designer; New York City Transit Authority, copyright 1974.*

5.20

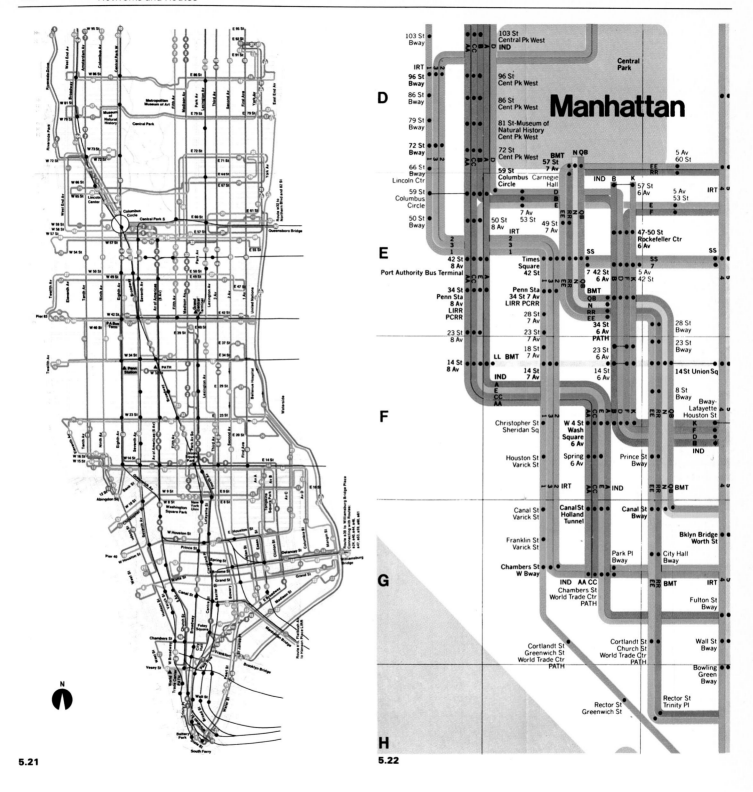

5.21

5.22

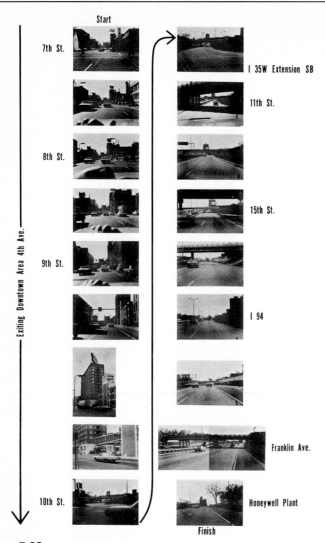

Start

7th St.

8th St.

9th St.

10th St.

I 35W Extension SB

11th St.

15th St.

I 94

Franklin Ave.

Honeywell Plant

Finish

Exiting Downtown Area 4th Ave.

5.23
Photographic Route Sequence:
Exiting Downtown Area via Fourth Avenue, Minneapolis

Route sequences of still photos or film are useful in environmental analysis and design and can also be effective in route learning. In still-photograph sequences it is important that each photograph contain a repetition of some identifiable element from the previous photograph so there is no confusion about the relations between them. The ninth photograph down on the left indicates that one is going to turn a corner. Although photographic sequences provide good route information, there is no sense of what is outside the picture frames. In addition they normally have to be annotated with such information as street names and addresses, which are not usually dominant enough in a photograph. *Department of Planning & Development, City of Minneapolis, 1969.*

5.24
Proposed Image Structure for a Highway: Minneapolis

Visual experience along a highway is symbolized here. Landmarks are shown by asterisks, open fields of view by long arrows, enclosure and tunnels by heavy black. Diagrammatic sectional views accompany the route on the right. The map is to be read from the bottom up; time-distance intervals are given for each minute of travel. Perceptual maps such as this have been useful in highway design and evaluation. *Department of Planning & Development, City of Minneapolis, 1969.*

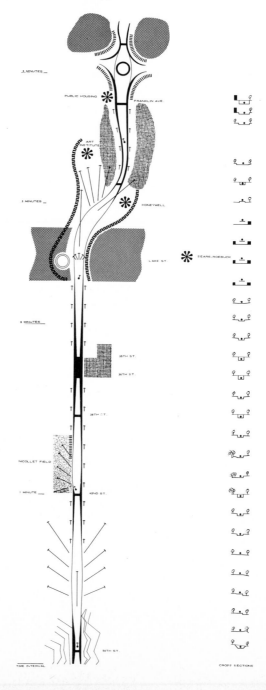

5.25
Sequence from I-35W
Bridge to Nicollet Mall
In many respects sketch sequences of a route are more effective than photo sequences because they allow emphasis and editing. What is most important can be highlighted and what is not informative or merely distracting, eliminated or simplified. Since the interpretive element is strong, caution must be taken so style does not predominate over information. Sketch sequences, in addition to having low production costs, are useful in simulating the visual impact of proposed environmental changes as perceived from a highway or street. *Department of Planning & Development, City of Minneapolis, 1970.*

1. Tall landmarks symbolizing Metro Center loom on the horizon from the highway near the western boundary of Minneapolis

2. getting larger and clearer as the separating distance lessens;

3. curves cause changes in the scope of vision

4. when suddenly the basilica on the right and the skyline ahead signal the entrance into Downtown;

5. onto the Third Avenue N. distributor where the western elevation of Downtown is so apparent;

6. then the highway depression far below the street level obliterates the view

7. and momentarily all that can be seen is the large parking ramp over the distributor;

8. direct access from roads to parking to skyway

9. where the rest of the trip to work is by foot in the comfort of the second-level skyways and arcades;

10. a pleasant walk where diversity is everywhere — from the domed courts

11. to the cheerful cafes

12. and shops along the route and below on the street where new vistas are achieved from the glass-walled bridges

High-Speed and Commuter Rail System

Southeastern Pennsylvania Transportation Authority

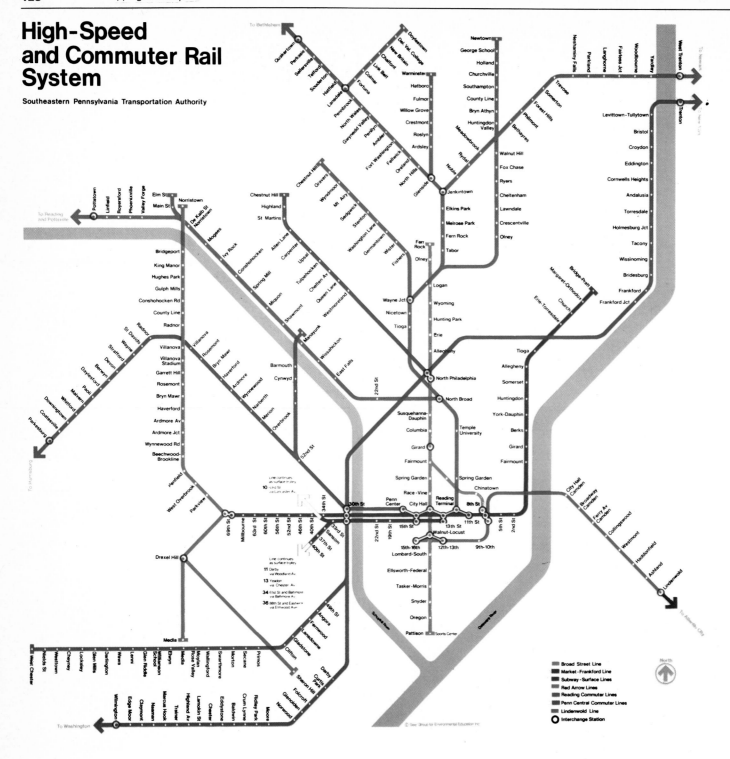

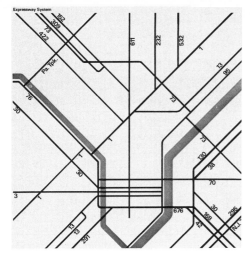

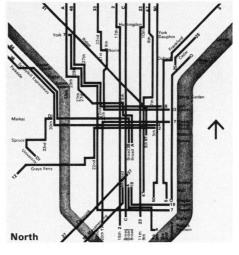

North

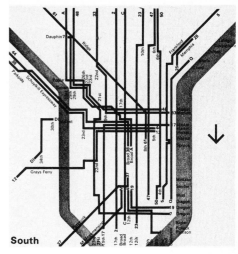

South

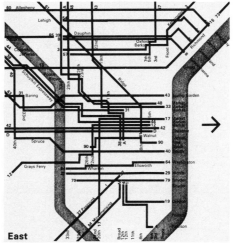

East

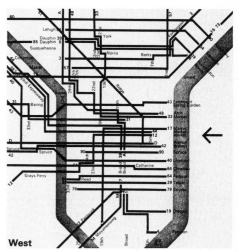

West

5.26
Subway, Bus, and Expressway Maps: Philadelphia

Dissection, distortion, and simplification in these maps have helped make the Philadelphia transportation system more understandable. The subway map, based on the London Underground map, uses the skeletal system approach. Routes are regularized and simplified and station names are emphasized. As in London, only the rivers are shown for geographic orientation. Because no other landmark data are given, the routes appear to exist in a vacuum.

While comprehension of the subway system is made simple, relating that system to the rest of the city is difficult for strangers. Other maps—including mental maps—must be used in conjunction with system maps such as these.

The bus system map uses similar principles. To simplify the system, north, south, east, and west buses have been shown on two separate maps. No stops are shown but street names and bus numbers are given. Despite the elegant graphics and clarity, the map might still be difficult to use. Without landmarks or a street grid, one is at a disadvantage and must find one's own route in the tangle of possibilities. *Richard Saul Wurman and John Andrew Gallery,* Man-Made Philadelphia: A Guide To Its Physical and Cultural Environment *(Cambridge, MA: MIT Press; copyright GEE! 1972).*

5.27
Route-Intersection Maps
Entries, exits, and intersections are the main sources of confusion on highways. Thus, these strip maps give detailed information for each decision point. Intervening segments of highway are compressed. Note that the entire route is represented as a straight line, ignoring any curves, since these are not particularly important in highway orientation. Little information is given about the environs; without environmental backup information one must know exactly which intersection is needed. The strip system allows much more compact presentation of a route than conventional techniques. Reader's Digest AA New Book of the Road *(London: copyright © 1975 The Reader's Digest Association Limited; based upon Ordnance Survey; Crown copyright reserved).*

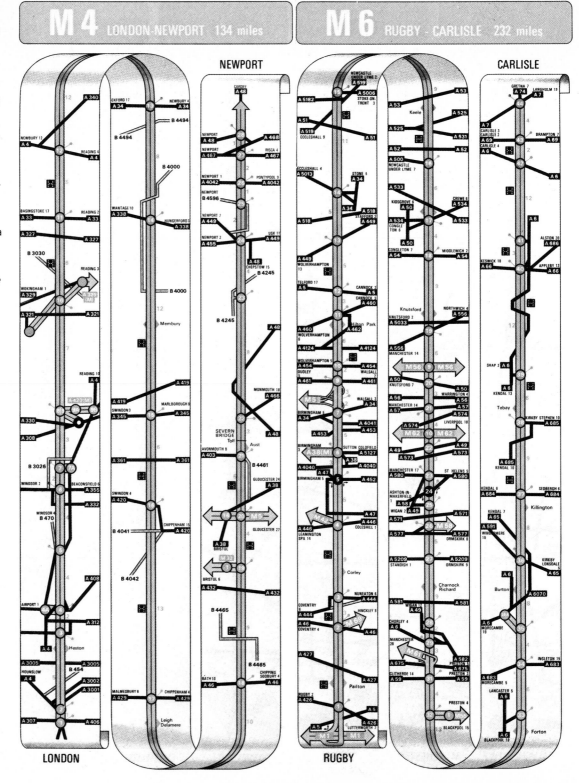

5.28
Strip Map: York to West Chester

Unlike the diagrammatic strip map (5.27), this rendition attempts to show slight changes in direction as well as some landmarks along the way. One must recognize, of course, that the road system was far simpler and without complex interchanges when this map was made; it appeared in John Ogilby's *Britannia* in 1675. The graphic device of showing the road on a continuous ribbonlike strip is appealing; one reads the map from bottom to top, and from left to right. *Edward Lynam,* The Mapmaker's Art: Essays on the History of Maps *(London: Batchworth Press, 1953).*

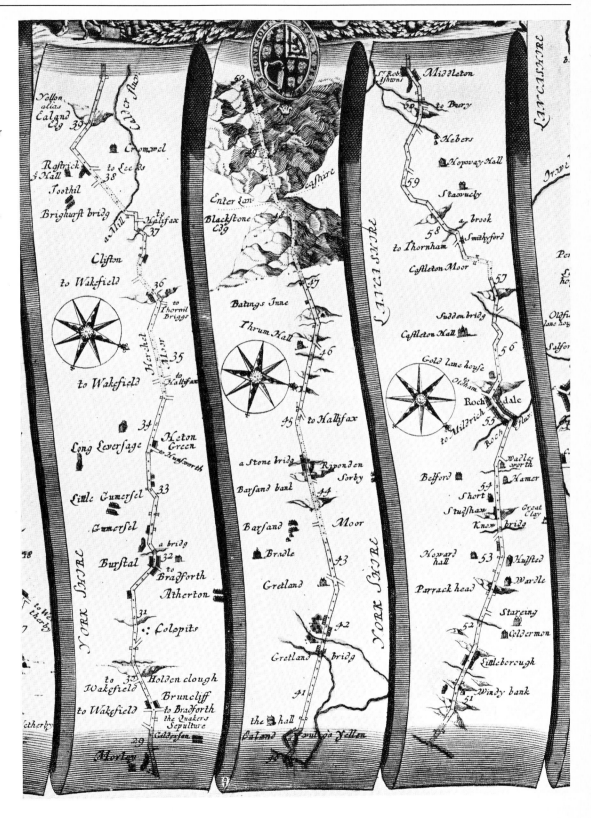

5.29
Road Map
Neither innovative nor graphically exciting, conventional road maps concentrate on circulation systems and place-names. Roads are graphically coded by type. Little information is given on topography and landmarks. No attempt has been made to make the map more attractive and legible by streamlining the road network through elimination of meaningless curves and bends, as in the London Underground (5.13) and many other public transit maps. Nor have other approaches to graphic simplification, such as separation of different systems into separate maps, been employed. Chicago and Vicinity.
Copyright © AAA. Reproduced by permission.

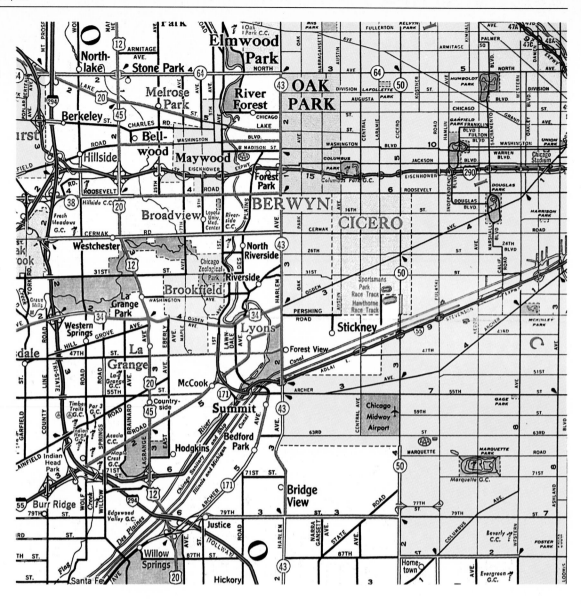

5.30
Official Road Map for Allied Forces: France

Excellent information on road types and conditons is provided on this military map by means of color and line quality. In addition, the map emphasizes national boundaries. Note that no topographic data are given. For its purpose—travel by highway—the map is very successful. *USAREUR, Engineer Topographic Center, Washington, DC.*

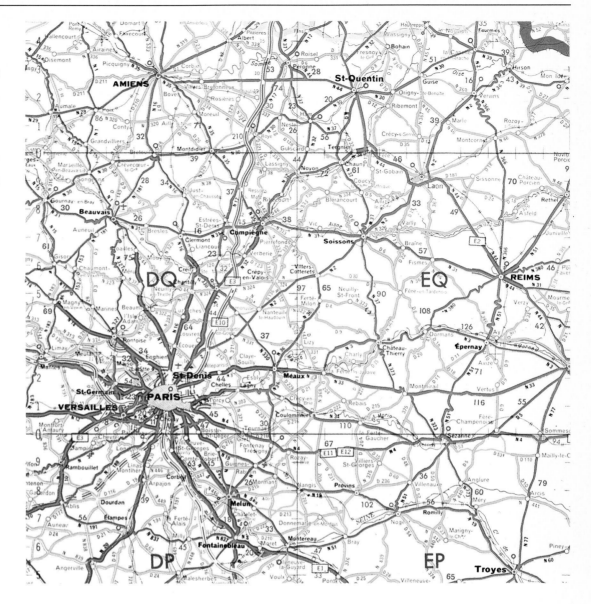

English	Deutsch	Français	English	Deutsch	Français
Roads	**Straßen**	**Routes**	**Road numbers**	**Straßennummern**	**Numéros de routes**
Signification	**Bedeutung**	**Signification**	E70 International	E70 Europastrasse	E70 International
Autobahn	Autobahn	Autoroute	27 National road	27 Bundesstraße	27 Route nationale
Autobahn under construction	Autobahn im Bau	Autoroute en construction	123 National road	123 Bundesstraße	123 Route nationale
Super highway (more than 7 m)	Fernverkehrsstraße (über 7 m)	Grande route (plus de 7 m de large)	**Principal Localities**	**Wichtige Verwaltungssitze**	**Sièges administratifs importants**
Arterial road (6—7 m)	Hauptstraße (6—7 m)	Route principale (6—7 m de large)	Country capital	Staatshauptstadt	La capitale de l'Etat
Main road (4—6 m)	Verbindungsstraße (4—6 m)	Route de relation (4—6 m de large)	State capital	Landeshauptstadt	La capitale de province
Secondary road (3—4 m)	Nebenstraße (3—4 m)	Route secondaire (3—4 m de large)	County capital	Regierungs-bezirkshauptstadt	La capitale de région
By-road (less than 3 m)	Fahrweg (unter 3 m)	Chemin carrossable (moins de 3 m de large)	**Other Symbols**	**Sonstige Angaben**	**Autres indications**
Condition	**Zustand**	**Etat des routes**	Major airport	Wichtiger Verkehrsflughafen	Aéroport important
Road with hard surface	Straße mit befestigtem Belag	Route avec revêtement consolidé	Mountain pass	Paß	Col
Road with loose surface	Straße ohne befestigten Belag	Route avec revêtement non consolidé	Shipping lane	Schiffahrtslinie	Ligne de navigation
Gradients	**Steigungen**	**Montées**	Car ferry	Autofähre	Bac pour autos
Road with many steep grades	Bergige Straße mit vielen Steigungen	Route accidentée avec de nombreuses montées	Air transport of vehicles	Luftfähre für Fahrzeuge	Embarquement de voitures par avion
Sharp isolated ascent in the direction of the arrow	Plötzliche stelle Steigung in Pfeilrichtung	Montée raide isolée dans le direction de la flèche	Railway single track	Eisenbahn, eingleisig	Chemin de fer – à voie unique
			Railway, multiple tracks	Eisenbahn, mehrgleisig	Chemin de fer – à plusieurs voies
			State boundary	Landesgrenze	Frontière nationale

5.31
Pictographic Maps:
Mexico City Metro and
National Zoo

Pictographs can be very useful in guiding large crowds of people efficiently around a city. The Mexico City system was particularly appropriate for the 1968 Olympics visitors since it is equally comprehensible to foreigners. Pictographs were developed to symbolize landmarks located near each station of the Mexico City Metro system. They have been arranged to represent the order of stations and the overall pattern (**A**).

Sources for several pictographs are illustrated in **B**. As long as the pictographs suggest the correct destinations to most users, the graphic system is easy and direct to use. In this system, the airplane and train are more likely to be understood by strangers than some of the other pictographs. *Mexico City Metro graphic design and photography by Lance Wyman.*

A

B

B (con.t)

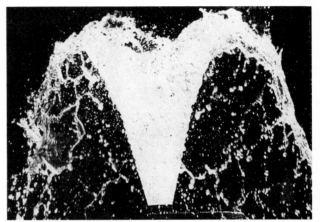

5.31 (cont.)
National Zoo

Pictographic signing for the National Zoo is illustrated in **C** and **D**. Stylized heads and footprints of animals are used to guide visitors through the zoo. Pictographs are arranged vertically on directional "totems" along the footpaths. *National Zoo map and graphics program by Wyman and Cannan, New York City.*

c

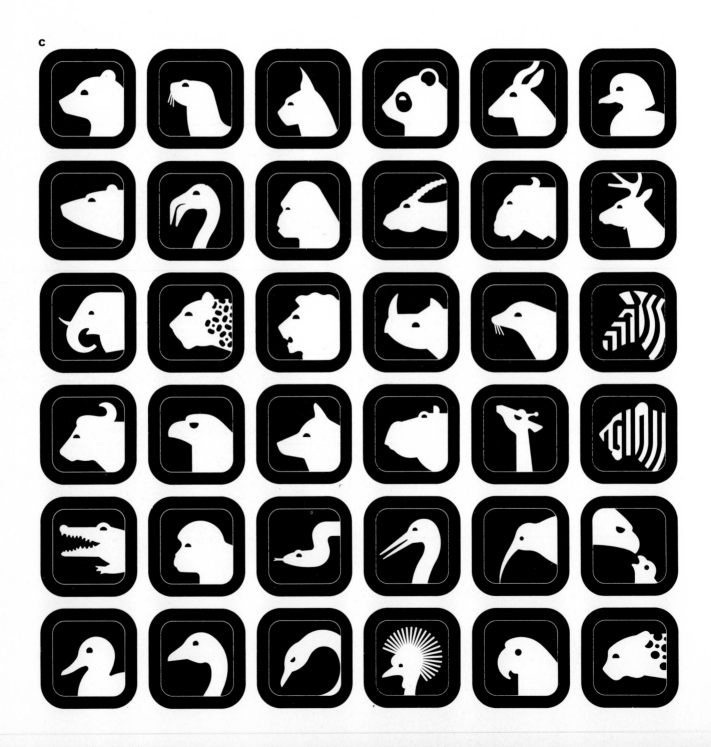

D

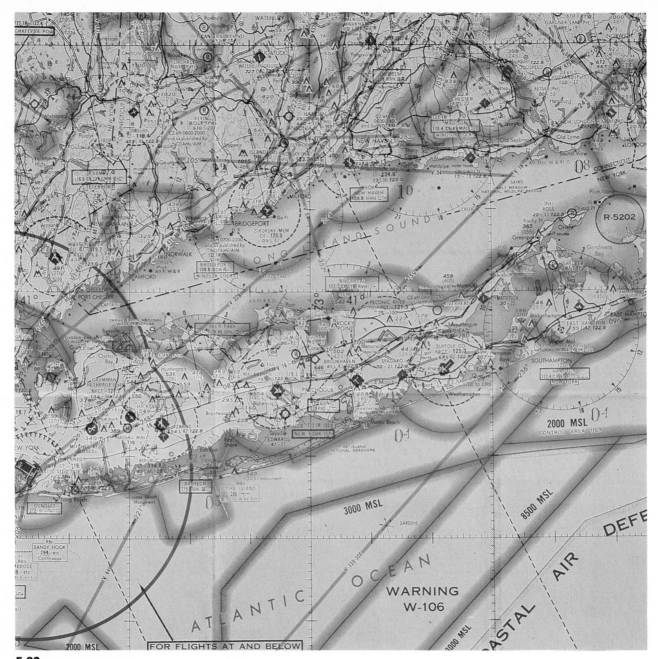

5.32
Sectional Aeronautical Chart

In contrast to map 5.33, this flight map shows extensive ground information. Air fields are classified by type using symbols that require learning. Boundaries of controlled airspace are shown by vignette bands. In addition, information is given about radio aids, special airways, parachute jumping areas, obstructions, and beacons. The map is difficult to read and actually seems more usable to the highway motorist than to the pilot. The problem is that graphic dominance does not correlate with information priorities; for example, highways in dark blue dominate the map, while low-altitude federal airways are in faint blue bands.

Note: Not to be used for navigation.

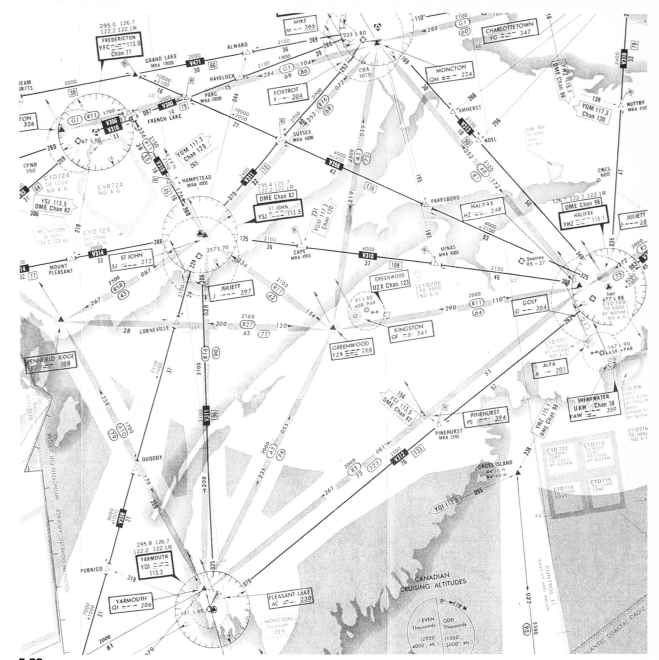

5.33
Flight Map
For the layman, this flight map of northeastern United States and Canada is a maze of unintelligible symbols. Place-names and faint coastline markings are the only commonly understood ground references. Routes radiate from compass roses giving exact directions for each airway. Much of the map information concerns radio aids to navigation.

6.1
Selected Techniques for Communicating Quantity, Density, and Percentage

Several attractive techniques for illustrating density, quantity, and percentage are seen in these maps of France. In **A** percentage is shown by a series of equidistant horizontal contour bands. The blacker a region is, the more of a certain quantity it possesses. **B** communicates percentage by dots of varying size spaced on a grid. This system permits easier interpretation of data by district or subre-

gion than does **A**. In **C** both absolute quantity and percentage are given by *département*. Each *département* has its own rectangle with the length of the base proportional to population within the district. Height of the rectangle is proportional to the percentage of quantity *x* in the district. Thus, the total area of each rectangle is proportional to the absolute quantity of *x*. **D** represents quantity or density

by means of equally spaced horizontal contour lines. The resulting effect is one of peaks, plateaus, and valleys. Finally, **E** uses columns of varying heights, one for each municipality, to represent quantity.
Jacques Bertin, Sémiologie Graphique *(Paris: Éditions Gauthier-Villars; Paris, New York, The Hague: Mouton Publishers; Paris: École des Hautes Études en Sciences Sociales, 1967).*

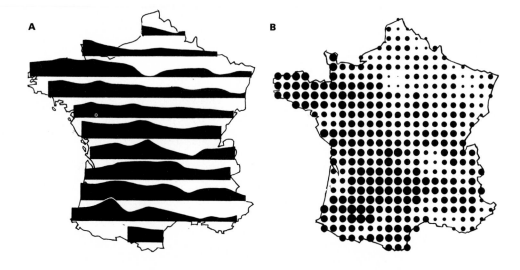

A   B

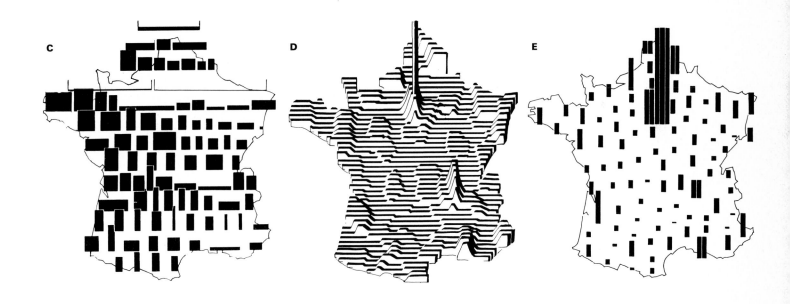

Data maps aid understanding of phenomena on a large scale by showing quantity, density or intensity, and distribution of any characteristic over a region. Information normally presented in charts or graphs is often more meaningful when conveyed on a map. Data maps are useful in research, planning, policy development, and other fields. Any data with spatial dimensions, from marriage or income statistics to population of an endangered species, can be mapped. Data maps can range from the very simple to the highly complex, and they can be made for the child learning elementary sociological facts or for the city planner concerned with the impact of a new highway system.

Many techniques are available to the data mapmaker. A map may show one or more variables, using an abstract technique such as dots, bars, or columns, or a representational system such as pictograms or cartoons. Data maps need not be sterile and boring to be accurate; to be most effective they should also be appealing to look at. In general, the larger and more diverse one's audience, the more care and attention the mapmaker must devote to creating an attractive yet meaningful image by selecting the best mapping technique.

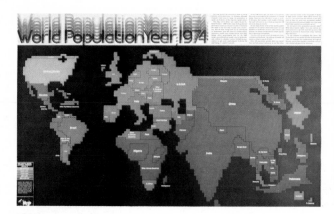

6.2
World Population
World population is vividly portrayed by making the size of each country proportional to its population, not its actual area. Thus, Canada is a narrow band bordering the United States, India is larger than Africa, and Japan is nearly as large as South America. Reducing the irregularities of countries to block patterns, yet retaining their general shapes and geographic relationships, makes them simple and easy to compare (see 7.6).
Courtesy of Hal Aber Graphics, Inc., Congers, NY.

6.3
Ninety-fifth Congress
The geographic shapes of the states are rounded and regularized, producing a simplified background for the political information communicated in colors, symbols, and numbers. Political party is designated by color, circles represent senators, squares are representatives, and numbers give the quantity in each party. Elimination of distracting, nonessential detail is important for clarity and ease of communication in data maps. *Courtesy of Hal Aber Graphics, Inc., Congers, NY.*

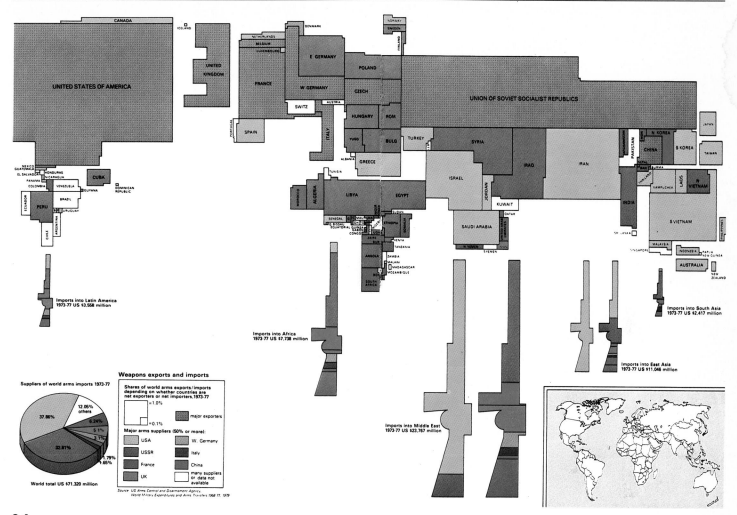

6.4
Weapons Exports and Imports

The volume of worldwide weapons exports and imports is effectively shown in this map. Each country is reduced to a simple rectangular shape, its size proportional to its share of world arms imports and exports. By comparing this map with the geographic map in the lower right, we find that some very large geographic areas play small roles in the arms race — for example, Canada, Africa, and South America — while several other areas appear disproportionately large in terms of arms business — the United States, Europe, Israel, Iran, and South Vietnam, for instance. The gun graphs show the proportional amount of weapons imported into Latin America, Africa, the Middle East, East Asia, and South Asia. *Michael Kidron and Ronald Segal*, The State of the World Atlas *(copyright © 1981 by Pluto Press Ltd.; reprinted by permission of Simon & Schuster, a Division of Gulf & Western Corporation).*

6.5
Computer Maps: ASPEX, TRIDIGRAM, SYMAP, PRISM, and ODYSSEY

This set of computer-generated maps illustrates various data-mapping techniques. **A** ASPEX: The relief lines dramatically portray the population of the United States at nine points in time, from 1790 to 1960. **B** TRIDIGRAM: In this technique, the population of the country is divided into cells; the height of the column in each cell is proportional to the number of people within that cell. **C** SYMAP: Typeface characters are used to illustrate metropolitan boundaries and percentages of built structures after 1950. **D** ODYSSEY (PRISM MODULE): Here each state is projected prismatically to illustrate the amount of alcoholism per 100,000 persons. **E** ODYSSEY: The basic map of the United States is transformed by the computer to represent the distance from St. Louis, Missouri, in terms of long-distance telephone rates—rather than miles—at three points in time: 1940, 1960, and 1970. The maps show how strikingly the long-distance rates have decreased over the thirty-year period, bearing no linear relationship to the physical distances. *Maps reprinted by permission of the Laboratory for Computer Graphics and Spatial Analysis, Harvard Graduate School of Design.*

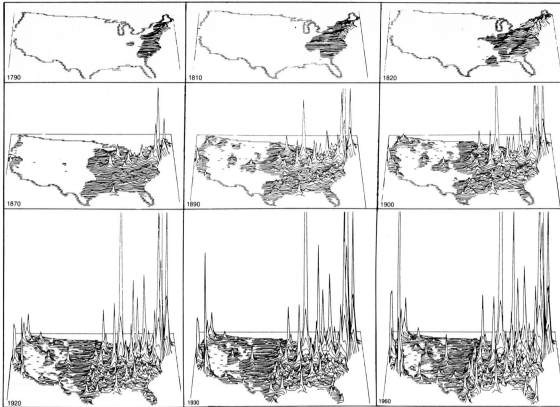

A

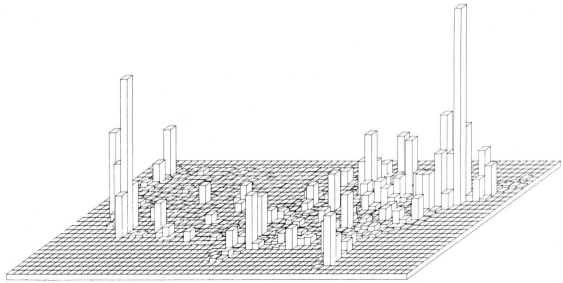

B

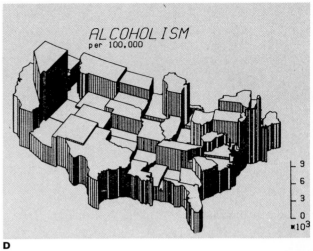

C

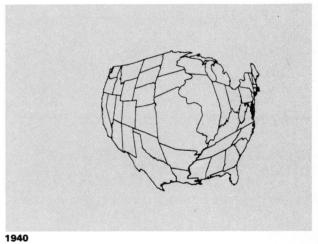

D

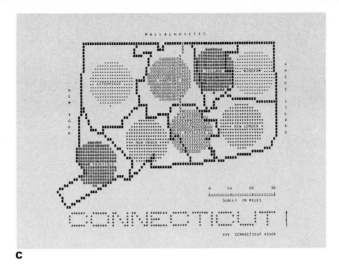

Basic map

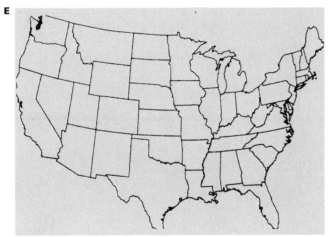

1940

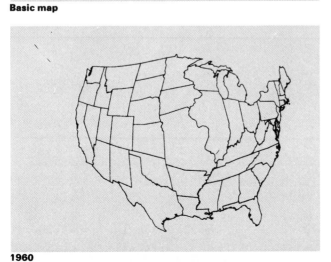

1960

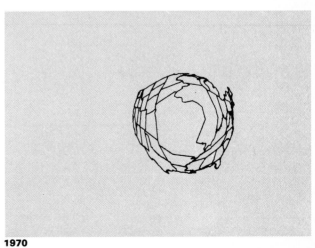

1970

6.6
Pie Map: Potential Voters by Race in Metrolina

The "pie circle," a conventional technique and not very exciting graphically, shows both quantity and percentage. On this map, the size of the pie is proportional to population, while the size of the wedge indicates percentage of registered Negro voters. Thus, the biggest pieces of pie indicate the largest number of potential Negro voters. A further layer of information is given by color of county, telling percent change in Negro registration between 1960 and 1968. *James W. Clay and Douglas M. Orr, Jr., Metrolina Atlas (Copyright 1972 The University of North Carolina Press). Reprinted by permission of the publisher.*

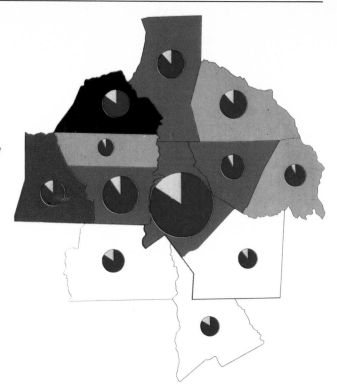

% Change in Negro Registration (1960–68)

- Over 8%
- 4–8%
- 2–4%
- 0–2%
- Decline

Total Registrants

- Negro Registrants
- White Registrants

- 150,000
- 50,000
- 25,000
- 15,000
- 10,000

6.7
Metrolina Population Density Pattern

An alternative to the dot map, color or texture mosaic, or graph map for representing density and distribution is this variation on the standard method of indicating topography. Here, the highest population densities occur at "peaks" and lowest in "valleys." Color is not essential, but aids rapid interpretation of levels. *James W. Clay and Douglas M. Orr, Jr., Metrolina Atlas (Copyright 1972 The University of North Carolina Press). Reprinted by permission of the publisher.*

Number of Persons per Square Mile

- 1000 above
- 800–1000
- 600–800
- 400–600
- 200–400
- 0 200

6.8
Bar Map: Average Metrolina Wind Direction and Speed

A variation of the bar graph, the wind rose gives direction, duration, and speed of wind. Length of bar segments is proportional to percentage of time that wind of varying velocities occurs for each of sixteen directions, averaged over three-month periods. This technique is appropriate only for data that involve directional movement, such as weather, transportation, migration, or trade. *James W. Clay and Douglas M. Orr, Jr.,* Metrolina Atlas *(Copyright 1972 The University of North Carolina Press). Reprinted by permission of the publisher.*

Miles Per Hour

——— 0–3
▬ 4–7
▬ 8–12
▬ 13–18
▬ 19–24
▬ 25+

0 1.0 2.0 3.0 4.0 5.0 6.0 7.0 8.0 9.0 10.0

Percent of Time

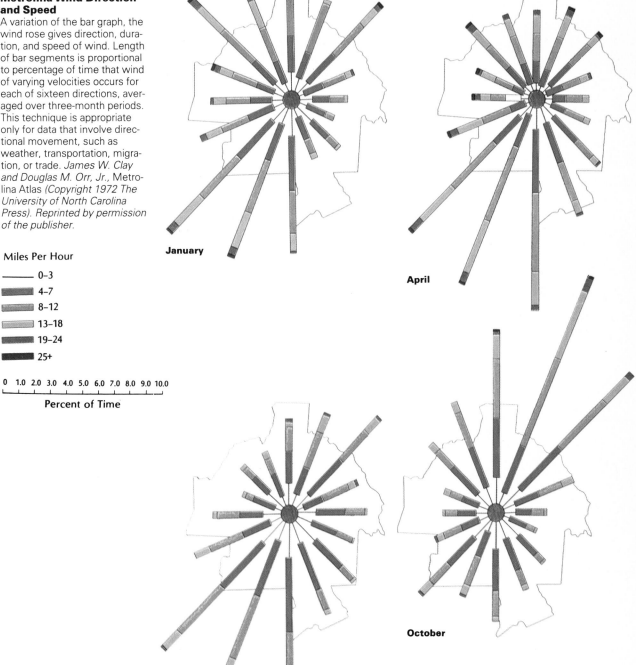

January

April

July

October

6.9
Circle Map: Average Number of Daily Telephone Messages per 100,000 Persons between Boston` and Selected Cities for April 1958
Black circles of varying sizes indicate quantity of events taking place at a given time. The overlapping patterns, however, leave one unsure of the locations, since geographic references are obscured by the black circles. *Neil C. Gustafson in Jean Gottmann,* Megalopolis *(Cambridge, MA: MIT Press, 1961).*

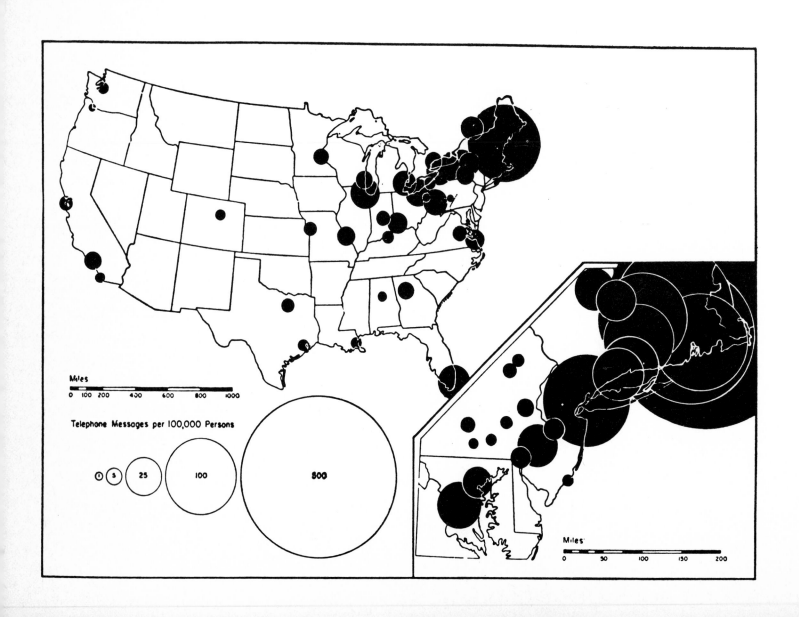

6.10
**Dot Map: Value of All Farm
Products Sold**

Dots are used to indicate high
and low concentrations of quan-
tities, in this case sales of farm
products in dollars. The technique is simple, direct, and understandable to a wide audience. Without looking at the
key it is apparent where concentrations and scarcities exist.
This is an important aspect of
quick comprehension in data
mapping.

The technique is old and
still usable because the symbol—the dot—has minimal distracting features. This kind of
map often shows concentrations by the build-up of complex
symbols, which become more
attention-demanding than the
overall patterns of density (compare 6.12). *U.S. Bureau of the
Census.*

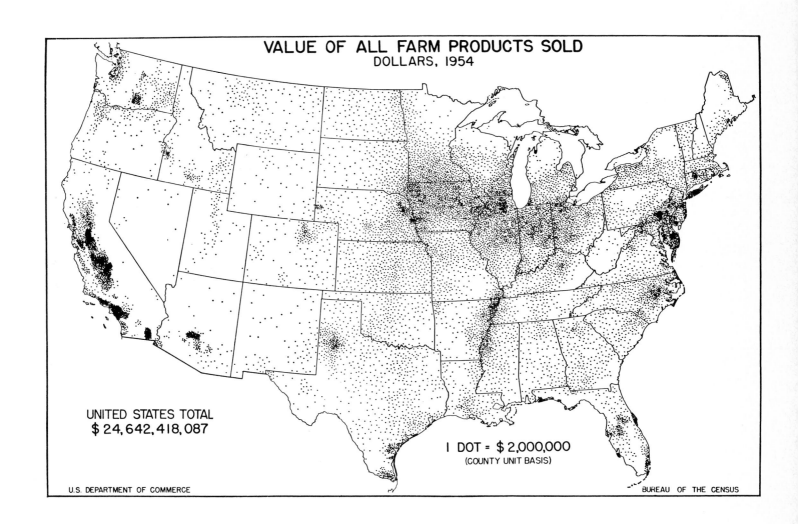

VALUE OF ALL FARM PRODUCTS SOLD
DOLLARS, 1954

UNITED STATES TOTAL
$ 24,642,418,087

I DOT = $ 2,000,000
(COUNTY UNIT BASIS)

U.S. DEPARTMENT OF COMMERCE

BUREAU OF THE CENSUS

6.11
Flash Maps: New York Music Centers and Libraries

The concept of flash maps is appropriate for complex environments with diverse users. Mapmaking and using are simplified by presenting only one category of information at a time. Thus, one must consult several maps during a typical day of traveling: for example, shops, restaurants, transportation systems, theaters, and parks would each be on sepa-

rate maps. While a single map with all the information would be nearly useless because there would be too much for clarity, a series of simple maps is understandable. *Reprinted from FLASHMAPS—New York (copyright by FLASHMAPS Publications Inc.); Toy Lasker, Publisher/Editor; Timothy W. Lasker, Director of Cartography.*

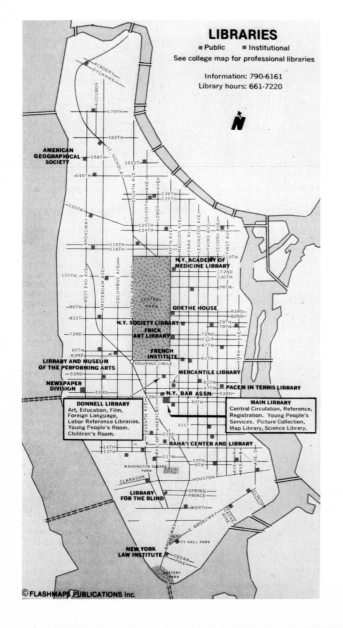

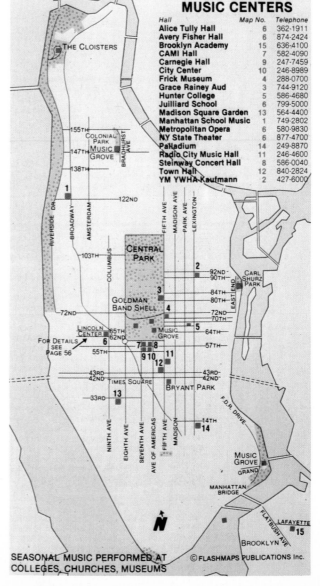

Hall	Map No.	Telephone
Alice Tully Hall	6	362-1911
Avery Fisher Hall	6	874-2424
Brooklyn Academy	15	636-4100
CAMI Hall	7	582-4090
Carnegie Hall	9	247-7459
City Center	10	246-8989
Frick Museum	4	288-0700
Grace Rainey Aud	3	744-9120
Hunter College	5	586-4680
Juilliard School	6	799-5000
Madison Square Garden	13	564-4400
Manhattan School Music	1	749-2802
Metropolitan Opera	6	580-9830
NY State Theater	6	877-4700
Palladium	14	249-8870
Radio City Music Hall	11	246-4600
Steinway Concert Hall	8	586-0040
Town Hall	12	840-2824
YM YWHA Kaufmann	2	427-6000

6.12
Whale Chart
This mid-nineteenth-century
map provides information on
the location of various types of
whales and the best seasons
for finding them. Continents are
simply outlined and named and
a few cities are identified.
Whales are shown by pictographs. The map is simple, yet
handsome and informative.
*M. F. Maury, A.M., Lieutenant,
U.S. Navy; published at the
National Observatory, 1851.*

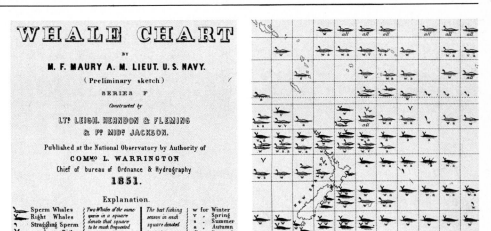

Detail

Detail

6.13
Three-Dimensional
Pictograph: The Balance
of Power, 1914

Three-dimensional pictographs standing on a map of Europe and Russia convey population, number of soldiers, battleships, submarines, quantity of steel production, railway mileage, and other power-related factors.

Abstract data are thus made simple, attractive, and understandable to most people.
Bruce Robertson, History of the Twentieth Century *(London: Purnell Reference Books, Phoebus).*

6.14
Cartoon Map: Futureworld
The population problem is emphatically expressed in this cartoon map showing great piles of people on North America. No explanation or key is necessary to communicate the intended point to any age group. The idea of showing quantity through exaggerated drawings of the unit of measure—people in this case—overlaid on the geographic territory is useful. Obviously, the technique is not precise and can treat only relative distribution. *Frank Marchiciano, "Headline Focus Wall Map 18,"* Scholastic Magazines, Inc. *(Dayton, OH; copyright 1976).*

7.1
Comparative Maps: Population, Income, and Land Use
Twenty cities are presented at the same scale in terms of population density, income, and land use. The unique value of these maps lies in the opportunity they afford to compare the same variables in different cities. Data were mapped in a system that potentially could be automated. USGS maps provided the base, upon which population and income data were overlaid. Although the majority of the maps are large—17½ by 17½ inches (**A**)—the most interesting ones are the small maps at the end of the atlas (**B**). These are arranged side by side; comparison is quite easy and not much detail is lost. However, the background base map is not included. Limitations of the dot technique become apparent when population and income are overlaid together, making it nearly impossible to interpret either variable. *Joseph R. Passonneau and Richard Saul Wurman,* Urban Atlas: 20 American Cities *(Cambridge, MA: MIT Press; copyright 1968 by Passonneau and Wurman).*

7 Relation and Comparison

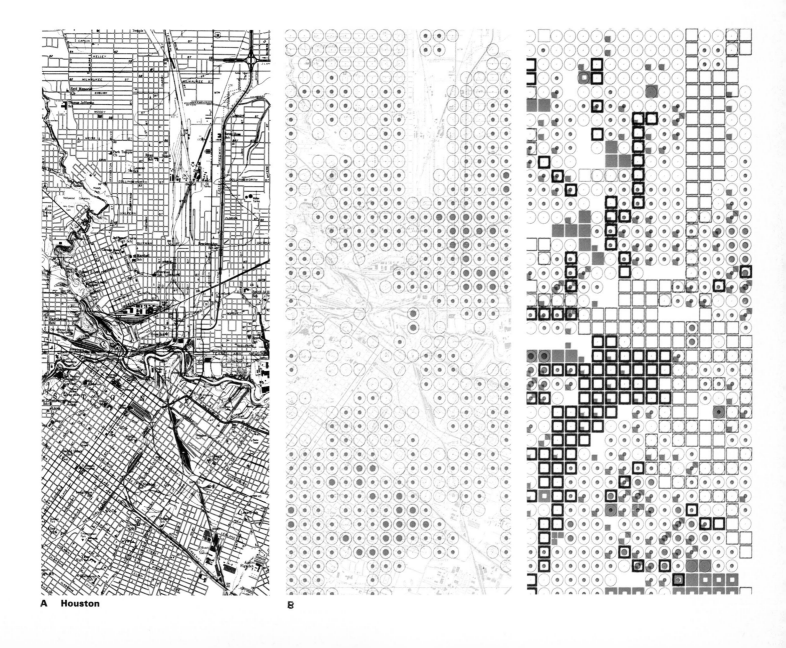

A Houston

B

Comparison is a basic learning technique that can be effectively applied to maps. One way is to juxtapose the known with the unknown, as in the North American climatic analogs for USSR crop regions, where the strange becomes both familiar and understandable (7.4). Similarly, the immense population of New York City becomes more comprehensible by making the Upper East Side equivalent to Austin, Texas (7.3). Simplification and abstraction are other useful techniques for making comparisons. By reduc-

ing complex information to simple forms, comparison becomes easier, as when the irregular shapes of countries are reduced to block form (7.6). Diagrammatic maps of travel distance help one understand one's location in relation to the larger world, relations that might not be fully grasped in a standard map (7.2). Presentation of several maps in the same scale, size, and graphic system is another technique that facilitates comparative study (7.1).

7.1B

Detroit

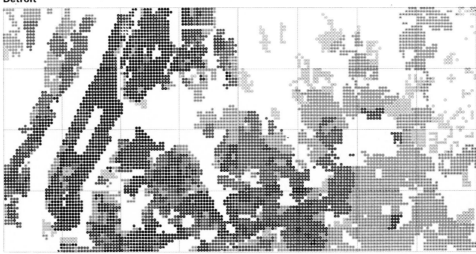

New York

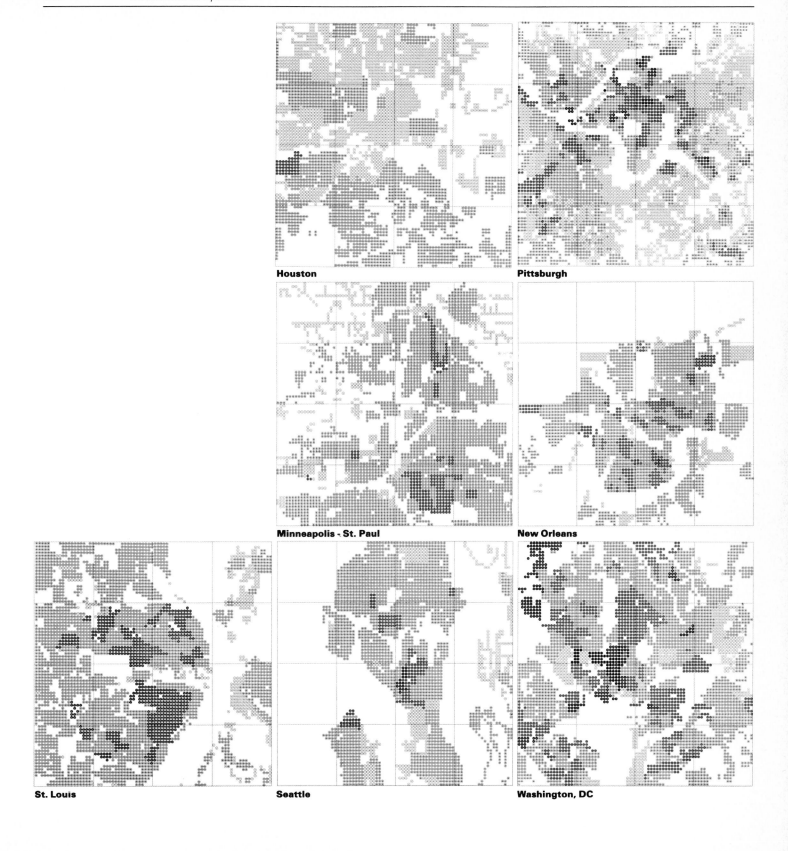

Houston

Pittsburgh

Minneapolis - St. Paul

New Orleans

St. Louis

Seattle

Washington, DC

7.2
Zoom Maps: Aspen, Colorado
By means of a series of maps, one has the effect of zooming in from the scale of the earth, through the country and state, down to the small town of Aspen. All of the maps are drawn with Aspen as the focus. *Richard Saul Wurman and Joel Katz of Murphy, Levy, Wurman, Aspen Visible (Aspen International Design Conference; copyright 1972 IDCA).*

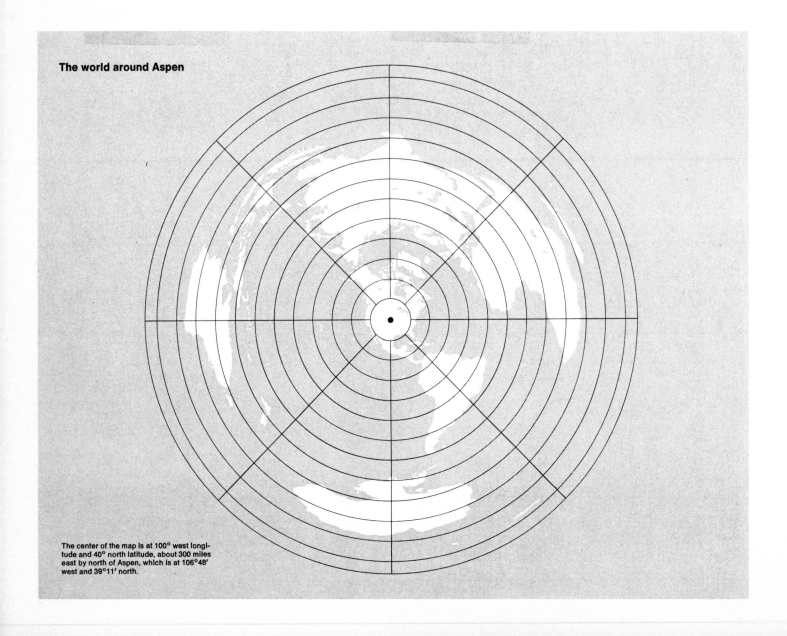

The world around Aspen

The center of the map is at 100° west longitude and 40° north latitude, about 300 miles east by north of Aspen, which is at 106°48′ west and 39°11′ north.

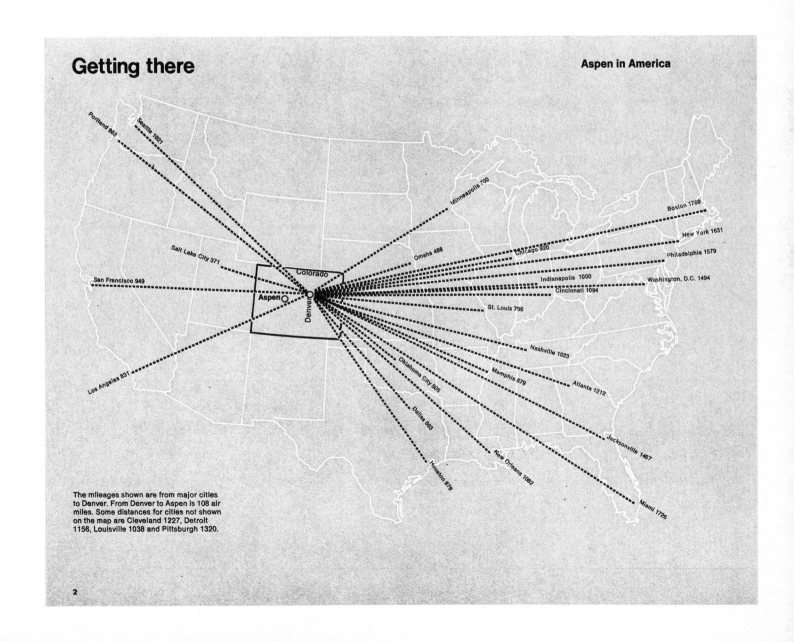

Getting there   **Aspen in America**

Portland 982
Seattle 1021
Minneapolis 700
Boston 1769
New York 1631
Salt Lake City 371
Omaha 488
Chicago 920
Philadelphia 1579
Indianapolis 1000
Washington, D.C. 1494
San Francisco 949
Colorado
Cincinnati 1094
Aspen
Denver
St. Louis 796
Nashville 1023
Oklahoma City 505
Memphis 879
Atlanta 1212
Los Angeles 831
Dallas 663
Jacksonville 1467
Houston 879
New Orleans 1082
Miami 1726

The mileages shown are from major cities
to Denver. From Denver to Aspen is 108 air
miles. Some distances for cities not shown
on the map are Cleveland 1227, Detroit
1156, Louisville 1038 and Pittsburgh 1320.

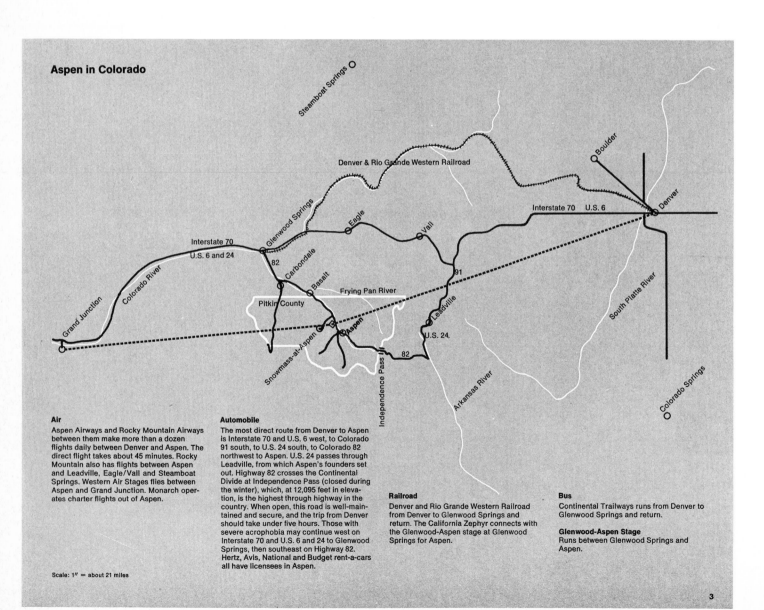

Aspen in Colorado

Steamboat Springs

Denver & Rio Grande Western Railroad

Boulder

Glenwood Springs

Eagle

Vail

Interstate 70   U.S. 6

Denver

Interstate 70

U.S. 6 and 24

Colorado River

82

Carbondale

Basalt

91

Frying Pan River

South Platte River

Pitkin County

Grand Junction

Leadville

U.S. 24

Snowmass-at-Aspen

Aspen

82

Independence Pass

Arkansas River

Colorado Springs

Air
Aspen Airways and Rocky Mountain Airways
between them make more than a dozen
flights daily between Denver and Aspen. The
direct flight takes about 45 minutes. Rocky
Mountain also has flights between Aspen
and Leadville, Eagle/Vail and Steamboat
Springs. Western Air Stages flies between
Aspen and Grand Junction. Monarch oper-
ates charter flights out of Aspen.

Automobile
The most direct route from Denver to Aspen
is Interstate 70 and U.S. 6 west, to Colorado
91 south, to U.S. 24 south, to Colorado 82
northwest to Aspen. U.S. 24 passes through
Leadville, from which Aspen's founders set
out. Highway 82 crosses the Continental
Divide at Independence Pass (closed during
the winter), which, at 12,095 feet in elevation, is the highest through highway in the
country. When open, this road is well-main-
tained and secure, and the trip from Denver
should take under five hours. Those with
severe acrophobia may continue west on
Interstate 70 and U.S. 6 and 24 to Glenwood
Springs, then southeast on Highway 82.
Hertz, Avis, National and Budget rent-a-cars
all have licensees in Aspen.

Railroad
Denver and Rio Grande Western Railroad
from Denver to Glenwood Springs and
return. The California Zephyr connects with
the Glenwood-Aspen stage at Glenwood
Springs for Aspen.

Bus
Continental Trailways runs from Denver to
Glenwood Springs and return.

Glenwood-Aspen Stage
Runs between Glenwood Springs and
Aspen.

Scale: 1″ = about 21 miles

3

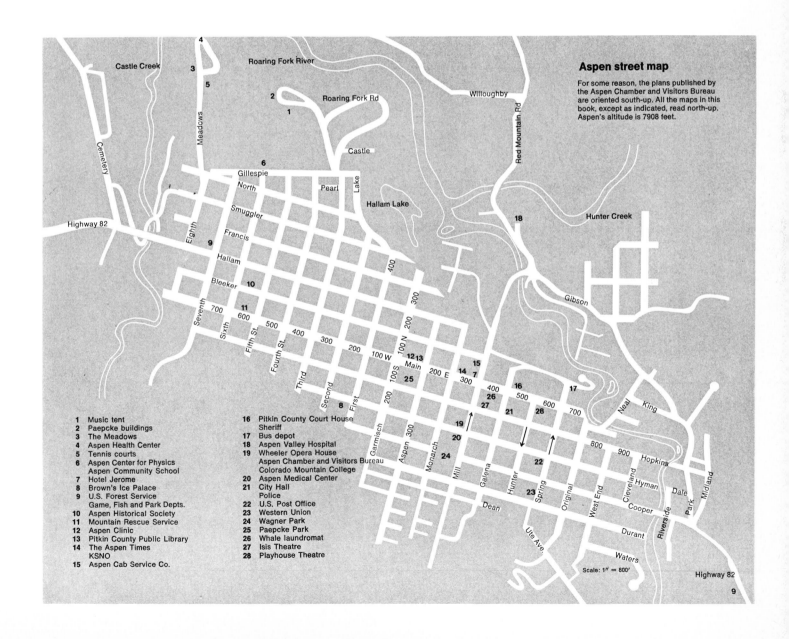

Aspen street map

For some reason, the plans published by the Aspen Chamber and Visitors Bureau are oriented south-up. All the maps in this book, except as indicated, read north-up. Aspen's altitude is 7908 feet.

1 Music tent
2 Paepcke buildings
3 The Meadows
4 Aspen Health Center
5 Tennis courts
6 Aspen Center for Physics
   Aspen Community School
7 Hotel Jerome
8 Brown's Ice Palace
9 U.S. Forest Service
   Game, Fish and Park Depts.
10 Aspen Historical Society
11 Mountain Rescue Service
12 Aspen Clinic
13 Pitkin County Public Library
14 The Aspen Times
   KSNO
15 Aspen Cab Service Co.

16 Pitkin County Court House
   Sheriff
17 Bus depot
18 Aspen Valley Hospital
19 Wheeler Opera House
   Aspen Chamber and Visitors Bureau
   Colorado Mountain College
20 Aspen Medical Center
21 City Hall
   Police
22 U.S. Post Office
23 Western Union
24 Wagner Park
25 Paepcke Park
26 Whale laundromat
27 Isis Theatre
28 Playhouse Theatre

Scale: 1″ = 800′

Highway 82

9

7.3
Comparative Map:
New York = 62 Cities from
50 States
To make the huge population of
New York City and its neighborhoods more concrete, it has
been divided into areas identified as other familiar cities in
the United States having equivalent populations. The map
would be even more informative if the population of each
superimposed city were given
under its name. Such comparisons are helpful in conceptualizing the population size and density of New York, since large
numbers and statistics often
mean little to most people. In
any situation where large numbers are to be communicated
this technique might be effective. *New York City Planning
Commission,* Plan for New York
City, Volume 1 *(Cambridge,
MA: MIT Press, 1969; copyright © 1969, Department of
City Planning, City of New York).*

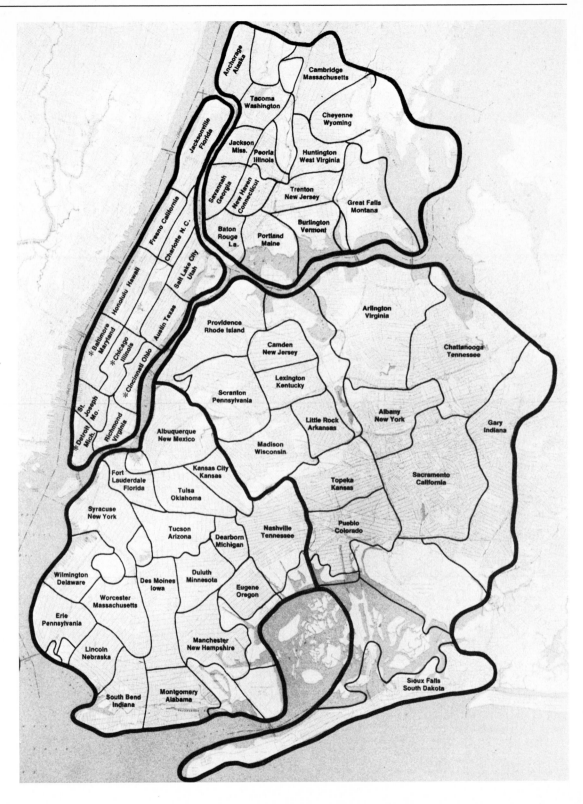

7.4
North American Climatic Analogs for USSR Crop Regions

To communicate rather technical information about crop regions in the Soviet Union, North American place-names having equivalent climates are superimposed on the map of the Soviet Union, creating some odd conjunctions. Imagine how Montana would feel to wake up and find itself south of Moscow! But precisely this startling impact is helpful in making the point. To make the unfamiliar country less strange, familiar equivalents describe it more effectively and quickly than technical terms. Obviously, the technique depends on use of equivalents that are familiar to the map user. The map on the left compares the area and latitude of the Soviet Union with the United States' by superimposing one map on the other. Thus, the comparison becomes vivid and direct. *Central Intelligence Agency,* USSR Agriculture Atlas, *1974.*

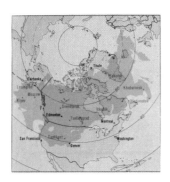

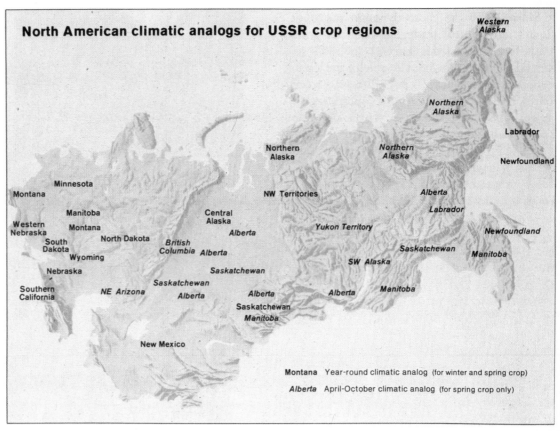

North American climatic analogs for USSR crop regions

Montana	Year-round climatic analog (for winter and spring crop)
Alberta	April-October climatic analog (for spring crop only)

7.5
Distances from Autun to Other Points in France and Europe

A highly simplified "spider" diagram presents relative distances from Autun to several regional destinations. Only the road numbers and altitudes are indicated as additional information. In a geometric band around the perimeter the distances from Autun to various prominent French and other European cities are listed. The whole diagram is highly stylized and selective, with no descriptive verbal backup.

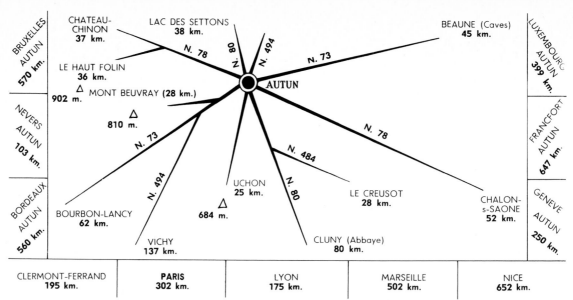

CHATEAU-CHINON 37 km.
LAC DES SETTONS 38 km.
BEAUNE (Caves) 45 km.
LE HAUT FOLIN 36 km.
MONT BEUVRAY (28 km.) 902 m.
810 m.
N. 78
N. 80
N. 494
N. 73
AUTUN
N. 73
N. 78
N. 484
N. 80
UCHON 25 km.
684 m.
LE CREUSOT 28 km.
CHALON-s-SAONE 52 km.
BOURBON-LANCY 62 km.
VICHY 137 km.
CLUNY (Abbaye) 80 km.

BRUXELLES AUTUN 570 km.
NEVERS AUTUN 103 km.
BORDEAUX AUTUN 560 km.

LUXEMBOURG AUTUN 399 km.
FRANCFORT AUTUN 647 km.
GENEVE AUTUN 250 km.

| CLERMONT-FERRAND 195 km. | PARIS 302 km. | LYON 175 km. | MARSEILLE 502 km. | NICE 652 km. |

7.6
Comparative Maps: Size of Main Regions of the Soviet Union; World Map of Population and Income

In map **A**, the irregular boundaries of the several republics in the Soviet Union are converted to rectangular shapes to facilitate comparision of administrative regions in 1944. Map **B**, a map of the world, converts countries to blocks with areas proportional to population and heights proportional to per capita income. Thus, the volume of each block represents gross national product. The technique is extremely effective for a variety of comparative studies. **A** *Arthur Lockwood,* Diagrams *(New York: Watson-Guptill; London: Studio Vista; copyright 1969).* **B** *Erwin Raisz,* General Cartography *(New York: McGraw-Hill, 1948; adapted from Colin Clark,* The Conditions of Progress, *1940).*

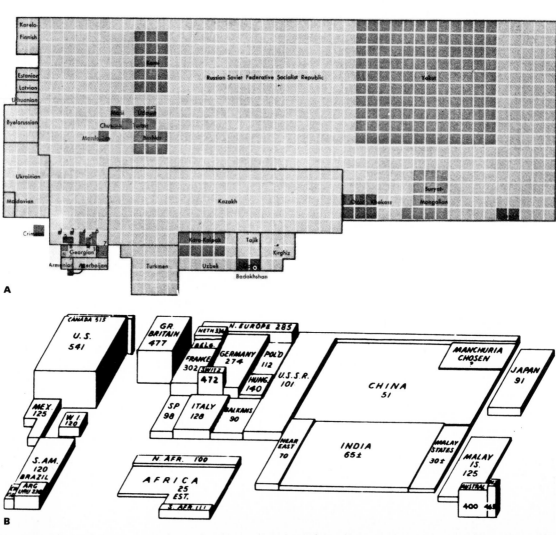

7.7
Point of View: Azimuthal Equidistant Projection Centered Near San Antonio

The world is seen in a different perspective when an unusual center is used—San Antonio in this example. All distances and azimuths measured from point of tangency are true. Measurements may be made from any point within one hundred miles of San Antonio, the point of tangency, with an error of less than 1 percent. *Reprinted by permission of the American Geographical Society.*

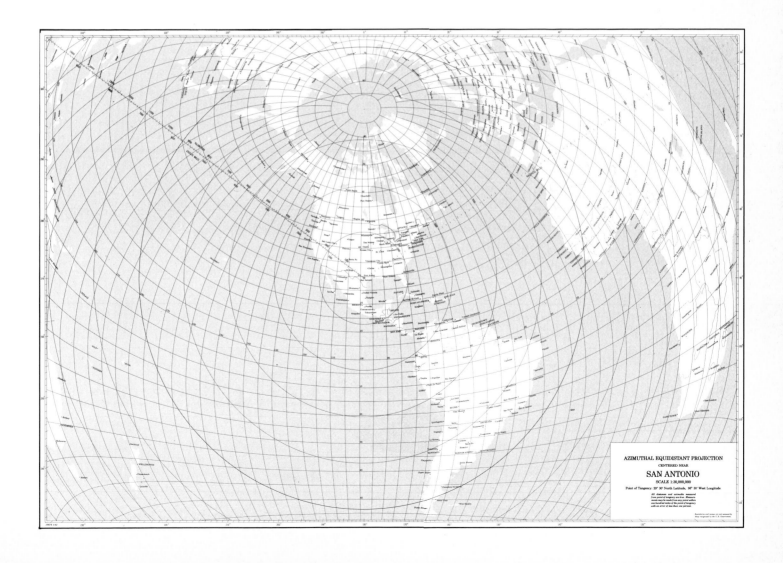

AZIMUTHAL EQUIDISTANT PROJECTION
CENTERED NEAR
SAN ANTONIO
SCALE 1:30,000,000
Point of Tangency: 29° 30′ North Latitude, 98° 30′ West Longitude

7.8
Comparative Panoramic
Perspectives of the Earth:
China and Japan

Comparative views from different vantage points help one understand relations not apparent on a single map. Unlike flat maps, these panoramic perspectives of the earth draw the observer into the view, helping him feel part of the scene. Topographic features—mountains, rivers, roads—are exaggerated to make the map communicate. In contrast to the Taiwan view of China (9.17), the view of China from the east (left) focuses on China with the white-tipped peaks of the Himalayas crowning the scene. Taiwan is small and gray in the foreground. In the second view (right) we see Japan from Siberia and Manchuria with the vast Pacific Ocean, dotted with islands, curving over the horizon. *Richard Edes Harrison,* Look at the World: The FORTUNE Atlas for World Strategy *(New York: © Time Inc., 1944. All rights reserved).*

China from the East

CHINA, from the standpoint of internal communication, is one of the least developed of the great nations. Even before the fall of Allied areas in the Pacific limited her to a tenuous supply line across Sinkiang and to a hazardous air route along the Himalayas, her only coastal supply centers, besides Rangoon, were the small smuggling ports indicated on the map by blue arrows. These were linked to Free China by the system of roads, rivers, footpaths, and railroads outlined in blue.

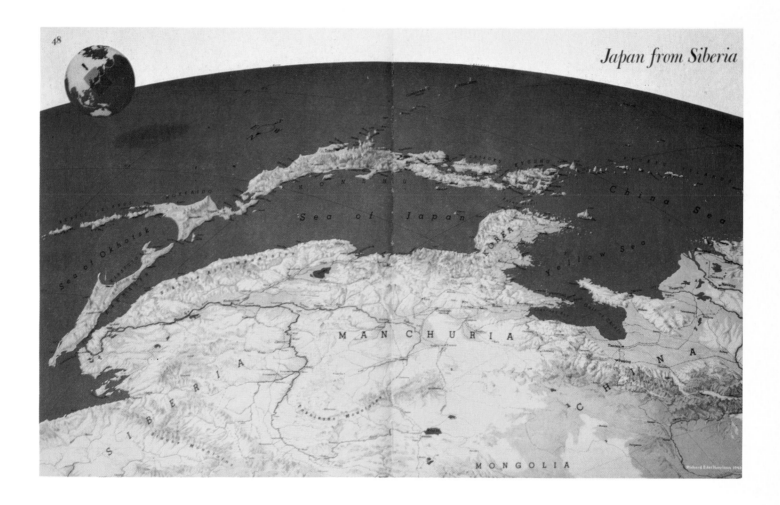

7.9
Perspective-Section: Diagram of an Oil-Prospecting Program
By combining a diagrammatic section with an aerial perspective above the seascape, the relationships between the surface and undersea activities are established (compare 4.25).
Tanguy de Rémur/Pétrole Progrès—Esso Standard S.A.F., in Graphis Diagrams, *1974. Courtesy GRAPHIS Press Corp., Zurich, Switzerland.*

7.10
Multiple Viewpoints:
Facade, Section, and
Plan-Perspectives of Two
Buildings

Because any single view gives only partial information about a building, Rasmussen shows three views of the same thing— a traditional facade view of the outside front, then a cut-away section showing half of the interior, and finally a cut-away plan-perspective showing the walls and columns and spaces they form inside and outside.

In the drawing of the Banlieues the inside and outside of a whole city block are combined in a ground-level perspective with a cut-away section in the foreground. Below is the cut-away perspective-plan showing large blocks and tiny flats. The multiple points of view technique is also appropriate to mapping of nonarchitectural large-scale environments, such as a river valley or mountain pass. *Steen Eiler Rasmussen, Towns and Buildings (Cambridge, MA: MIT Press, 1969; copyright 1949 and 1951 by Steen Eiler Rasmussen).*

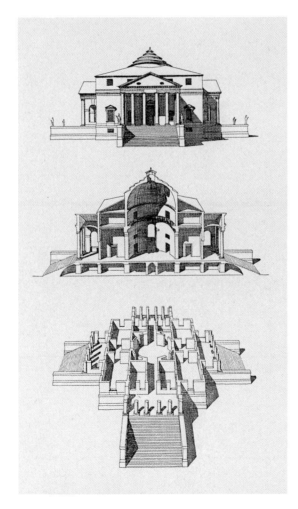

8.1
Synchronological Map: A Chronological Chart of Ancient, Modern, and Biblical History

This map depicts the time and place of major milestones in history, from the dawn of civilization to modern times. The stream of time is represented by the long black line extending from left to right. Each hundred years is marked by an upright black pillar and every decade is indicated by a red pillar. Flowing with the stream of time are colored areas that show the world's geopolitical structure for any given period. Time lines are amplified with notes and illustrations. The map is about fifteen feet long. The section reproduced on this page represents about four feet of the entire map, from which a detail is enlarged and shown on the facing page. Sebastian Cabot Adams (1825-1898), a pioneer Oregon educator and minister, developed the map and first issued it in 1871. *By Sebastian Cabot Adams. Copyright Samuel J. Ferelli 1978.*

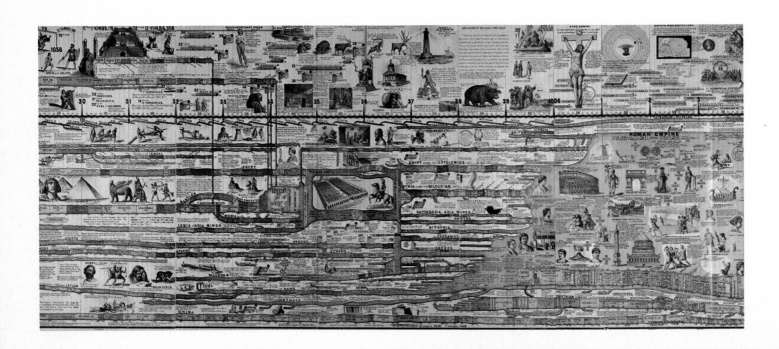

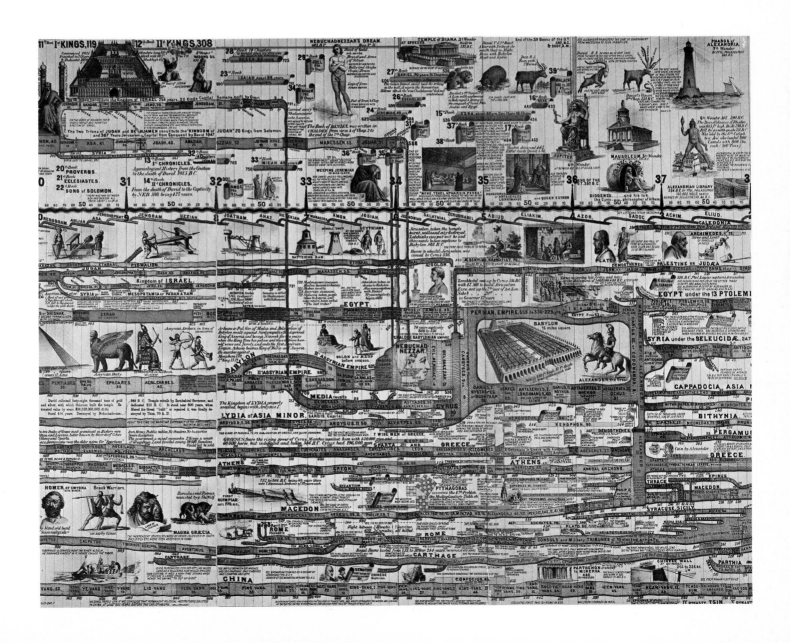

Just as space can be mapped, so can time. In the twentieth century, with many travel modes of varying speeds available, time distance is often more important than physical distance. High-speed transportation has made certain distant places more accessible in time than many closer locations. The time-distance map of Japan addresses this new reality (8.4). Maps of time are also used to study growth, change, and history. Time-lapse maps or photographs are one effective technique, as seen in the sequence of maps on London's growth (8.3) and the

time-lapse film of the American road edge (8.7). Time lines are another approach, as in the weather recorder (8.9), the monumental, richly detailed synchronological chart (8.1), and the Genghis Khan spiral (8.12). Direction and intensity of flows, for traffic or migration, can be communicated by directional symbols and varied densities of line width (8.8, 8.11, 8.13). Film and video maps offer many possibilities for maps of time, change, and movement by allowing the user to study change in real time rather than in static representations.

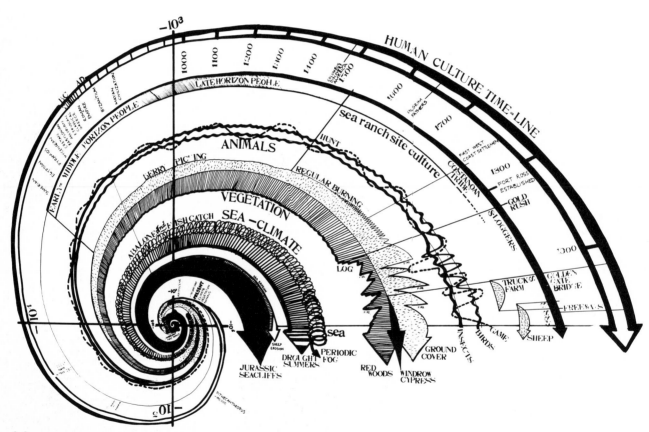

8.2
Time-Line Spiral

The evolution of Sea Ranch—a California residential and recreational development—and its environs is mapped as a time spiral. Beginning at the primeval core, the spiral progresses and expands through time quadrants—one hundred million years ago, ten million and so on down to a hundred years ago. As modern times approach, the spiral presents four aspects of the area's evolution: sea-climate, vegetation, animal life,

and human culture. The same information could have been shown as well in a straight line, although the spiral is space-saving and arresting. Compare this spiral with the Genghis Khan time circle (8.12) and the synchronological map (8.1). *Lawrence Halprin*, RSVP Cycles: Creative Processes in the Human Environment *(New York: George Braziller, Inc., 1969).*

8.3
Growth and Change: London—Area Built Over 1840, 1860, 1880, 1900, 1914, 1929

Consecutive mapping of the same geography over time can be used to compare any aspect of growth, consumption, production, and so on, that is linked to geography. This series dramatically shows the growth of London between 1840 and 1929. The simple graphic style is highly effective. *Steen Eiler Rasmussen,* London: The Unique City *(Cambridge, MA: MIT Press; copyright 1934 by Steen Eiler Rasmussen).*

London: Area built over 1840

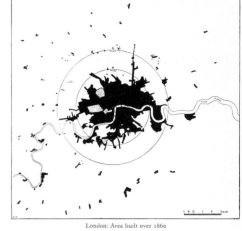
London: Area built over 1860

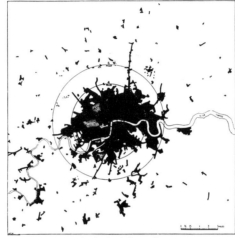
London: Area built over 1880

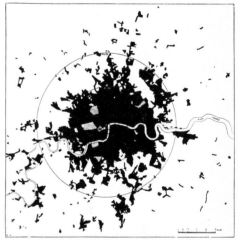
London: Area built over 1900

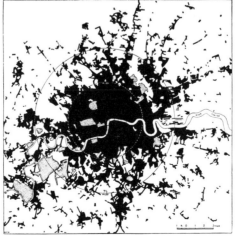
London: Area built over 1914

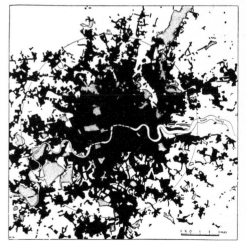
London: Area built over 1929

8.4
Time-Distance Map: Travel Time, Japan
In this unusual map, the configuration of Japan is warped according to travel time rather than distance from Tokyo. Thus, a near point that takes a long time to reach appears farther away from Tokyo than another point that can be reached more quickly. The bands of concentric circles represent the time frames for location of the various points. The time distances are based on the shortest travel times via airplane and train as found in time tables. *Cho Shinta et al.*, Shukan Asahi magazine, Tokyo, May 9, 1969.

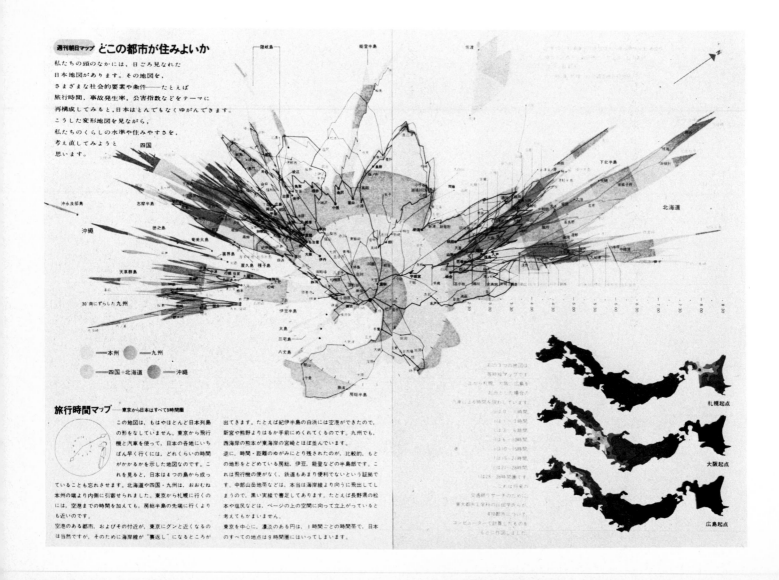

8.5
Time-Lapse, Mixed-Media Map: A Slice through Central Park, 1870 and 1970s

This slice through Central Park is a collage of three pieces of a recent aerial photograph and two pieces of a nineteenth-century engraving, fitted together to create a single image, and printed in different colors to differentiate the time shifts back and forth. The strip is sur- rounded by seven views of areas of the park shown in the slice, similarly color-keyed. *Richard Saul Wurman, Alan Levy, Joel Katz,* The Nature of Recreation *(Cambridge, MA: MIT Press; copyright 1972 by The American Federation of Arts and GEE!).*

8.6
Photographic Time-Lapse: A Day in the Life of Three Persons and Two Spaces at Hourly Intervals

Time-lapse photographs map changes in activity and space. Through photographs of various spaces and individuals in a school taken at hourly intervals between 7:00 A.M. and 5:00 P.M., the life of the school is illustrated nonverbally. This technique is useful for quick in-depth descriptions of an environment and its users. It can be a valuable tool to administrators and planners in considering use of resources. The technique has also been applied to career counseling; time-lapse photos of people doing different jobs can give a better sense of what is involved in that job than job descriptions alone. The essential ingredient of the technique is the rigid schedule of photos. *Richard Saul Wurman and Joel Katz,* Opt *(copyright 1973 by GEE!). Photography by Howard Brunner, Scott Miller, and David Lebe.*

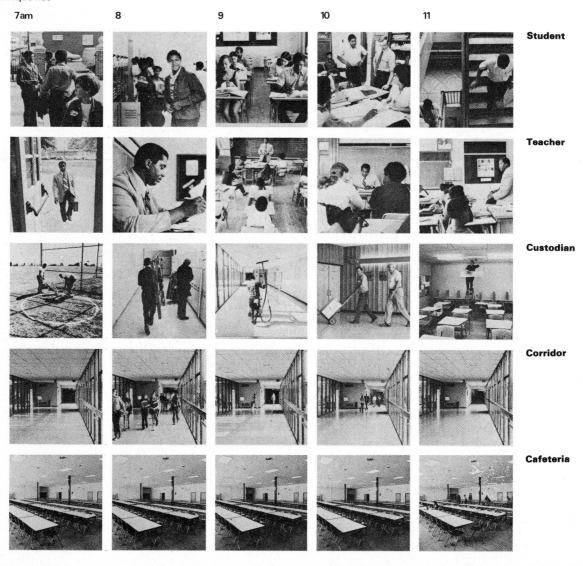

7am	8	9	10	11	
					Student
					Teacher
					Custodian
					Corridor
					Cafeteria

8.7
**Photographic Time-Lapse:
The American Road Edge**
The road edge from Philadelphia City Hall to Buffalo City Hall
is documented in this novel and
highly specialized map. Using
time-lapse photography, a
frame was shot every thirty seconds, resulting in a total of 1700
frames. Each frame covers approximately one-half mile. The
technique is useful for studying
changes over a large territory.
Joel Katz, 1974.

8.8
Vehicle Traffic Volume in Metrolina

One effective and commonly used technique for representing intensity or volume of movement—traffic in this case—is found in this regional map of Charlotte, North Carolina. Bands proportional in width to amount of traffic are superimposed on the highway network. One drawback of the approach is the difficulty of working with dense networks where there is no space to put the bands. *James W. Clay and Douglas M. Orr, Jr., Metrolina Atlas (Copyright 1972 The University of North Carolina Press). Reprinted by permission of the publisher.*

Vehicles per Day

0

5,000

10,000

15,000

20,000

8.9
Time and Temperature Chart

Not a map of space, but of time and temperature, this weather recorder is typical of many devices designed to make a permanent record of weather patterns. A stylus continuously marks the temperature over the course of a week and produces a round chart. Other systems use rolls, producing linear charts that can record several weeks. Weather instruments such as these convert the tran-sitory measurements of thermometers into automatically written history. The temperature at the most recent hour becomes less important than the pattern of temperature variation over the previous days—the times of day that have been warmest and coolest, the speed or extent of the changes, or the warmest or coolest days. *Courtesy Bacharach Instrument Company, Pittsburgh, PA.*

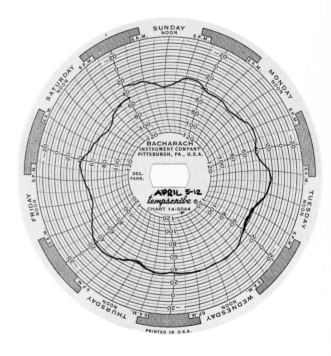

8.10
Star Finder

The star finder is designed to locate and identify the fifty-seven numbered stars listed in the air and nautical almanacs, as well as the sun, moon, and planets from any point on the earth. The instrument consists of a star base map for the northern and southern hemispheres, a meridian angle-declination template, and nine transparent altitude-azimuth templates. The appropriate disks are overlaid on one another and rotated to conform to the observer's location and date. The approximate altitudes and azimuths of celestial bodies above the horizon are then indicated by the curve. *Manufactured by Simulux.*

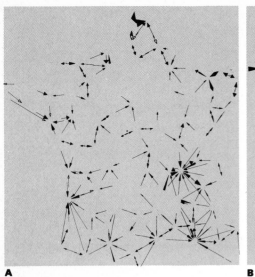

A

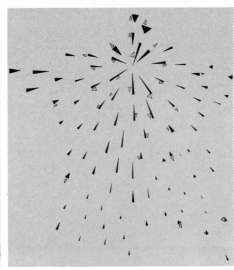

B

C

8.11
Migration Map: France

Population migration in and out of French cities is shown by means of arrows. The sizes of the arrows are proportional to the number of people migrating. Map **A** shows migration into cities throughout France; Map **B** shows migration from these cities into Paris; and Map

C is a composite of **A** and **B**. The technique is graphically elegant and easy to interpret.
Jacques Bertin, Sémiologie Graphique *(Paris, Éditions Gauthier-Villars; Paris, New York, The Hague: Mouton Publishers; Paris: École des Hautes Études en Sciences Sociales, 1967).*

8.12
Family Map: Genghis Khan and His Descendants

Relations of Genghis Khan to his descendants are mapped in circular heredity charts starting from the central point representing Genghis Khan and radiating outward through successive generations. Like the pattern inside a tree, the outer ring represents the most recent growth and the inner rings are the preceding generations. This approach is a useful alternative to the time line; it is a more compact presentation and allows mapping of more information as time progresses.
Jacques Bertin, Sémiologie Graphique *(Paris: Éditions Gauthier-Villars; Paris, New York, The Hague: Mouton Publishers; Paris: École des Hautes Études en Sciences Sociales, 1967).*

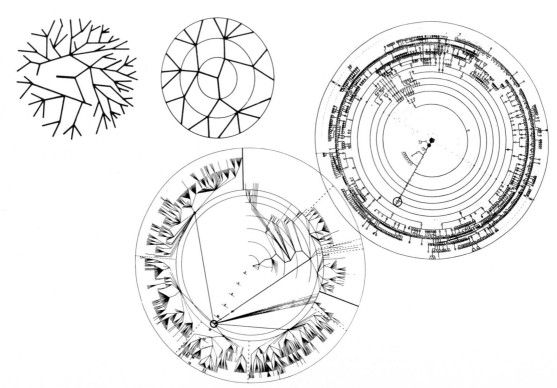

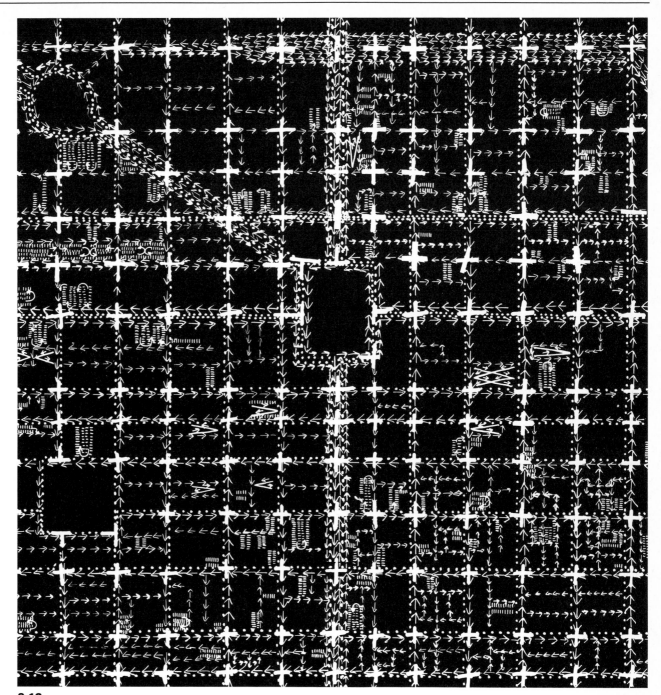

8.13
Traffic Movement and
Vehicle Storage

One aspect of Philadelphia's city form, the circulation system, is expressed in terms of moving and parked vehicles. Arrows symbolize both direction and relative density of moving vehicles. Short lines indicate parked cars. The technique is direct and understandable, as well as graphically exciting. *Louis I. Kahn,* The Notebooks and Drawings of Louis I. Kahn, *Richard Saul Wurman and Eugene Feldman, editors and designers (Philadelphia: The Falcon Press, copyright 1962).*

9.1
Pictorial Map:
Covarrubias's America
Miguel Covarrubias's fascinating impression of America, a mural created for the Golden Gate International Exposition in San Francisco in 1939, has influenced many a school child's image of the country. Covarrubias painted pictographs in his unique style to epitomize each region. Hollywood has glamorous movie stars, Texas has oil wells, Boston has beans. The result is very personal and also very dated, but all of this makes it more evocative and nostalgic to viewers several decades later. *Miguel Covarrubias.*

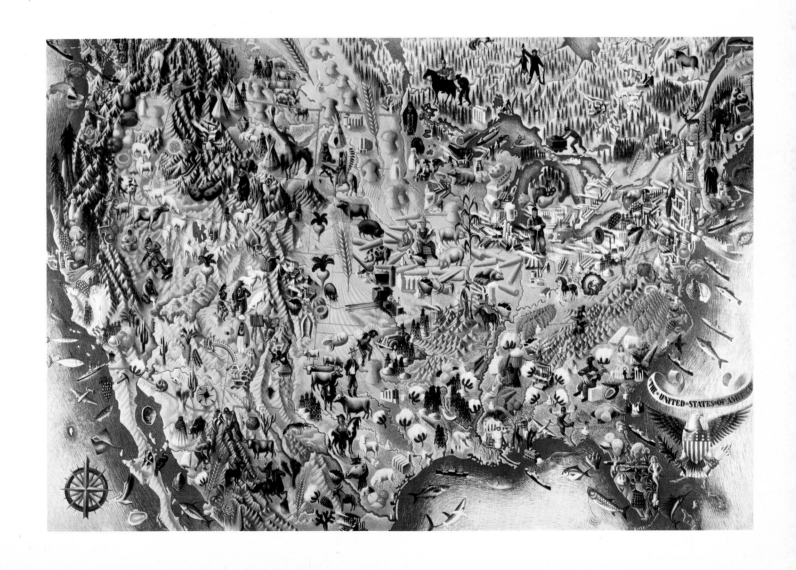

This group of maps looks at the world, not as it is, but as particular people see it. "Image" maps focus on the mental reality rather than the geographic fact. Our interpretation of geography may be shaped by our values, our activities in the environment, and our memories and imagination. Maps of individual geographic images and behavior have many uses: in the social sciences for understanding human spatial behavior, and in education, advertising, journalism, and political propaganda. Subjective maps can communicate through words, pictures, cartoons, or symbols, or all these means.

The concerns of conventional cartography, such as scale, projection systems, distortion, and accuracy, are not usually important in making these maps. Rather, the emphasis is on expression and individual perceptions instead of geographic description. By understanding how individuals conceive the environment, cartographers can make better maps and planners can design better cities.

9.2
Activity Map
Several graphic techniques convey information about activity types and their users in various districts of Boston. Boundary patterns symbolize activity type—for example, insurance offices, entertainment, government. Vertical and horizontal lines relate to regularity of use patterns and familiarity of users with the area, while the density of cross-hatched lines expresses intensity of use or number of users. Pie graphs, divided into halves, communicate social class and age of users. Although symbolic techniques can encode a lot of information, one must learn the "language" to interpret them (compare 4.22). *Donald Appleyard and Michael Southworth, General Motors Urban Transportation Project, unpublished.*

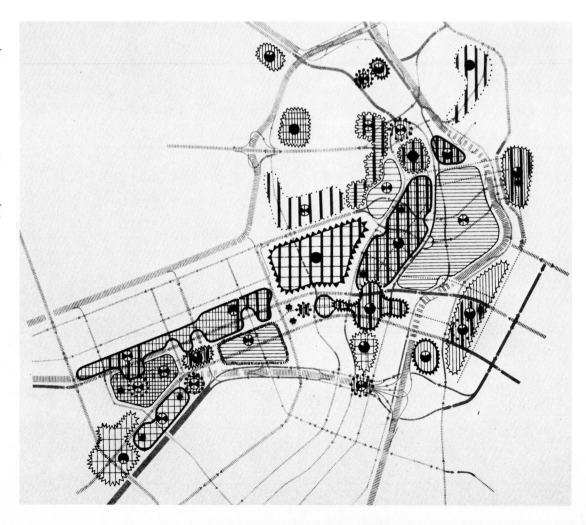

9.3
Neighboring and Visiting: San Francisco

Study of this innovative social interchange map suggests that heavy traffic is detrimental to neighboring and visiting. The lines connecting buildings on three different streets represent the patterns of neighboring and visiting. The amount of friendly social encounters is proportional to the number of lines, with the largest amount of encounters occurring on the street at the top, which has light traffic. The dots on the sidewalks represent intensity of sidewalk social activity. The opposite facades on each block are shown by sketches on each side of the street. Typical comments from residents of each street reinforce the social picture of the streets. The technique makes social data, normally presented in a dry, unengaging manner, meaningful to almost anyone. *San Francisco Department of City Planning, Donald Appleyard, Consultant,* Street Livability Study *(San Francisco, 1970).*

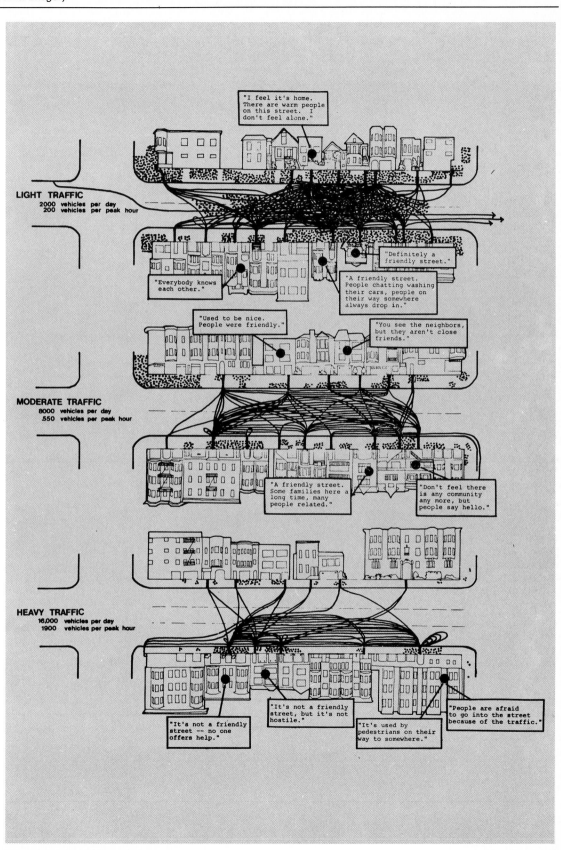

9.4
Montage Map: Bermuda Triangle

Through a montage of surprisingly varied techniques, this map expresses more about the Bermuda Triangle than a conventional map could. A photographic view of the area is superimposed on the sinister triangle, surrounded by photographs of doomed airplanes and a drawing of a sea monster. One understands the location and size of the area, what it looks like, and the aura of threat and mystery that surrounds it. While the technique is successful in conveying emotional concepts and symbolic character of a place, it is not appropriate to most practical uses. *Courtesy of Hal Aber Graphics, Inc., Congers, NY.*

Gateway To Orient   Denny   Mt. Rainier   Hills
Mountains   Rainfall   Overcast   Sunsets   Mist
American Dream   Outdoors   Puget Sound
Waterways   Cascades   Perimeter Mountains
Sailboats   Madrona Trees   Fog   City of Hills
International Commerce   Mt. Baker   Potlatch
Family Life   Historical   Boldness   Middle-Class
Seaport   International Fountain   Mild Climate
Pike Street   Sawmills   Waterbound City   Fish
Wood Houses   Monorail   Winter Roses   Alki
Rhododendron   Gardens   Water   Gold Rush
The Good Life   Salmon   Canal   Olympics Firs
Foliage   Pioneer Spirit   Chief Seattle   Boeing
Wholesome Surroundings   Cultural Heritage
Seafair   Airplanes   Great Northwest   Chinook
University of Washington   Floating Bridge   Ships
Salt Water   Education   Theater   Homes Views
Pioneer Square   First Avenue   Sports   Ferries
Aurora   Houseboats   Fireboats Gray   Seagulls
Front Lawns   Deck   Great Outdoors   Huskies
Skiing   Sails   Waterways   Home Ownership
Queen City   Green   Hilly   University   District
Ballard   Pier 91   Frederick and Nelson   Ridges
Valleys   Skid Road   Alaskan Way   Portage Bay
Highway 99   Ship Canal   Leschi   Greenlake
Totem Poles   Alaska Trade   Leisure   Drizzle
Mercer Girls   Market   Harbor Island   Nature
The Downtown   Timber   Sea-First   Arboretum
USS Decatur   Bardahl Denny Regrade   Wawona
Alaska Yukon Exposition   Ivars   Forward Thrust
World's Fair   Montlake Fill   Evergreens   Cedar
Smith Tower   Duwamish Waterway   Indians
Salt Water   1869   Alaskan Way   Space Needle
747   Seattle University   Dexter Horton   Metro
Schooner Exact   B-17 'Doc' Maynard   Bell Town
Pleasure Craft   City Light   Central District   1851
King County   Shilshole   Pioneer Building   Port
Fire of 1889   The Freeway   King Street Station
Pike and Pine   Lakes   Northgate   Elliott Bay   5th Ave

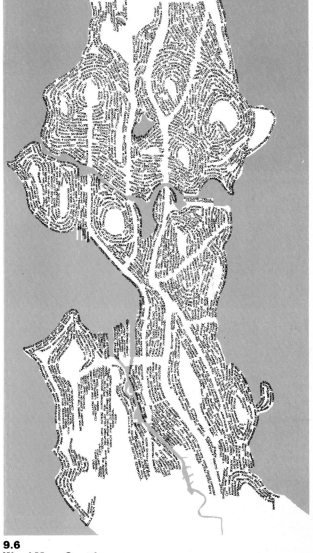

9.5
Word-Collage Map: Seattle
Place-names, slogans, and other imageable words, printed in an overall undifferentiated pattern, characterize Seattle, creating a verbal poster of city souvenirs. One can dive in at any point and come up with suggestive verbal pictures. It is unnecessary to read the entire "map" as one would read a book, line by line from left to right. Rather, one scans it and lands on "Wood Houses/Monorail/Winter Roses," for example. It can be looked at as a straight list of attractions in the conventional sense and thus can provide possible destinations for the stranger, but it is more successful as a suggestion of the impressions the city gives. The "map" is not an operational orientation device for planned movement through the environment; the locations of names of sites bear no relation to their positions in the landscape. *Urban Design Section,* Seattle Urban Design Report *(Seattle: Department of Community Development, 1971).*

9.6
Word Map: Seattle
This unusual verbal map does in fact locate activities and sites in the geography, and in theory one could navigate with it, but its primary value is in its ability to evoke place-related imagery. Words and phrases are located at the points they refer to and follow topographic contours and streets. Street names are given as well as such descriptive terms as "water tower/asphalt/driftwood/picnics/small homes/moorage/sail boat races." In some ways this might prove to be a most useful map for a stranger to Seattle, but it does take time and close attention to "read." For the armchair traveler who never gets to Seattle it is a rich source of impressions of the city. *Urban Design Section,* Seattle Urban Design Report *(Seattle: Department of Community Development, 1971).*

9.7
Street Analysis: Detroit
Analysis is one important function of maps in planning and strategy. Here a city street is evaluated in terms of several qualities, including pedestrian volume, barriers to movement, accessibility, detail, apparent characteristics of people, and mood. Independent of content, the format used here is valuable. Presenting the analyses in separate but adjacent maps at the same scale facilitates comparison and comprehension. *Urban Design Division, Detroit City Plan Commission, ''Central Business District Study'' (unpublished, 1970).*

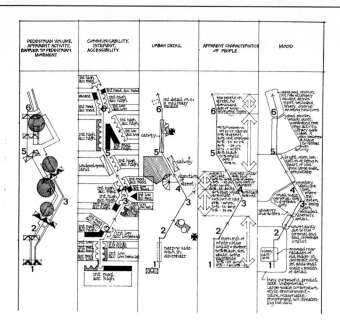

9.8
Evaluation of the Soundscape: Boston
A composite view of the variety of city sounds as perceived along a sequence of streets in Boston by numerous subjects is graphically represented in map form. Symbols were developed to represent qualities of sounds as much as possible, for example, soft, intense, roaring, muffled, sharp, echoing, expansive. Nevertheless, a legend is still needed to understand the map fully. *Michael Southworth, ''The Sonic Environment of Cities'' (unpublished MIT Thesis, 1967).*

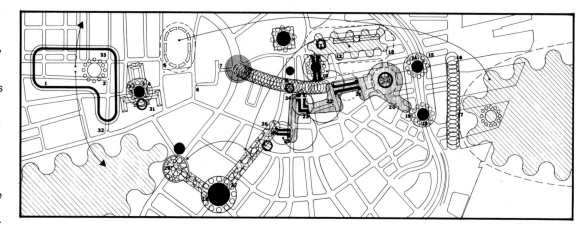

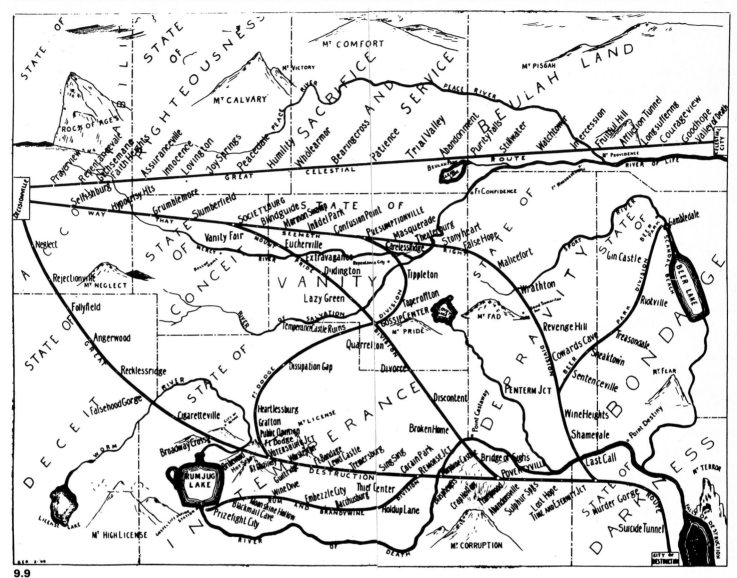

9.9
Fantasy Map: Gospel
Temperance Railroad Map

As in medieval T-in-O maps, geography is the vehicle for expressing religious ideals in this early twentieth-century map. The attitudes of the Gospel Temperance movement are forcefully communicated in a visual metaphor. The Railroad of Life, leaving from Decisionville, can go down through a host of sinful stops, past Mount Terror, into the State of Darkness. In the State of Bondage one finds Wine Heights, Shamevale, and Gambledale. Or one can take the northern route through Bearingcross and Beulah Land to reach the Celestial City. Moral choices and obligations are depicted with all the concreteness of the puritanical mind. *Copyright 1908 G. E. Bula, in J. B. Post,* An Atlas of Fantasy *(Baltimore: Mirage Press, Ltd., 1973).*

9.10
Symbolic Maps: Images and Physical Form, St. Paul

Another example of symbolic mapping, these maps treat ''images'' and ''physical form'' in a redevelopment plan. The problem of symbols is particularly apparent in the physical form map. Although a rather delightful abstraction is created, it is meaningless without careful cross-referencing to the legend. Unfortunately, the symbols used bear little relation to the qualities being represented. In general, it is wise to develop symbol systems that evoke the qualities represented to achieve greater intelligibility. *Michael Southworth, Alan Melting; unpublished redevelopment plan for St. Paul, MN.*

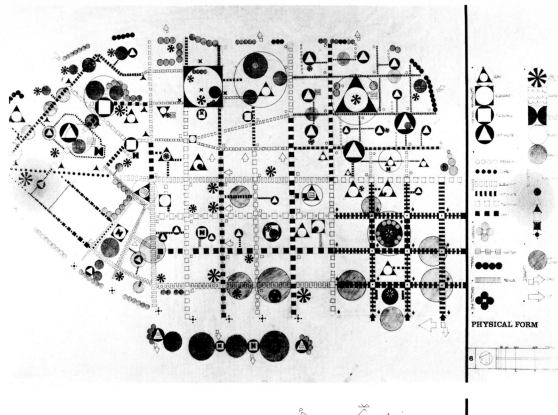

PHYSICAL FORM

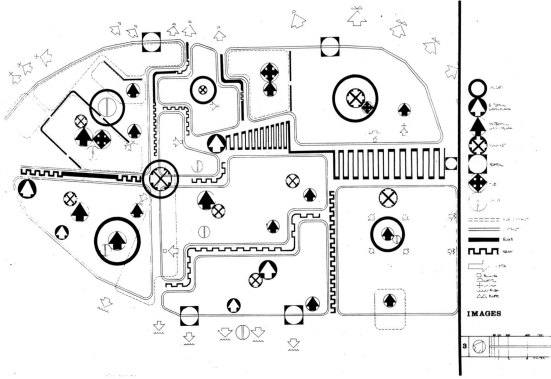

IMAGES

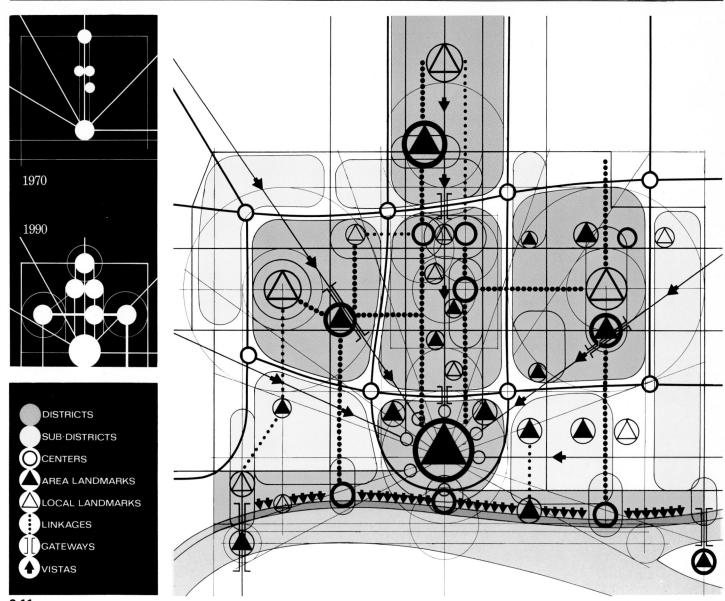

DISTRICTS
SUB-DISTRICTS
CENTERS
AREA LANDMARKS
LOCAL LANDMARKS
LINKAGES
GATEWAYS
VISTAS

9.11
Symbolic Diagrams:
Detroit—Character, 1970
and 1990

Diagrams represent symbolically the perceived character of
the city in the present and as
proposed in the future. Elements include districts, centers,
landmarks, major routes, gateways, and vistas. The large map
details the anticipated future
image. Symbolic diagrams can
powerfully convey concepts
that would be lost in the detail
of conventional maps, but their
meaning is often not apparent
without study. *Urban Design Di-*
vision, Detroit City Plan Com-
mission, Detroit *1990 (Detroit,*
1969).

9.12
Motion-Sequence Map:
Visual Character of a
Highway Network

The experience of vision and motion along a highway network is represented in this map used in highway planning and design. Qualities of the highway experience such as spatial containment, views, sense of motion, and field of view are represented. Although economical, the technique requires far more imagination and interpretation from the user than simulation techniques such as models or film. *MIT Student Project, Robin Moore, Department of City Planning, 1966.*

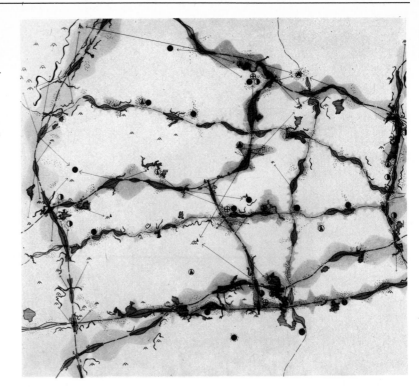

9.13
View Sequence Along
Major Streets

The changing views seen by drivers are shown in map form by connecting individual views along routes into a chain. Activity and form are depicted schematically. The technique is useful in highway design and analysis, but routes can be "traveled" in only one direction. Street networks must be widely enough spaced to accommodate the view chains (compare 5.24, 5.25). *Donald Appleyard and Michael Southworth, General Motors Urban Transportation Project, unpublished.*

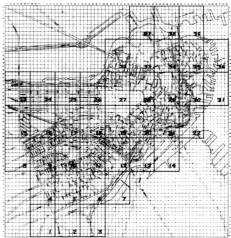

9.14
Eye-level Photo Grid Map:
Central Boston

Central Boston was arbitrarily divided into a grid of small equal-size cells about 150 by 150 feet. A single photograph was then taken from one point within each cell to show its character. Photos were mounted in the same pattern as the cell grid, creating a photo-montage map. The technique provides a strong sense of the character of city districts but cannot be used for orientation. It is most useful when overlaid with a transparent street grid to provide reference points (compare 5.23). *Carl Steinitz, "Congruence and Meaning" (unpublished MIT dissertation, 1967).*

9.15
Counter-Intuitive Map:
Hard-to-find Quality
Shops, Midtown
Manhattan

Alerting prospective shoppers to the hidden or unknown quality shops located just off the main shopping streets is the purpose of this map and the accompanying set of thirty-six slides. Commonly known shops and landmarks are ignored in favor of little-known but worthwhile places. The shopper first views slides of store fronts in rapid succession before leaving on a shopping trip. He retains the image of facades, signs, and windows that interest him and is alerted to look for them on the street. On the map the continuous red line indicates the primary shopping streets. The small red rectangles located off these streets correspond to the hidden or difficult-to-find shops. The long, narrow Manhattan block has been intentionally distorted to an even more elongated shape to represent the way it is perceived on the street. Similarly, block lengths are shown as equal, even though they are in fact unequal. *Dr. Craig Fields, graphics by Rand McNally; unpublished.*

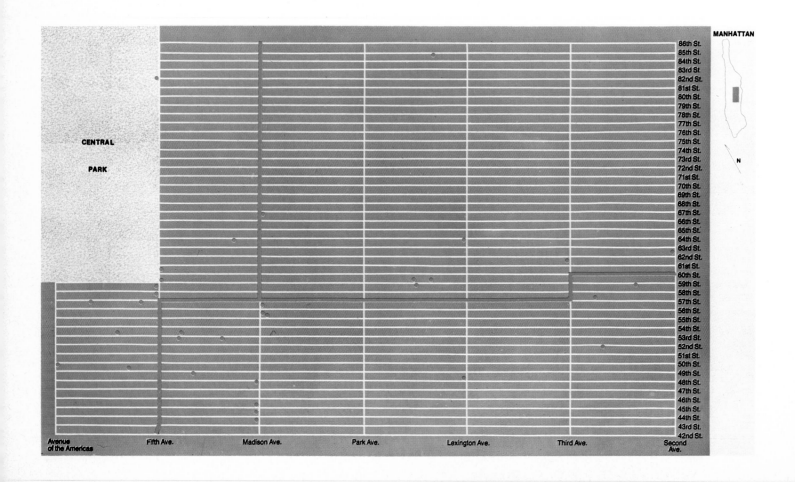

9.16
Cartoon Image Map: New York versus Los Angeles

Sunny Los Angeles and urban New York battle each other's values with dart missiles. Los Angeles is a sunbaked movie set, an unreal world adorned with sunglasses, towel, palm tree, and telephone pole. New York, in contrast, is a dark, massive fortress of nearly impenetrable masonry with the top of the Chrysler Building poking up. The Statue of Liberty seems to be sinking as she struggles up to her knees in water. *Mike Sell (© 1979 The Bantam Gallery, A Division of Bantam Books, Inc.)*

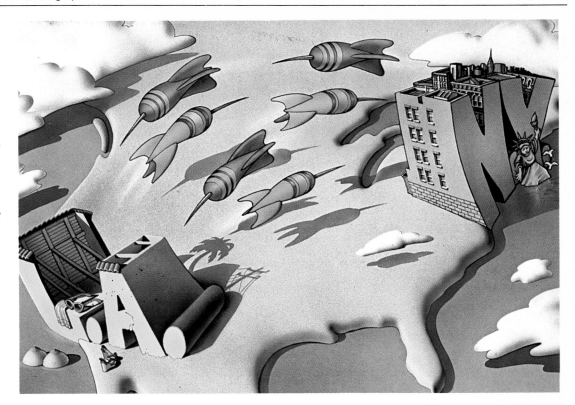

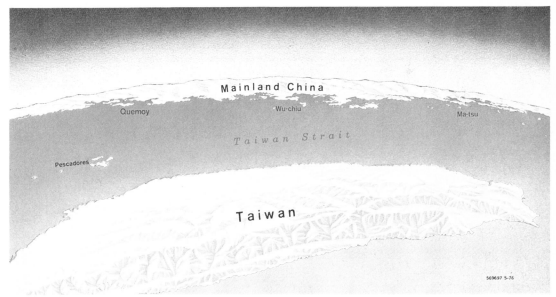

9.17
Point-of-view Map: China and Taiwan

The importance of point of view in mapping is well illustrated in this bird's-eye perspective. Taiwan looms large and powerful over China in a political-military map designed to convey the strategic importance of Taiwan. By exaggerating the relative size of Taiwan, and by locating the viewer above Taiwan and allowing mainland China to disappear over the horizon, the significance of Taiwan is enhanced and the importance and size of China diminish. New attitudes or understanding can be developed through artful selection of vantage points.

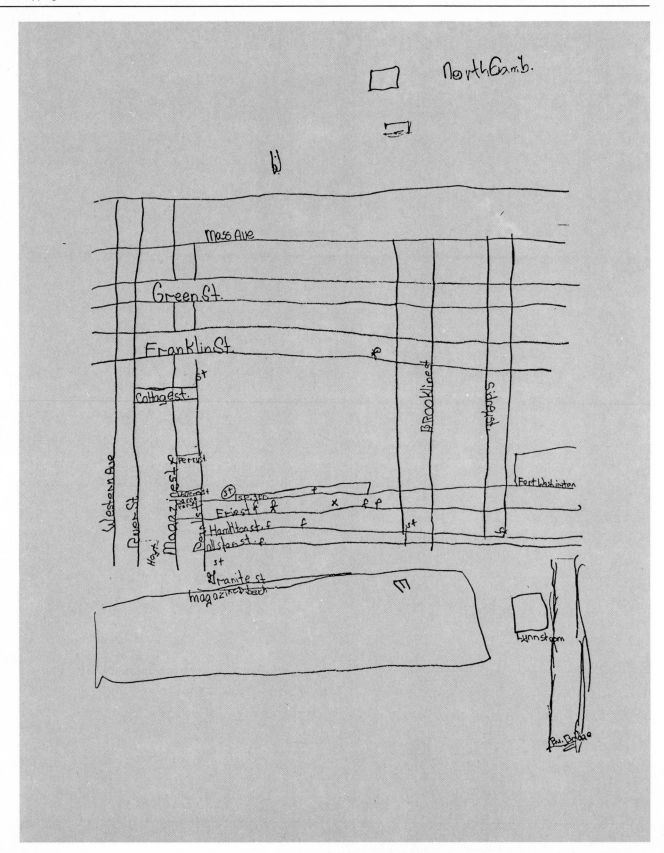

**9.18
Personal Image Maps:
Cambridgeport—Two
Boys' Maps of the Same
Neighborhood**

Two twelve-year-old boys drew these maps of their own neighborhoods, which were used in studying their knowledge and use of the city. Maps drawn from memory provide insights into the way space is organized mentally and the kinds of landmarks and other environmental cues we depend upon in thinking and traveling. Study of such maps can help cartographers create maps that are easier for the general public to use. Although there is wide variation in style and content of personal image maps of the same neighborhood or city, certain landmarks, streets, or other references appear repeatedly and thus are considered important orientation cues. Similarly, other areas might be confused or distorted in image maps, or might be devoid of information; here, the cartographer must pay special attention to providing additional orientation cues or clarifying a confusing pattern. *Michael Southworth,* An Urban Service for Children Based on Analysis of Cambridgeport Boys' Conception and Use of the City *(MIT Dissertation, 1970).*

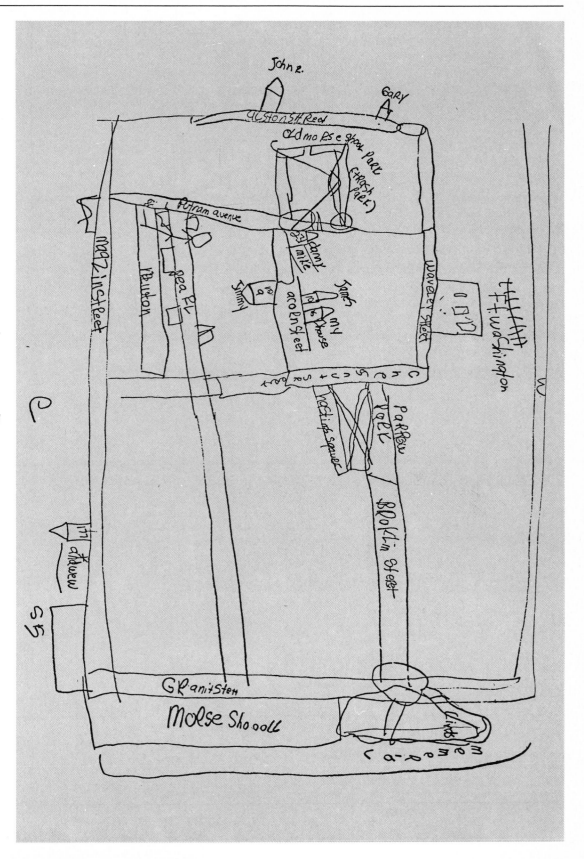

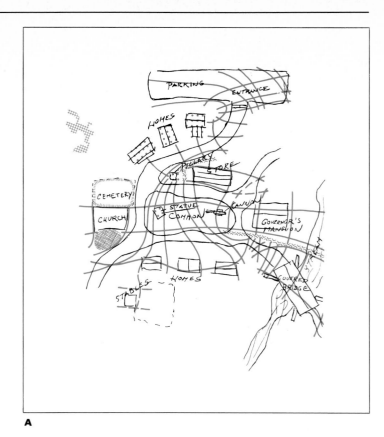

A

9.19
Mental Maps:
Old Sturbridge Village

As part of a program to develop a new visitor map for Old Sturbridge Village, several people were asked to draw maps of the Village as they imagined or remembered it. Some people had never been there, nor had they seen a map; however, they had preconceptions of what a typical New England village was like (map **A**). Others had never been there, but had seen maps (maps **B** and **C**).

Maps **D** and **E** were made by people who had some experience with the Village. The "cognitive" maps have been analyzed in terms of displacement, nonexistent objects, warps, mirror images, and duplication. Such mental maps provide insights into conditions that are important in visitor behavior and map use. Personal image maps have been used in solving a variety of problems in planning and cartography. They can help clarify community values and problems and can provide insights into making maps better suited to the user. *George F. McCleary, Jr., and Nicholas Westbrook,* Recreational and Re-Creational Mapping *(Worcester, MA: Clark University Cartographic Laboratory, 1974; monograph).*

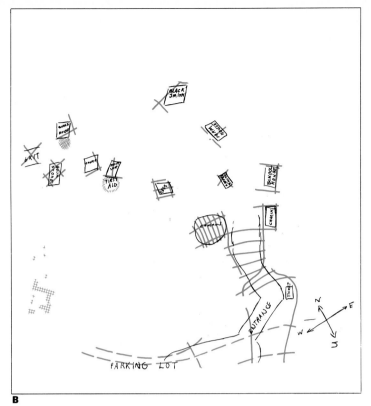

B

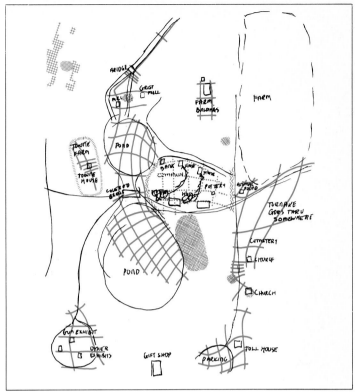

C

D

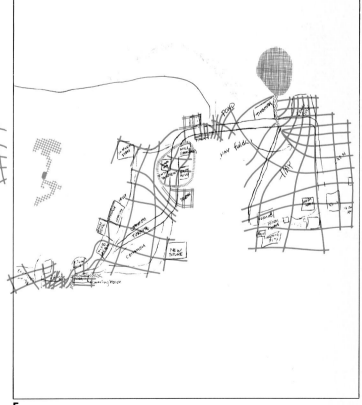

E

9.20
Superfeature Map:
University of California,
Santa Cruz

Distinctive features of this landscape and its buildings are exaggerated and distorted to create a composite "superfeature"
that will be recognized by most
people. The graphic result
resembles cubist art. The Santa
Cruz campus is particularly difficult to map and to orient one-
self in because it is heavily
wooded, highly dispersed, and
hilly. Topography is communicated by means of a warped
grid. A transparent forest overlay texture was developed to
allow visibility of the terrain grid.
Four stages in the development
of the map are illustrated: topography (**A**), vegetation (**B**), circulation (**C**), and buildings (**D**).

   The technique is not appropriate where quantifiable, accurate information is required, as
in navigation or construction. It
is particularly useful, however,
to the user who knows nothing
about the area he is about to explore. *Dana Charlene Cuff and
Kristina Hooper, University of
California, Santa Cruz.*

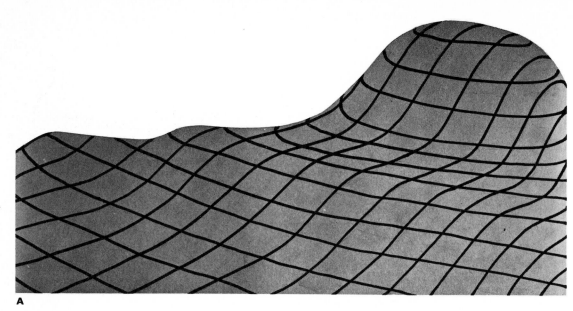

A

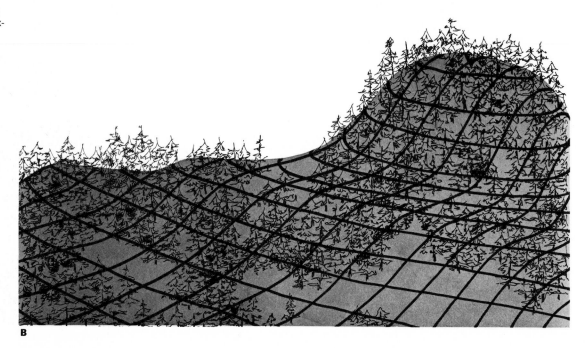

B

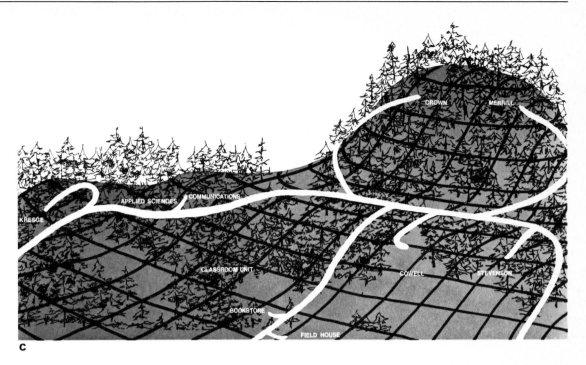

C

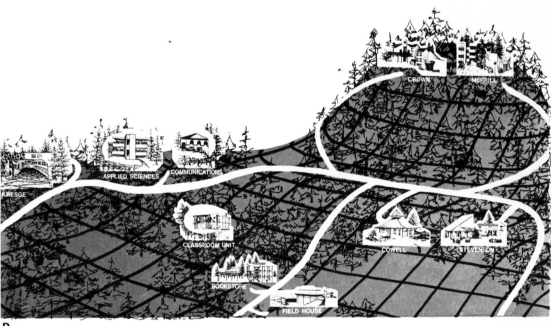

D

10.1
Computer Movie Map:
Dar-El-Mara

Dar-El-Mara is a fictional sea-side town in North Africa created as an exercise in computer simulation of an environment. Computer maps begin with a "digital data base" describing the geographic and cultural features of the mapped locale. If the data base is sufficiently detailed, it can be used to create three-dimensional pictures that reproduce the major visual as-

pects of the environment. A series of pictorial views, arranged sequentially, is then used to produce a computer movie map. The viewer of such a movie has the feeling of being driven through or flown over the mapped area. The natural appearance of the scenes, combined with the dynamic cues given by the movement, give a strong sense of place, facilitat-

ing both learning and orientation. This sequence of pictures is from a movie tour of Dar-El-Mara. View **A** is an aerial view from an elevation of 1600 feet. An aerial view looking north from a height of 250 feet is seen in **B**, while **C** is a street-level view. *Perceptronics, Inc., Woodland Hills, Ca.*

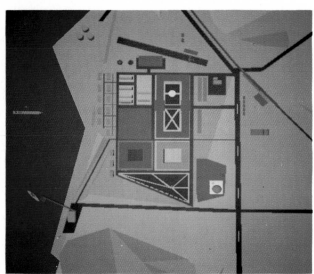

A 1600 feet

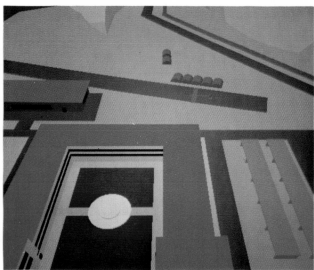

B 250 feet

C Street-level

Putting control in the hands of the map user to allow selection or manipulation of the map is a significant development that has greatly expanded with the technical possibilities of the computer and video disk. The wave of user control and input in many fields may be partially responsible for the current popularity of interactive mapping. Interactive computer-video maps allow high-speed, low-cost acquisition of information in map form. Moreover, the user may select and eliminate data as he chooses, or even annotate or change the data base. But some kinds of interactive mapping predate these sophisticated technologies. The Paris Métro light-up route maps, for example, have delighted and informed subway travelers for years, although their technology is about as basic as that in a string of Christmas-tree lights (10.7).

Simulation of environmental experience is another important function of many maps and allows one to learn much about an environment without actually being there. Simulation maps are therefore useful in training, travel, and planning. Early examples of simulation are walk-through model-maps (10.8, 10.9). Computer-video disk simulations present the possibility of going beyond real experience to the superreal by including added layers of information not normally available in real-world travel (10.15). The future possibilities of home video map disks are one exciting direction this technique could take, allowing the armchair traveler to go almost anywhere.

**10.2
Computer Representations
of Airplane
Landings**

Landing at an airport is simulated by a computer-generated film of the sequence. This is a useful training or planning tool, allowing one to move through an important sequence ahead of time. It has particular value in

simulating motion experiences that cannot be easily practiced in reality—for example, military operations or pilot training. Whether films of route views are more efficient than conven-

tional maps in teaching a route to a stranger is not clear, but they would be useful in museums, shopping centers, or cities in response to the ubiquitous "How do I get there?" *William*

Fetter in Richard Saul Wurman, Design Quarterly 80, Making the City Observable (Walker Art Center and MIT Press; copyright 1971 by Walker Art Center).

 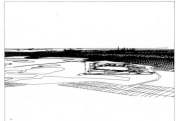  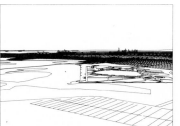

 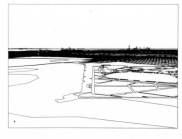  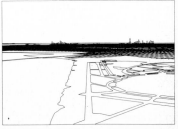

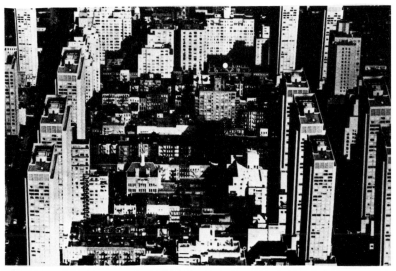

10.3
Photomontage: How Much High-Density Development Should be Permitted in Midtown Residential Areas?

Photomontage techniques can create convincing representations of future possibilities. Here we see three views of midtown Manhattan. On top is an actual photograph; in the middle is a photomontage of the same area as if it were covered with high-rise buildings, and on the bottom is a photomontage of the same area with high-rise buildings built only along the avenues. The technique creates a feeling of reality and is valuable for testing hypotheses or the impact of alternative policies. *New York City Planning Commission,* Plan for New York City: Manhattan *(Cambridge, MA: MIT Press, 1969; copyright © 1969, Department of City Planning, City of New York).*

10.4
CAORF Navigation Simulator

The CAORF (Computer Aided Operations Research Facility) simulator re-creates with considerable realism the experience of navigating a ship through a busy harbor. A twenty-five-foot cylindrical screen portrays ships and shorelines, navigational aids and docking area, bridges, and buildings as full-color television pictures. Six moving ships can be displayed at once, with the scene changing in real time in response to the ship's own movement and that of other ships, As the picture text states: "Illumination from daylight to moonless night, passing ship and harbor lights, haze and fog can all be simulated. Any geographic area, any port, any ship can be generated by a computer with a data base of three-dimensional coordinates and characteristics. As the ship handler changes course or speed, the 240-degree visual scene automatically changes, and CAORF radar and instrument readings adjust accordingly."

The simulator is used in teaching and research, including collision analysis, bridge systems design, analysis of harbor designs and restricted waterways, and ship control, navigation, and operational procedures. *National Maritime Research Center, Kings Point, NY.*

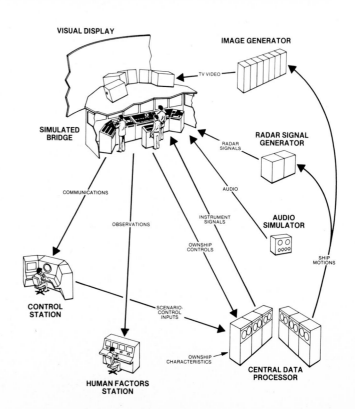

10.5
Computer Simulation
Tanks and terrain were constructed mathematically using a computer and the Synthevision® system developed by MAGI. This example has three-dimensional qualities but is a static simulation. *Mathematical Applications Group, Inc., Elmsford, NY, 1974.*

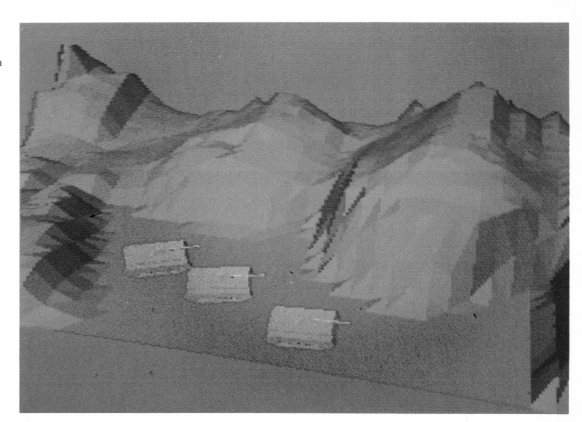

10.6
Walk-Through Map of Lowell
This design proposal for an outdoor musuem of the city is a schematic walk-through model of the streets and major sites on a one-acre plot. Intended as an educational tool for use by school children and tourists, it allows quick conceptualization of a large area in very real terms. *Michael & Susan Southworth, City Design and Architecture, Boston, MA.*

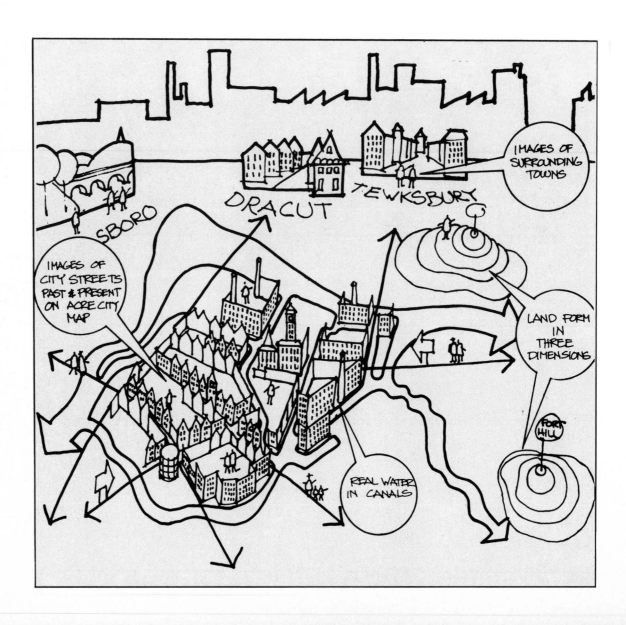

10.7
Paris Métro Light-up
Route Map
For the Paris Métro system, the most extensive subway system in the world, with a complex spiderweb of routes, the light-up electric map is a very useful device. Most destinations in the system can be reached by at least two routes from any given starting point; several transfers are often necessary. Finding the most efficient route could be a time-consuming effort. Using the electric map, a rider simply pushes the button for his destination on the panel below the map. The destination and the most efficient route to it then light up. An electric map is applicable to any transportation system: bus, airplane, train, highway, as well as subway. It is also useful in complex office buildings, art museums, or college campuses. Computer technology can make electronic routing maps very sophisticated by allowing route selection using criteria other than efficiency—for example, a scenic route, the safest route, the least crowded route. Personalized itineraries and route maps may also be printed out by such computer terminals. *In Richard Saul Wurman,* Design Quarterly 80, Making the City Observable *(Walker Art Center and MIT Press; copyright 1971 by Walker Art Center).*

10.8
Walk-through Globe:
Mapparium
The Christian Science Publishing Building Mapparium allows one to walk on a bridge through the center of a giant illuminated stained-glass globe thirty feet in diameter and to look at it from the inside. Peculiar acoustic properties result from the spherical space. Oddly, continents are represented as one would see them on the outside of a globe. The major value of the technique is for education and exhibition. *The Christian Science Publishing Society, Boston, MA.*

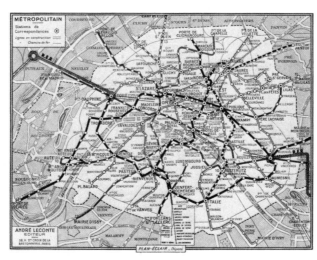

**10.9
Walk-through Model:
Guatemala**

The entire country of Guatemala is simulated in this large
outdoor topographic model of
concrete. Vertical scale is exaggerated. Mountains, rivers, and
towns are identified by flags.
One may view the model from
ground level or from several
high viewing towers. *Photograph by Michael Southworth.*

**10.10
Touch-Sensitive Auditory
Map**

By touching any point on the
map, the user hears a description of the place he is touching.
Sonars (piezo ceramic transduc-
ers) located on two sides of the
frame locate the coordinates
where the user's finger is pointing. The corresponding data set
is then retrieved from the disk
where auditory data is stored
digitally. A map such as this
would be particularly valuable to
the sight-impaired, nonreaders,
or children. *Architecture
Machine Group, MIT.*

10.11
Participatory Simulation Map: Mapping by Yourself

A hand-held 12-by-12-inch mapping "window" is capable of presenting computer-stored images of an environment from multiple vantage points. In effect, the user can travel through the modeled environment, controlling path, speed, angle of approach, and scale. Touch-sensitive layers on the panel allow the user to input requests and to manipulate information displayed by using the fingers. Other aspects of the "Mapping by Yourself" project include amplifying maps with sound, representing uncertain information, and making surfaces such as the ground penetrable, "transparent." *Architecture Machine Group, MIT.*

10.12
T-Shirt Map

The user need not worry about losing or storing this map, "The Revised Wearable Guide to the West Side." Although it is intended as an advertisement and souvenir for the West Side, it does locate several boutiques, restaurants, museums, concert halls, and other amusements. These are identified verbally and illustrated with a logo superimposed on the block outlines from Seventy-second to Eighty-sixth streets and Central Park to the Hudson River. *Made in France for Charivari.*

10.13
Participatory Map:
Community-Made Map,
Hill District, Pittsburgh

Rarely does one encounter such a large map—25 by 40 feet. Produced piece by piece by community residents in a Pittsburgh neighborhood, it is a walk-on map. The intention was not precision but identification and expression of resources, problems, and attitudes in the neighborhood; it is filled with judgment, preferences, and omissions. The participatory development and large scale of such maps make them valuable in community planning and education. *Community Design Associates: Troy West, Douglas Cooper, Jay Greenfield, Richard Ridley, Ed Goff, and many community participants.*

Detail

10.14
Image Model:
Ruckus Manhattan
An artist's conception of Lower Manhattan, this topsy-turvy model fills a large room and rises to a height of thirty feet. Although it is based on real buildings, simplification, distortion, and selection result in a surreal or cartoon sense of the city. The section illustrated is the World Trade Center. Materials are wood, steel, and plastic. *Red Grooms and The Ruckus Construction Company; photograph by Robert Mates and Gail Stern; courtesy Marlborough Gallery, New York City.*

10.15
Interactive Movie Map: Aspen

This experimental mapping system attempts to simluate "being there" and gives the user the ability to "drive" through the environment, selecting his own route and speed. The viewer "drives" by means of a joystick or a touch-sensitive video screen that has a control area at the bottom for forward, reverse, top, left and right turns, slow and fast (**A, B, C**). The user may also enter many buildings and explore them or obtain more information. For example, one may stop at a restaurant and look at its menu, or at a hotel and view its rooms (**D**). Buildings and streets may be seen at different seasons or at different points in their history (**E**). Self-documentation is another aspect of the system; users may annotate views with notes or sketches, thus creating personalized maps. The technique is useful in familiarizing people with an environment before they actually visit it and has obvious entertainment value for the armchair traveler. The entire photographic base was digitized to eliminate distractions and to enable users to simulate aerial travel and make changes in architectural form (**F**).

Optical video-disk technology, which allows storage and random access to 54,000 television frames, is used to store views of all streets. In this case, Aspen was photographed from a truck with a camera mounted eleven feet above the road (**G**). Photographs were taken every ten feet and in four directions—left, right, ahead, and behind.

An audio track provides street names, compass directions, confirmation of turns and other commands, information about landmarks, and distance information. The same streets were also photographed using an anamorphic lens, which records a 360-degree doughnut-shaped panorama that can be projected on cylindrical walls surrounding the user, enhancing the sense of reality. *Architecture Machine Group, MIT.*

A

C

B

E

F

D

G

References

Bagrow, Leo. *History of Cartography,* revised and enlarged by R. A. Skelton (Cambridge, MA: Harvard University Press, 1964).

Bertin, Jacques; *Sémiologie Graphique* (Paris: Éditions Gauthier-Villars; Paris, New York, The Hague: Mouton Publishers; Paris: École des Hautes Études en Sciences Sociales, 1967).

Brown, Lloyd A. *The Story of Maps* (Boston: Little, Brown and Company, 1949).

Centre Georges Pompidou. *Cartes et Figures de la Terre* (Paris: Centre Georges Pompidou, 1980).

Crone, Gerald Roe. *Maps and Their Makers* (London: Hutchinson, 1966).

Downs, Roger M., and David Stea, editors. *Image and Environment: Cognitive Mapping and Spatial Behavior* (Chicago: Aldine Publishing Company, 1973).

Downs, Roger M., and David Stea. *Maps in Minds* (New York: Harper and Row, 1977).

Greenhood, David. *Down To Earth: Mapping for Everybody* (New York: Holiday House, 1951).

Hooper, Kristina. *The Mapping Process* (University of California, Santa Cruz: monograph, 1977).

Lynam, Edward. *The Mapmaker's Art: Essays on the History of Maps* (London: Batchworth Press, 1953).

Post, J. B. *An Atlas of Fantasy* (Baltimore: Mirage Press, Ltd., 1973).

Raisz, Erwin. *General Cartography* (New York, Toronto, London: McGraw-Hill Book Company, 1948).

Robinson, Arthur H., and Barbara Bartz Petchenik. *The Nature of Maps* (Chicago and London: University of Chicago Press, 1976).

Skelton, R. A. *Explorers' Maps* (New York: Frederick A. Praeger, 1958).

Thrower, Norman J. W. *Maps and Man: An Examination of Cartography in Relation to Culture and Civilization* (Englewood Cliffs, NY: Prentice-Hall, Inc., 1972).

List of Maps and Illustrations

1
Maps, Map Users, and the Milieu
1.1 Anthropomorphic Map
1.2 Signs as Maps
1.3 Ancient Babylonian Map
1.4 Illuminated T-in-O Map

2
Landmarks in Mapmaking
2.1 Coastal Profile
2.2 Dutch Map of Africa
2.3 Mental Maps
2.4 Babylonian World Map
2.5 Korean World Map
2.6 Roman World Map
2.7 Tabula Peutingeriana, A Roman Road Map
2.8 Ptolemy's World
2.9 T-in-O and Zone Maps
2.10 Hereford Map
2.11 Medieval Road Map
2.12 Map of al-Idrisi
2.13 Portolan Chart
2.14 Sketch Map by Christopher Columbus
2.15 Gerardus Mercator
2.16 Jean Dominique Cassini
2.17 Triangulation of France

3
Land Form
3.1 Computer-Generated Topographic Map
3.2 A Variety of Map Projections
3.3 Geodesic Globe
3.4 Landsat View: The Baluchistan Desert
3.5 Computer-Generated Topography and Concealment Maps
3.6 Digitized Topographic Map of Mount St. Helens
3.7 Bryson: Air Landing Graphic
3.8 Bryson: Topography and Vegetation

3.9 Raised Relief Topographic Maps
3.10 Stereo Map: Lycoming and Clinton Counties, Pennsylvania
3.11 Topographic Map of Switzerland
3.13 Military Maps: Columbus
3.13 Ground Tactical Data: Manati, Puerto Rico
3.14 Pictorical Map Graph: Eight Landscape Types
3.15 Eskimo Coastline Relief Carvings
3.16 Computer-Generated Map: Lake Istokpoga, Florida
3.17 Geological Map: Soviet Union
3.18 Nighttime Satellite Photograph
3.19 Satellite Photograph with Graphic Overlay
3.20 Orienteering Map: Bear Brook State Park
3.21 Red Sea Diver's Guide
3.22 Seattle: Shadow Patterns
3.23 Seattle: Sequential Sections
3.24 Weather Charts
3.25 Infrared Reflectance

4
Built Form
4.1 Panorama: Florence
4.2 Panoramic Perspective: Penn Mutual's Philadelphia
4.3 Aerial Perspective Drawing: Disneyland
4.4 Distorted Bird's-Eye Perspective View: New Orleans
4.5 Sailing Chart and Coastline Views: Annapolis
4.6 Photographic Panoramas: Monument Valley and New York City

4.7 Baedeker's Genoa
4.8 Florence: Plan of the City
4.9 Plan-Perspective: La Terra de Hochelaga nella Nova Francia
4.10 Plan-Panorama: Mexico-Tenochtitlán
4.11 Plan-Perspective: Mexico-Tenochtitlán
4.12 Brussels
4.13 Athens
4.14 Pictorial-Elevation Map: Jerusalem, 1584
4.15 Paris: Plan Turgot, 1734
4.16 Archaeological Map: Delos
4.17 Development of Miletus
4.18 Aerial Photograph: Manhattan
4.19 Lower Manhattan Plan
4.20 Axonometric Pictorial Map: Manhattan
4.21 Fish-eye Aerial Photo of Manhattan
4.22 Symbolic Map: Philadelphia
4.23 Annotated Schematic Map: Washington, DC, Capitol Hill
4.24 Tourist Map: Cologne
4.25 Cross-Section Map: New York Underground
4.26 Section-Plan Map: Novanoah II
4.27 Pictorial Map: Dry Dock Country
4.28 Pictorial Landmark Map: Boston Discovery Map
4.29 Elevation-Plan Map: Park Mall, Detroit
4.30 Pictorial Map: Nagasaki Harbor
4.31 Historic Mantorville, Minnesota
4.32 Zoom Map: Yeshiva University
4.33 Floating Landmark Map: Cambridge

4.34 Floating Landmark Map: Jerusalem
4.35 Soft Manhattan #1: Postal Zones
4.36 Relief Maps: Peking and Rome
4.37 Casablanca: Building Type
4.38 Casablanca: City Perspective
4.39 Address Finder: *Répertoire des Rues*
4.40 Environmental Control Map: Management of Main Street
4.41 Sanborn Insurance Map: Spokane, Washington
4.42 Vine Grove, Kentucky
4.43 Stuttgart and Environs
4.44 Model: Detroit
4.45 Tactile Model for the Blind: Philadelphia, Independence Hall Block
4.46 Braille-Tactile Map: Boston and Cambridge
4.47 Braille Map: MBTA System Tactile Route Map
4.48 Compact Map: London
4.49 Pop-Out Map: Yellowbird Migration Guide
4.50 Embossed Map: Buffalo
4.51 Relief Map: Washington Mall

5
Networks and Routes
5.1 Pictorial Subway Guide for Children
5.2 Route Map: The Procession of the Empress Elizabeth, 1742
5.3 Pictorial Route Map: The Nile
5.4 Verbal Strip Map: A Trip down the Grand Canal, Venice
5.5 Verbal Route Program: Angers-Gien or Gien-Angers

5.6 Navigational Stick Chart: Marshall Islands
5.7 Diagrammatic Strip Map: Los Angeles
5.8 Bus Chart: Los Angeles
5.9 Route Map: Place St. Michel to the Pont Sully, Paris
5.10 Verbal Map: Guide to the Appalachian Trail in Maine
5.11 Line Diagram for Helsinki Subway
5.12 Pictorial Bus Route
5.13 London Transport Underground System
5.14 Verbal Route Guide: Up the Coast to Malibu
5.15 Triptik
5.16 System Diagram with Landmarks: Washington, DC, Metro
5.17 Bus Routes: Seattle-King County
5.18 Strip Maps: Paris Buses
5.19 Highway Intersection Map: Detroit
5.20 New York Subway Map
5.21 Manhattan Bus Guide
5.22 New York Subway Guide
5.23 Photographic Route Sequence: Minneapolis
5.24 Proposed Image Structure for a Highway: Minneapolis
5.25 Sequence from I-35W Bridge to Nicollet Mall, Minneapolis
5.26 Subway, Bus, and Expressway Maps: Philadelphia
5.27 Route-Intersection Maps
5.28 Strip Map: York to West Chester
5.29 Road Map
5.30 Official Road Map for Allied Forces: France
5.31 Pictographic Maps: Mexico City Metro and National Zoo
5.32 Sectional Aeronautical Chart
5.33 Flight Map

6
Quantity, Density, and Distribution
6.1 Techniques for Communicating Quantity, Density, and Percentage
6.2 World Population
6.3 Ninety-fifth Congress
6.4 Weapons Exports and Imports
6.5 Computer Maps
6.6 Pie Map: Potential Voters by Race in Metrolina
6.7 Metrolina Population Density Pattern

6.8 Bar Map: Average Metrolina Wind Direction and Speed
6.9 Circle Map: Average Number of Daily Telephone Messages between Boston and Selected Cities, April 1953
6.10 Dot Map: Value of All Farm Products Sold
6.11 Flash Maps: New York Music Centers and Libraries
6.12 Whale Chart
6.13 Three-dimensional Pictograph: The Balance of Power, 1914
6.14 Cartoon Map: Futureworld

7
Relation and Comparison
7.1 Comparative Maps: Population, Income, and Land Use
7.2 Zoom Maps: Aspen, Colorado
7.3 Comparative Map: New York - 62 Cities from 50 States
7.4 North American Climatic Analogs for USSR Crop Regions
7.5 Distances from Autun to Other Points in France and Europe
7.6 Comparative Maps: Main Regions of the Soviet Union; World Map of Population and Income
7.7 Point of View: Azimuthal Equidistant Projection Centered Near San Antonio
7.8 Comparative Panoramic Perspectives of the Earth: China and Japan
7.9 Perspective-Section: Diagram of an Oil-Prospecting Program
7.10 Multiple Viewpoints: Facade, Section, and Plan-Perspectives of Two Buildings

8
Time, Change, and Movement
8.1 Synchronological Map: Ancient, Modern, and Biblical History
8.2 Time-Line Spiral
8.3 Growth and Change: London
8.4 Time-Distance Map: Travel Time, Japan
8.5 Time-Lapse, Mixed-Media Map: Central Park, 1870 and 1970s

8.6 Photographic Time-Lapse: A Day in the Life of Three Persons and Two Spaces
8.7 Photographic Time-Lapse: The American Road Edge
8.8 Vehicle Traffic Volume in Metrolina
8.9 Time and Temperature Chart
8.10 Star Finder
8.11 Migration Map: France
8.12 Family Map: Genghis Khan and His Descendants
8.13 Traffic Movement and Vehicle Storage

9
Behavior and Personal Imagery
9.1 Pictorial Map: Covarrubias's America
9.2 Activity Map
9.3 Neighboring and Visiting: San Francisco
9.4 Montage Map: Bermuda Triangle
9.5 Word-Collage Map: Seattle
9.6 Word Map: Seattle
9.7 Street Analysis: Detroit
9.8 Evaluation of the Soundscape: Boston
9.9 Fantasy Map: Gospel Temperance Railroad Map
9.10 Symbolic Maps: Images and Physical Form, St. Paul
9.11 Symbolic Diagrams: Detroit — Character, 1970 and 1990
9.12 Motion-Sequence Map: Visual Character of a Highway Network
9.13 View Sequence along Major Streets
9.14 Eye-level Photo Grid Map: Central Boston
9.15 Counter-intuitive Map: Hard-to-find Quality Shops, Manhattan
9.16 Cartoon Image Map: New York versus Los Angeles
9.17 Point-of-view Map: China and Taiwan
9.18 Personal Image Maps: Cambridgeport — Two Boys' Maps
9.19 Mental Maps: Old Sturbridge Village
9.20 Superfeature Map: University of California, Santa Cruz

10
Simulation and Interaction
10.1 Computer Movie Map: Dar-El-Mara
10.2 Computer Representations of Airplane Landings
10.3 Photomontage: How Much High-Density Development Should be Permitted in Midtown Residential Areas?
10.4 CAORF Navigation Simulator
10.5 Computer Simulation
10.6 Walk-Through Map of Lowell
10.7 Paris Métro Light-up Route Map
10.8 Walk-Through Globe: Mapparium
10.9 Walk-Through Model: Guatemala
10.10 Touch-Sensitive Auditory Map
10.11 Participatory Simulation Map: Mapping by Yourself
10.12 T-Shirt Map
10.13 Participatory Map: Community-made Map, Hill District, Pittsburgh
10.14 Image Model: Ruckus Manhattan
10.15 Interactive Movie Map: Aspen

Index

abstraction, 158
accuracy, 14, 16, 20, 21, 22, 25, 33
activity maps, 178, 184-185, 186, 187
Adams, Sebastian Cabot, 172
address finder, 94
Aegean Sea, 23
aerial perspective drawing, 65
aerial photographs, 33, 40, 44, 46, 78, 79, 177
aeronautical maps, 140, 141, 206
Africa, 20, 21, 23, 25, 26, 27, 33
agricultural maps, 151, 165
Alexander VI, Pope, 32
Alexandria, Egypt, 23, 24, 25
Alfonzo, King of Portugal, 31
analysis, analytical maps, 15, 190
Anaximander of Miletus, 23
Anaximenes, 23
Angers-Gien, France, 110
Annapolis, MD, 66
annotated schematic map, 80
anthropomorphic map, 8-9
Appalachian Trail map, 115
Arab maps, 24, 28, 29
Aral Sea, 28
archaeological maps, 76, 77
Aristotle, 23
armchair travel, 11-12, 75, 108
Asia, 23, 25, 26, 28, 31, 168, 169
Aspen, CO, 160-163, 216-217
ASPEX, 146
assessors' maps, 12
Athens, Greece, 73
Atlantic Ocean, 31
auditory maps, 14, 212, 216-217
Austria, 8
Autun, France, 166
axonometric projections, 71, 75, 79
Aztecs, 12, 71

Babylonia, 12, 13, 22, 25
Baedeker, Karl, 68, 110
Balboa, Vasco Núñez de, 32
balloon surveys, 33
Baluchistan, 41
Banlieues, 171
bar maps, 149
Bear Brook State Park, ME, 56
Bermuda Triangle, 188
bicycling maps, 106, 118
bird's-eye perspective, 65
blind, maps for, 12, 14, 99, 100
Boston, MA, 21, 85, 100, 104-105, 116, 150, 186, 190, 195
Braille maps, 99, 100
Britain, 24, 25
Brussels, Belgium, 72
Bryson, CO, 44, 45
Buddhist maps, 23
Buffalo, NY, 102, 179
building data, 92, 93, 95, 97, 171
bus maps, 113, 116, 121, 122, 125, 129

cadastral maps, 12, 13
California, 21, 118, 174
Calvin, John, 25
Cambridge, MA, 88, 100, 198-199
CAORF, 208-209
Cape Cod, MA, 21
Cartier, Jacques, 70
cartoons, 84, 88, 155, 197, 215
Casablanca, Morocco, 92, 93
Cassini, César François, 32
Cassini, Jean Dominique, 20, 32, 34
Central Park, New York City, 177
Cervantes, Miguel de, 11
change, maps of, 15, 174, 175
Charlotte, NC, 148-149, 180
Chicago, IL, 132
children: maps for, 12, 104-105; maps by, 198-199
China, 22, 168, 169, 197
Christian Science Publishing Building Mapparium, 211

chronological chart, 172-173, 174
circle map, 150
circulation system map, 183
cities, representing, 64
clay maps, 12, 13, 22
climate: analog map, 165; in zone maps, 28
Clinton County, PA, 46
Colbert, Jean Baptiste, 32
Cologne, Germany, 81
color, 16: in land-form maps, 40, 41, 44, 45, 48, 49, 53, 61; in built-form maps, 73, 77, 81, 92, 133; in network maps, 100, 104-105, 113, 116, 117, 120, 124-125; in data maps, 144-145, 148-149
Columbus, Bartolomeo, 31
Columbus, Christopher, 31
Columbus, OH, 48
compact map, 101
comparison, mapping of, 12, 15, 90-91, 145, 146-151, 156-159, 164-169
compass, magnetic, 30, 31
computer mapping: simulation, 12, 16, 204-206, 208-209; for analysis, 15; interactive, 17, 206, 211, 212-213, 216-217; topographic, 36-37, 40, 42, 43, 52, 61; data, 146-147
construction maps, 16
contour lines, 15, 40
Coronelli, Père Vincenzo, 32
Cortes, Hernando, 71
counter-intuitive map, 196
Covarrubias, Miguel, 185
Crates of Mallus, 24-25
cross-section maps, 59, 82, 83, 170
cylindrical equal-area projection, 38
Cyprus, 23

Dar-El-Mara, 204-205
data maps, 15, 142-161
data storage, 12, 15, 206. See also computer mapping
definitions of map, 10, 11
Delapointe, F., 47
Delos, Greece, 76
density, 142-143, 144, 148, 151, 153, 157-159, 180, 183
design of maps, 16-17
Detroit, MI, 87, 98, 123, 158, 190, 193
diagrams, diagrammatic maps, 106, 112, 116, 124-125, 126, 158, 160-163; "spider," 100, 104-105, 117, 120, 128, 166
Dicaearcus of Messana, 23
disk maps, 22, 23
Disneyland, CA, 65
distance maps, 161, 166, 176
distortion, 20-21, 65, 79, 88, 124-125, 128-129, 196
distribution, 144, 145, 148, 150-153
diver's guide, 57
Don River, 26, 27
dot maps, 151, 157-159, 187
Dover, England, 29
Dufour, Guillaume Henri, 47
Dutch maps, 20, 21, 106

earthquakes, 40
Ebstorf map, 12, 28
Eckert projection, 38
educational maps, 210, 211
egocentric maps, 22, 23
Egypt, 12, 23, 24, 108-109
electric map, 211
elevation maps, 64, 70, 71, 74, 81, 86
elliptical equal-area projection, 39
embossed maps, 100, 102
England, 8, 29, 130, 131
English Channel, 29
Entebbe, Uganda, 10, 11
environment, and map use, 12, 14, 15, 16

Eratosthenes of Cyrene, 23-24, 26
Eskimos, coastline carvings, 51
Eudoxus, 24
Europe, 8-9, 23, 25, 26, 27, 154; surveyed, 32
exaggeration, 20, 197. *See also* distortion
experience, and maps, 11-12, 20, 22
exploration, 31-32

facades, 86
fantasy maps, 191-197
films, time-lapse, 174, 178-179
fish-eye aerial photograph, 79
flash maps, 152
floating landmark maps, 88, 89
Florence, Italy, 62-63, 69
folding of maps, 16, 101
France, 8, 20, 32, 34, 110, 133, 142-143, 166, 182
Frederick the Great, 12
Fuller, Buckminster, 40
functions of maps, 11-12

Gall cylindrical projection, 38
Gama, Vasco da, 32
Ganges River, 24, 25
Gastaldi, Giacomo, 12
genealogical chart, 182
Genghis Khan, 182
Genoa, Italy, 68
geodesic globe, 40
Geographica (Ptolemy), 25, 26, 30
geological map, 53
geology, geologists, 12, 40, 41
Germany, 32
Gibraltar, 23
Gien-Angers, France, 110
globes, 24-25, 32, 38
Goode's interrupted homolographic projection, 39
Good Hope, Cape of, 32
graphic overlays, 55, 57
graphic scale, 15
Greece, 23-26, 28, 76, 77
grid, warped, 36, 40, 42, 43, 202-203
growth, urban, map, 175
Guatemala, walk-through map, 212

hachures, 15, 40, 47
Haldingham, Richard of, 28
Harrison, John, 32
Helsinki, Finland, 116
heredity chart, 182
Hereford map, 12, 28
Herodotus, 23
highway maps, 16, 24, 25, 97, 119, 123, 126, 127, 129, 130, 132, 133, 162, 194
hiking maps, 56, 106, 115
Hipparchus, 24, 26, 32
historical development map, 77
Hochelaga, La, map of, 70

Holland, 8
Holy Land, 26, 28, 29
Homer, 23
Houston, TX, 157, 159

Idrisi, al-, 28, 29
image maps, 126, 189, 192. *See also* personal image maps
inch-to-mile scale, 15
income, maps of, 157-159, 166
India, 25, 32
infrared reflectance map, 61
insurance maps, 12, 95
interactive maps, 17, 206, 212, 213, 216-217
International Cartographic Association, 10
intuitive mapping, *see* personal image maps
Ireland, 8
isopleths, 40
Istokpoga, Lake, FL, 52

Japan, 168, 169, 176
Jerusalem, 26, 28, 74, 89

Kazakhstan, Soviet Union, 53
klimata, 27, 28
Korea, 22, 23

Lambert equal-area projection, 39
landmarks, 64, 65, 66, 67, 69, 85, 87, 88, 89, 103, 107, 110, 114, 115, 116, 124, 129, 132, 134-139, 193
Landsat map, 41
land-use maps, 157-159
language, map, 14, 15, 16
latitude, 23-24, 25, 26, 28, 32
Laussedat, Aimé, 33
legend, map, 14
Lehmann, Johann George, 47
line quality, 97, 133
London, England, 29, 101, 175; Underground, 116, 117, 124-125, 128-129
longitude, 23-24, 25, 26, 28, 32
Los Angeles, CA, 112, 113, 197
Louis XIV, 20, 32, 34
Lowell, MA, walk-through map, 210
Lycoming County, PA, 46

Magellan, Ferdinand, 32
Maine, 115
Malibu, CA, 118
Manati, Puerto Rico, 49
Mantorville, MN, 87
Manhattan, *see* New York City
Mapparium, 211
map testing, 124
map use, 10-17
Marcus Agrippa, 25

Marshall Islands, 111
Martha's Vineyard, MA, 50
Massachusetts Bay, 21
medieval maps, 12, 14, 24, 26-28, 29, 30, 106
Mediterranean Sea, 25, 26, 27
memory maps, 198-199
mental maps, 11, 12, 20, 21, 129, 200-201
Mercator, Gerardus, 32, 33; projection, 15, 32, 33, 38
meteorology, 12
Metrolina, maps of, 148-149, 180
Mexico City, 134-137
Mexico, Tenochtitlán, 71
Middle East, infrared reflectance map, 61
migration maps, 101, 174, 182
Miletus, Greece, 77
military maps, 12, 16, 33, 40, 42, 44-45, 48-49, 133, 197, 206
Minneapolis, MN, 126-127, 159
Mississippi River, 65
models, 46, 98, 99, 103, 206, 212
montage map, 188
Mollweide projection, 39
Montreal, Canada, 70
Monument Valley, AZ, 67
motion, movement maps, 174, 180, 183, 194, 204-205, 206, 208-209, 216-217
Moscow, Russia, 107
Mount St. Helens, WA, 43
movie maps, 12, 204-205, 216-217

Nagasaki, Japan, 86
Naples, Museum of, 24
National Zoo, Washington, DC, 138-139
navigation, 12, 30-32, 33, 66, 111, 208-209
neighbors, neighborhoods, 22, 187, 214
New Orleans, LA, 65, 159
New York City, 67, 87, 152, 158, 164, 197; Manhattan, 78-79, 82, 84, 90, 124-125, 177, 196, 207, 213, 215
Nile River, 26, 27, 108-109
"Noachid" maps, 26
north, location of, 14, 22, 24
North America, 155
"Novanoah," 83
Nuzi, 13

oceanography, 40, 41
ODYSSEY, 146, 147
opisometer, 15
"orange-peel" projections, 39
orbis terrarum, see T-in-O maps
Oriental maps, 22, 23, 25, 86
orientation, orientation cues, 10-11, 12, 14, 15, 16, 22, 23, 24, 62, 85, 124,

129, 199. *See also* point of view
orienteering map, 56
ornament, 12, 14, 28
Ortelius, Abraham, 20
Oxford English Dictionary, 10

Pacific Ocean, 32
panoramas, panoramic perspectives, 62-63, 64, 67, 71, 168-169, 216
Paris, France, 75, 94, 114, 122; Observatory of, 20, 32, 34; Métro, 206, 211
participation maps, 17, 213, 214
Peirce projection, 39
Peking, China, 90
percentages, 142-143
perceptual map, 190
peripli, 30
personal image maps, 16, 21-22, 184-185, 198-199, 200-201, 215
perspective maps, 64, 65, 70, 71, 74, 93, 170, 171
Peutinger, Konrad, 25
Philadelphia, PA, 64, 80, 99, 128-129, 179, 183
Philip III, King of Spain, 32
photographic maps, 54, 55, 67, 126, 178, 179, 188, 206, 208-209, 216-217. *See also* aerial photographs
photo grid map, 195
photomontage maps, 195, 207
"physical form" map, 192
Picard's meridian, 32, 34
pictorial maps, 50, 69, 74, 75, 79, 84-89, 104-109, 114, 116, 126, 127, 172-173, 185, 187
pictographs, 134-139, 153, 154, 185
pie maps, 148, 186
pilots' training maps, 12, 40, 206, 208-209
Pisan chart, 30
Pittsburgh, PA, 159, 214
planning, 12, 15, 41, 42, 58, 94, 95, 96, 97, 190, 192, 200, 214
Plan Turgot, 75
plan views, 64, 68, 69, 70, 71, 73, 78, 83, 86, 92
Pococke, Edward, 29
point of view, 16, 22, 42, 86, 167, 168-169, 171, 197
political maps, 8-9, 22, 144, 154, 197
pop-out map, 101
population maps, 144, 146, 154, 155, 157-159, 164, 166
portolani, 30
Portugal, 32
Poseidonius, 26
Postel, Guillaume, projection, 38, 39
Prester John, 20
printing of maps, 30-31

projections, 26, 33, 38-39, 167
propaganda, 12, 16, 197
proportional scale, 15
Prussia, 8
Ptolemy, Claudius, 25, 26, 28, 30, 31, 32, 33
Ptolemy III, 23
Pythagoras, 23

quantity, 142-148, 150, 151, 153, 155, 156-159, 164, 166

Raisz, Erwin, 10
Ramusio, Giambattista, 70
"recognition views," 18
Red Sea, 57, 61
relations, *see* comparison
relief maps, 46, 51, 90-91, 100, 102, 103
religious maps, 26-28, 191
remote sensing, 33
Rhodes, 23
rhumb lines, 30
road maps, 24, 28, 123, 132, 133, 179. *See also* route maps
Robinson, A., and B. Petchenik, 10
Roger II, King of Sicily, 28, 29
Roman maps, 23, 24, 25, 26, 106
Rome, map of, 91
route maps, 24, 25, 28, 29, 106-107, 110, 113-133, 140-141, 211, 216-217
Russia, 8, 25, 32, 106-107, 154

sailing charts, 30, 32, 66, 111
St. Louis, MO, 159
St. Paul, MN, 192
St. Petersburg, Russia, 107
San Antonio, TX, 167
Sanborn map, 95
San Francisco, CA, 184, 187
Santa Cruz, CA, 202-203
satellite surveys, 33, 41, 54, 55, 61
satirical maps, 8-9, 21
scale, 14-15, 16, 28, 83, 90-91, 158, 212
Scarparia, Jacobus Angelus de, 30
scientific mapping, 26
sculpture map, 90
Scythia, 25
Seattle, WA, 58, 59, 121, 159, 189
section views, 59, 83, 126, 171
sequence maps, 59, 127, 194, 204-205, 206
Servetus, Michael, 25
shading, 15, 72, 78
shadow pattern map, 58
ships, and discovery, 31
signs as maps, 10, 11
simplification, 104, 106, 112, 113, 116, 117, 122, 123,

124, 127, 129, 130, 132, 158, 166
simulation, 12, 206-209, 213, 216-217
sinusoidal equal-area projection, 38
sketch maps, 31, 87, 127
social interchange map, 187
soundscape map, 189
South Africa, 22
Soviet Union, 53, 165, 166
Spain, 8, 32
sphere, concept of, 23, 24
"spider" diagrams, 100, 105, 117, 120, 128, 166
Spilhaus, Athelstan, 22
Spokane, WA, 95
star finder, 181
star projections, 39
stereographic projection, 38
stereoscopic aerial photographs, 40, 46
stick chart, 111
Strabo, 24, 26
Strait of Magellan, 32
streets: patterns, 64, 65, 80, 89, 97, 124, 194; maps, 69, 72, 73, 75, 79, 81, 85, 94, 95, 103, 112, 114, 121, 126, 127
strip maps, 24, 25, 28, 29, 106, 110, 112, 113, 119, 121, 130, 131
Sturbridge Village, MA, 200-201
Stuttgart, Germany, 97
subjective maps, *see* personal image maps
subway maps, 100, 104-105, 106, 116, 117, 120, 124, 125, 128-129, 134-137, 211
superfeature map, 202-203
surveying, 23, 24, 32-33, 34
Swift, Jonathan, 21
Switzerland, 8, 47
Syene, 24
SYMAP, 146, 147
symbolic maps, symbolism, 12, 14, 16, 46, 80, 134-139, 186, 188, 190, 192, 193
synchronological chart, 172-173, 174
systems, *see* networks

Tabula Peutingeriana, 24, 25, 106
tactile maps, 14, 99, 100
Taiwan, 197
Taoist maps, 22, 23
taxation, 12, 13
temperance map, 191
temperature chart, 181
Thales, 23
theology, 26-27
three-dimensional maps, 46, 154. *See also* relief maps
time, maps of, 10, 15, 172-173, 174, 181

time-distance maps, 16, 176
time-lapse maps, 174, 175, 177-179
T-in-O maps, 14, 26-28, 191
Tokyo, Japan, 176
topography maps, 36-37, 40-43, 45-47, 51, 56, 59, 96, 202-203
Toscanelli, Paolo dal Pozzo, 31
touch-sensitive maps, 212, 213
tourist map, 81
traffic maps, 180, 183, 187
triangulation, 32, 34
TRIDIGRAM, 146
Triptik, 106, 119
T-shirt map, 213
Turkey, 8
typefaces, 16, 72

United States Geological Survey, 43
users, map, and user needs, 11-12, 15, 16, 17, 200-201, 206

values: personal, 16, 21, 186; cultural, 20-22; community, 200-201
vantage points, 197, 213
vegetation, 16, 45, 49, 50
Venice, Italy, 12, 110
verbal maps, 94, 110, 115, 118, 189
video technology, 16, 17, 174, 206, 208-209, 216-217
Vine Grove, KY, 96
visual perception maps, 126, 194
volcanos, 40

walk-through maps, 12, 206, 210, 211, 212, 214
Washington, DC, 80, 103, 120, 159
weapons export-import map, 195
weather charts, 60, 149, 174, 181
West Chester, England, 131
whale chart, 153
"wheel" maps, 26
word maps, *see* verbal maps
world views, 20-33

Yeshiva University, NY, 87
York, England, 131

zone maps, 26-27, 28, 29
zoom maps, 87, 160-163